WHAT READERS ARE SAYING ABOUT
MAKE PEOPLE MATTER

"With *Make People Matter*, Cheri Tree gives leaders at all levels the ideas and tools to create great workplaces. Her insights are valuable and practical, leading your organization to its greatest impact."

— **Robin Sharma, #1 Worldwide Bestselling Author of *The 5AM Club* and *The Wealth Money Can't Buy***

"This book is money in the BANK—your bank! Salespeople who use BANK will replace salespeople who don't."

— **Jeffrey Gitomer, Author of *The Little Red Book of Selling***

"Humanity defined! 'Make People Matter' isn't just a fancy slogan; it's a way of being. This book has the power to transform your life if you'll let it. Bravo, Cheri!"

— **Art McCracken, Founder and CEO, Snake River Consulting**

"The intricate tapestry of individual journeys guided by the BANK methodology fosters a profound appreciation for the unique values shaping our perceptions and relationships. Each story not only enlightens but also invites introspection, illuminating the humanity that connects us all."

— **Anna Parker, Chief Learning Officer, Lucid AI Solutions**

"In *Make People Matter*, Cheri Tree empowers us to see the beauty in our differences and the strength in our connections. Her engaging storytelling and innovative use of the BANK personality science transform the way we communicate, inviting more joy, respect, and compassion into our lives and those around us. This book is a beacon for anyone seeking to enrich their personal and professional relationships."

— **Kathy Buckley, Comedian, Author, and Motivational Speaker**

"I've spent almost a decade mastering and sharing this methodology, but *Make People Matter* opened my eyes to new ways of applying it. The diverse perspectives in each chapter showed me just how powerful this work truly is—whether in business, love, or daily life. If you want to truly understand people and build deeper connections, this book is a must-read and *your* key to connection!"

— **Anne Lesperance, Realtor®, Certified and Licensed Trainer and Coach, Founder of Your Key to Connection**

"In a world where connections drive success, *Make People Matter* is the key to authentic engagement, offering a roadmap to ensuring people feel seen, heard, and valued. Whether in business or life, this book will help you understand personalities, deliver the right message to each audience, strengthen relationships, and lead with impact."

— **Dalia Harami, Certified and Licensed BANK Trainer and Coach, and Business Success Strategist**

"As an educator and trainer in personality development, I know that understanding people is key to effective teaching and leadership. *Make People Matter* provides powerful insights into communication and connection, offering practical tools to engage and inspire others. This book is a must-read for anyone in education looking to make a real impact!"

— **Deb Cash, Educator Coach Trainer**

"If you are looking for an *awesome* community to help you grow and share stories of triumph in helping the world be a better place by connecting with our fellow neighbors in such a way to make them feel amazing and valued, look no further and pick up this book now!"

— **Erik "Mr. Awesome" Swanson, 30 Time #1 Bestselling Author, Founder of Habitude Warrior International and Speaker Hearts International**

"People need to know they are important, significant, and have value. *Make People Matter* will show you how."

— **Esther Wildenberg, Co-Founder of Codebreaker Technologies and Author of *The Undermined Soul***

"Strong emotional intelligence will be the future of leadership in our companies, communities, and families. *Make People Matter* is a journey through impactful stories of resilience, success, and failure—all parts of the human journey. This book will help you reach new levels of success by elevating your mindset."

— **Jaime Taets, Founder and Chief Vision Officer of Keystone Group International, Three-Time Author, Speaker, and Podcast Host**

"When you harness the innate power of personality and intuition, you become an unstoppable force. *Make People Matter* is more than just a book—it's a community, a commitment, and a movement. Embracing its message has profoundly impacted my life, and it has the power to do the same for you."

— **Jon Kovach Jr., Award-Winning Speaker, Global Mastermind Leader, and Bestselling Author**

"From an early age, we recognize differences among people, but we are rarely taught to celebrate them. Instead, we often learn to view differences as something negative. *Make People Matter* and the BANK methodology will transform your perspective, helping you appreciate and celebrate each person's uniqueness."

— **Julie Stephens, Founder and CEO of Exclusive Association Management, Inc., Best-Selling Author, REALTOR®, Broker, Certified Coach**

"*Make People Matter* is a transformative collection of real-life stories that prove when we truly understand and honor the values of others, we unlock deeper connections, stronger businesses, and more fulfilling relationships. This book is a game-changer for anyone seeking to communicate with impact, lead with authenticity, and create meaningful change in both their personal and professional life."

— **Kathleen Vicenzotti, Co-Founder of The Selling Edge, Co-Owner of JAK Concrete Coatings, Business Consultant, Speaker, and Trainer**

"BANK has the power to revolutionize the educational system, enabling a transformative approach to teaching and student interaction. Implementing BANK in the classroom ensures that every student feels valued and understood, fundamentally changing the way we connect in the classroom. This marks a crucial step toward a more inclusive and effective educational framework, where every student truly matters."

— **Kelley Tenny, Founder of Teach Your Brilliance, Curriculum Strategist, Educator**

"Understanding BANKCODE has been a game-changer in both my personal and professional life. It's helped me communicate more effectively, build stronger relationships, and truly make people feel seen and valued. When you take the time to understand what matters most to others, you unlock deeper trust, better connections, and greater success in every area of life."

— **Kyle Fuller, Founder and CEO, Factum Financial**

"When people feel seen, heard, and valued, they rise."

— **Mamie Jean Lamley, BANK Master Trainer and Coach, Co-Founder of i3 Empowerment Solutions**

"When people feel seen, heard, and understood, the protective walls come down and we can reach into the human we want to serve, and let them know we're a safe space for their hopes, dreams, and vision."

— **Martha E. Krejci, Founder Krejci Media**

"I think we can all agree that it's important to make people matter. This book teaches you how to do so. It will help you live a happier life."

— **Michelle LaFrance, HVAC Marketing Expert, Creator of Winning at the Kitchen Table, Speaker, and Trainer**

"Communication is the key to unlocking your success in life and business. In a world with so much disconnect and misunderstanding, *Make People Matter* is a must read! It opens your eyes to truly understanding people and seeing the world through different lenses. This book is not just about transforming your communication skills; it's about transforming your life."

— Michelle Lee Myrter, International Bestselling Author, International Speaker, Certified and Licensed BANK Trainer and Coach

"In these pages, you'll learn to see and value people for who they truly are—the key to unlocking deeper connections, greater success, and a life of authenticity and impact. *Make People Matter* shows you how the quality of our relationships determines the quality of our lives, and how to harness the power of connection for lasting transformation."

— Monica Ritchey, Empowerment Coach

"*Make People Matter* is an extraordinary compilation of thought. This is well worth your time to read."

— Nick Ryan, Author of *From Jackass to Joy*

"The collection of experiences and lessons learned in *Make People Matter* vividly illustrates how unique we all are in showing up for better or worse. The very relatable stories will open your heart and mind wider than ever to help you serve the best of yourself and the best in others."

— Pam Kranhold, Award-Winning Business and Community Leader, Consultant and Trainer

"Want to create, experience, and realize your destiny? Start here! *Make People Matter* will help you live your life in service to others while making an impact on all of those who cross your path!"

— **Patrick Snow, International Bestselling Author of *Creating Your Own Destiny***

"*Make People Matter* is not only a book, but a movement that Cheri Tree started with her BANK methodology to make all people and all children feel seen, heard, important, and unique. What a unique collection of authors and stories to inspire and encourage us all to be better, and make others matter."

— **Patty Shih-Mei Lee Campbell, Founder and CEO of Abundance Group Inc., Entrepreneur and Educator, Real Estate Investor, Financial Fitness Coach, and Author of *Meilea's Chinese New Year***

"There is always a solution, and it involves making people matter. *Make People Matter* is a must read because we all need to be seen and heard. This is a book of encouragement and resilience with lessons of triumph."

— **Sue Mandell, Certified and Licensed BANK Trainer and Coach, Award-Winning Speaker, and International Best-Selling Author**

"I have found using BANK in all areas in my life builds trust, resolves issues more effectively in my personal life, and enhances customer satisfaction in my business. This approach creates a more personalized and positive customer experience, leading to stronger loyalty and retention."

— **Susan Gonzalez-Milliron, Certified and Licensed BANK Trainer and Coach, and Reiki Master**

"*Make People Matter* is essential in 2025. This tapestry of moments, woven around a mission that makes a difference, is a must-read for anyone searching to make impactful connections with others in a world that too often feels disconnected."

— **Tammy Quist, Founder and CEO Change Agent, Inc., National Leadership Speaker, Consultant, Coach, and Trainer**

"*Make People Matter* is a beautifully crafted collection of inspiring stories and actionable wisdom, aligning deeply with my mission to live abundantly and love boldly. This book is a powerful reminder that through intentional moments, meaningful movement, and shared purpose, we can elevate lives and transform the world."

— **Tara Ryan, Entrepreneur, Community Leader, and Author**

"Codebreaker has been truly life-changing. It's not only transformed my business and how I connect with clients, but it has had a profound impact on my relationships with family and friends. More than that, it helped me discover my deeper purpose—rescuing and saving animals. The BANK system gave me the tools to take action, inspire others, and bring people together to make a real difference."

— **Teresa Ryan, REALTOR®, SFR, e-PRO, CRS, CDPE, Managing Broker and Team Lead of Ryan Hill Group**

"This book is a wake-up call for healthcare. The BANK methodology offers real solutions to one of nursing's biggest crises—retention. When nurses feel understood, they stay, they thrive, and they make an impact."

— **Teresa Sanderson, Visionary Nursing Leader, Nurses Feed Their Young® and Thriving Nurse Network Founder**

"*Make People Matter* is more than just a book—it's a movement. Cheri Tree's BANK methodology has the power to transform not just individual relationships but entire communities, both personally and professionally. It's a must-read for anyone committed to making a positive impact."

— Tiffany Anderson, Create Success Coach

"By making people matter, everyone wins!"

— Tracie Hasse, Escrow Sales Executive

"To understand another is to venture beyond oneself. *Make People Matter* is an invitation to see, listen, and embrace difference. Through intentional connection, it reveals that true influence is not persuasion, but presence—a movement where understanding reigns and every soul is truly known."

— Vicki Parker, Global Speaker, International Best-Selling Author, Women's Empowerment Coach, Business Consultant and Innkeeper at the Inn at Brandywine Falls in the Cuyahoga Valley National Park, Ohio, USA

"*Make People Matter* is a transformative guide that underscores the core value of empathy in business. This book is a timely reminder of the power of kindness. It demonstrates that ethical leadership and heartfelt communication are keys to fostering lasting loyalty and success. A must-read for anyone looking to cultivate a community-centric approach."

— Winn Claybaugh, Dean and Co-Founder of Paul Mitchell Schools, and Author of *Be Nice (Or Else!)*

BASED ON THE REVOLUTIONARY BANK® METHODOLOGY
DESIGNED TO CONNECT AND EMPOWER HUMANITY

MAKE PEOPLE MATTER

CRACKING THE CODE TO INCREASE YOUR INFLUENCE, INCOME, AND IMPACT

CHERI TREE

FOUNDER & CEO | CODEBREAKER TECHNOLOGIES

MAKE PEOPLE MATTER
CRACKING THE CODE TO INCREASE YOUR INFLUENCE, INCOME, AND IMPACT
Copyright © 2025 by Cheri Tree. All rights reserved.

Print version published by: Digital version published by:
Aviva Publishing Integrity Publishing International
Lake Placid, New York Houston, Texas

All rights reserved. No part of this book may be used or reproduced in any manner whatsoever without the expressed written permission of the author. Address all inquiries to:

Cheri Tree
Telephone: (858) 997-7555
Email: cheri@codebreakertech.com
Web: MakePeopleMatter.com | CheriTree.com | CodebreakerTech.com | CrackMyCode.com

ISBN: 978-1-63618-385-5
Library of Congress Control Number: 2025906959

Editors: Jon Kovach Jr., Integrity Publishing International; Tyler Tichelaar, Superior Book Productions; Amanda Lauer, amandalauer.com; Dalia Harami, Certified and Licensed BANK Trainer and Coach
Cover Designer: Svetlana Hodoba
Interior Layout & Design: Fusion Creative Works, fusioncw.com
Author Photo: Adam Sternberg

Every attempt has been made to source all quotes properly.

Printed in the United States of America.

First Edition
2 4 6 8 10 12

DEDICATION

To my wife Esther and our son Kai—You are my everything, and I will always make you matter!

To our incredible community of Codebreakers—thank you for supporting our mission and movement to Make People Matter!

To humanity - YOU matter!

CONTENTS

PREFACE: THE BANK CODE **19**
INTRODUCTION: IS IT POSSIBLE FOR ONE IDEA TO CHANGE THE WORLD? **38**

SECTION 1: THE MISSION **46**
Chapter 1: The Human Family Is Broken 51
Chapter 2: Our Vision, Mission, and Mantra 57

SECTION 2: THE MOMENTS **68**
BLUEPRINT **72**
Chapter 3: Breaking Through: The Journey to Success
   by Julie Stephens 73
Chapter 4: Transforming Education Through BANK
   by Kelley Tenny 79
Chapter 5: Daring to Do Nursing Differently
   by Teresa Sanderson 93
ACTION **108**
Chapter 6: Your Key to Connection
   by Anne Lesperance 109
Chapter 7: Look for the Opportunity to Make Others Matter
   by Erik "Mr. Awesome" Swanson 127

Chapter 8: The Time Is Now to Empower Women
  by Esther Wildenberg.................. 145
Chapter 9: You Matter! You Are Significant!
  by Jon Kovach Jr................... 157
Chapter 10: Increasing Your Income Intelligence with BANK
  by Kathleen Vicenzotti.................. 167
Chapter 11: They Weren't Who I Thought They Were
  by Martha Krejci.................. 181
Chapter 12: The Assignment: Understanding Your Mother
  by Michelle LaFrance.................. 191
Chapter 13: Mastering Communication for Your Ultimate Success
  by Michelle Lee Myrter.................. 207
Chapter 14: Living Your Best Life with Connection
  by Monica Ritchey 215
Chapter 15: The Entrepreneur's Path to Success
  by Patrick Snow 233
Chapter 16: A Journey Toward Your Purpose and Passion
  by Teresa Ryan.................. 241

NURTURING **256**

Chapter 17: Enhancing Your Superpowers Using BANK
  by Deb Cash.................. 257
Chapter 18: Redefining Success Through Challenge
  by Jaime Taets.................. 269
Chapter 19: The Family Banking Business
  by Kyle Fuller.................. 279
Chapter 20: Emerging from the Shadows
  by Mamie-Jean Lamley.................. 293

Chapter 21: Lighten the F Up and Live Life Fully
　　　by Nick Ryan 311
Chapter 22: Serving the Best
　　　by Pam Kranhold 321
Chapter 23: Make People Matter Because They Matter to
　　　God
　　　by Patty Shih-Mei Lee Campbell 335
Chapter 24: Customer Appreciation: Everything You Need
　　　to Know to Succeed
　　　by Susan Gonzalez-Milliron 349
Chapter 25: Living Your Best Life Now
　　　by Tara Ryan 359
Chapter 26: Uncovering Your Path to Finding Your Purpose
　　　by Tiffany Anderson 373
Chapter 27: Connecting for Next Level Success
　　　by Tracie Hasse 385
Chapter 28: The Art of Intentional Connection
　　　by Vicki Parker 399
Chapter 29: Making People Matter in the World of Business
　　　and Making Money
　　　by Winn Claybaugh 417

KNOWLEDGE **436**

Chapter 30: The AI-Enabled Leader: Building Quality and
　　　Trust with BANK
　　　by Anna Parker 437
Chapter 31: Maximize Relationships, Build Teams, Skyrocket
　　　Results
　　　by Dalia Harami 453

Chapter 32: Deserving Second Chances
　　　　　by Sue Mandell..469
Chapter 33: Unleashing the Power of BANK in Education
　　　　　by Tammy Quist..483

SECTION 3: **THE MOVEMENT**.................................**498**
Chapter 34: The Code Breaker...503
Chapter 35: Join the Movement.......................................513

SECTION 4: **THE MATCH**...**519**
Chapter 36: Make Kids Matter..523
A FINAL NOTE: **MAKE PEOPLE MATTER**..................**529**

GETTING STARTED: **UNLOCK YOUR ACCESS**...........**533**

ACKNOWLEDGMENTS...**535**

ABOUT THE AUTHOR: **CHERI TREE**..........................**538**

"The definition of genius is taking the complex and making it simple."

— Albert Einstein

PREFACE

THE BANK® CODE

The Mission, the Moments, and the Movement shared in Make People Matter are all based on the BANK methodology created by Cheri Tree in the early 2000s. BANK is a powerful values-based assessment model rooted in personality science and based in the art and science of influence.

BANK was originally designed to predict buying behavior and reveal what makes someone say yes versus no in the sales process. Rather than being based in psychology like most personality assessment models, BANK was built using BUYology—the science of buying behavior or buy-IN behavior.

BANK is the only methodology in the world that has been scientifically validated to predict buying behavior in less than ninety seconds with its quick and reliable assessments, and now nanoseconds with Codebreaker AI. More than 500,000 people have taken our assessment and cracked their code from more than one hundred countries around the world and counting.

BANK is personality-based, profit-focused, people-centered, and purpose-driven.

WHAT ARE THE BANKCODES?

BANK is an acronym for the four primary personality codes in the system: Blueprint, Action, Nurturing, and Knowledge. Every person in the world is all four codes, simply prioritized based on each person's own set of values, creating something we like to call a BANKCODE.

As you can probably imagine, people are wired totally differently from each other. So differently, in fact, that I want you to imagine they are each powered by a different operating system. What motivates one person might completely de-motivate another. If you want to better understand people, it's critical to understand what their BANKCODE is and then learn how to interact with them accordingly.

Let's take a quick look at each of the four primary BANKCODES to better understand the main values and dominant behaviors that drive each code, and the strategies to optimize your communication with that code.

THE BLUEPRINT CODE

OVERVIEW

The Blueprint code is typically conservative by nature, risk-adverse, formal, and thinks "inside the box." I use the color blue to associate with this primary code because such people are typically colder to approach and more professional in nature. They are past-focused and believe that history repeats itself.

VALUES

Twelve core values motivate and drive the Blueprint code:

- Stability
- Structure
- Systems
- Planning
- Processes
- Predictability
- Responsibility
- Duty
- Rules
- Credentials
- Titles
- Tradition

BEHAVIORS

You can expect a Blueprint to regularly act out certain behaviors. Blueprint codes typically:

- Expect everyone to follow the rules and regulations.
- Require people to keep their word.
- Set up and implement predictable systems.
- Trust proven authorities.

- See everything in the world through the lens of right and wrong.
- Accept only a time-tested and proven establishment.
- Learn best through memorization, recall, and drill.
- Run agenda-driven, efficient meetings that start and end on time.
- Enjoy seeing people being held accountable for their wrong behavior.
- Dislike it when people question authority or do not obey.
- Work best with systems, routines, and procedures.
- Learn from past mistakes and proceed with caution.

COMMUNICATION

To communicate effectively with a Blueprint, we recommend you:

- Always tell the truth, the whole truth, and nothing but the truth.
- Focus on the facts, leaving unknowns out.
- Avoiding letting emotions cloud the conversation.
- Be clear and avoid gray areas of interpretation.
- Speak calmly and firmly.
- Stay polite and formal until you know them well.
- Be efficient and respect their timeline for the conversation.
- Structure your arguments well.

- Take important topics seriously.
- Follow a simple, easy-to-follow message organization.
- Act your age and behave responsibly throughout the interaction.
- Avoid surprises. If you're going to bring up an unpleasant subject, start there.

THE ACTION CODE

OVERVIEW

The Action code is typically full of energy, ambitious, driven, and thinks "outside the box." I use the color red to associate with this primary code because Action codes typically act like they just drank Red Bull for breakfast; they are explosive like a red-hot firecracker and expect red carpet VIP treatment. They are future-focused and believe the best is yet to come.

VALUES

Twelve core values motivate and drive the Action code:

- Freedom
- Flexibility
- Spontaneity
- Action
- Opportunity
- Excitement
- Attention
- Stimulation
- Competition
- Winning
- Fun
- Image

BEHAVIORS

You can expect an Action to regularly act out certain behaviors. Action codes typically:

- Negotiate skillfully and look for their own win.
- Are optimistic and act on instinct.

- Are competitive and have a propensity for sports and entertainment.
- Love beauty and anything aesthetically pleasing.
- Recognize and go after opportunity.
- Look to find a better way to do things.
- Rebel against rules, routine, and structure.
- Take risks getting things done.
- Act entrepreneurially and like to lead.
- Learn best through hands-on methods: Show me; don't tell me.
- Dislike boredom or waiting.
- Dislike abstract ideas, excessive details, and useless theories.

COMMUNICATION

To communicate effectively with an Action, we recommend you:

- Be enthusiastic when speaking.
- Make sure you look cool and put-together before starting the conversation.
- Make your point snappy.
- Get straight to the core of your argument without preamble.
- Avoid long, detailed explanations; bullet point the important issues.

- Make them the center of attention; don't split your focus.
- Let loose a bit.
- Know when it's okay to get loud or funny—and do so!
- Be flexible; let the conversation flow naturally in the style that appeals to them.
- Have fun! Entertain them to keep them engaged.
- Give them plenty of praise.
- Match their energy and share their excitement.

THE NURTURING CODE

OVERVIEW

The Nurturing code is typically kind in nature, excellent with people, friendly, and one to "recycle the box." I use the color yellow to associate with this primary code because Nurturing codes are typically warm like sunshine, sweet like honey, and have a heart of gold. They are present-focused and believe the only moment that exists is the here and now.

VALUES

Twelve core values motivate and drive the Nurturing code:

- Relationships
- Authenticity
- Personal Growth
- Significance
- Teamwork
- Involvement
- Community
- Charity
- Ethics
- Harmony
- Morality
- Contribution

BEHAVIORS

You can expect a Nurturer to regularly act out certain behaviors. Nurturing codes typically:

- Dislike inauthentic or fake people.
- Enjoy training, motivating, and coaching others.
- Need interaction with people, groups, and teams.

- Seek deeper meaning beyond material possessions.
- Show appreciation easily and in many ways.
- Avoid conflict, contention, and excessive competition.
- Are genuine, kind, and thoughtful.
- Are on a quest for self-actualization and want others to do the same.
- Believe in the greater good of people.
- Support and empower others to be their best.
- Are empathetic and intuitively understand others' needs.
- Are here to positively impact others.

COMMUNICATION

To communicate effectively with a Nurturer, we recommend you:

- Include them fully in the conversation; make sure you're speaking with them, not to them.
- Be honest and trustworthy.
- Give feedback kindly; don't hurt their feelings with brutal truth, but rather cloak it in the positive.
- Speak sincerely and authentically, sharing from the heart.
- Listen actively and remember what they said.
- Show your emotions openly, being sincere about how you're feeling, happy or sad.
- Be fully present and in the moment with them.

- Actively and genuinely listen to what they are saying; don't divide your attention.
- Maintain good eye contact.
- Use appropriate touch during a conversation to connect.
- Have empathy and avoid judgment—both of them and others.
- Share your passions and the causes that drive you.

THE KNOWLEDGE CODE

OVERVIEW

The Knowledge code is typically intelligent in nature, witty, introverted, and will "engineer the box." I use the color green to associate with this primary code because Knowledge codes would typically absorb themselves in data or computer code (Microsoft Excel's logo is green and the computer code in the Matrix is green). They are abstract thought-focused and often have their heads in space or the Metaverse.

VALUES

Twelve core values motivate and drive the Knowledge code:

- Learning
- Intelligence
- Logic
- Self-Mastery
- Technology
- Research and Development
- Science
- Universal Truths
- Expertise
- Competence
- Accuracy
- The Big Picture

BEHAVIORS

You can expect a Knowledge to regularly act out certain behaviors. Knowledge codes typically:

- Trust logic and reason above all.
- Map out strategy at the macro level.

- Are precise in speech and notice contradictions.
- Have a need for data and meaningful interpretation or analysis of it.
- Respect the power of nature and feel attracted to the sciences.
- Focus on long-term results with projections far into the future.
- Easily learn abstract ideas and process several issues at the same time.
- Dislike rote memorization without understanding.
- Resolve conflict logically and rationally without emotional reactions.
- Use diagrams and models to communicate abstractions.
- Can easily recognize truths and untruths.
- Dislike chitchat and instead seek conversations with substance.

COMMUNICATION

To communicate effectively with a Knowledge, we recommend you:

- Build your argument logically, avoiding long digressions into irrelevant information.
- Keep the emotions out of your reasoning.
- Stick to tangible information and trustworthy research.
- Don't take criticism personally.
- Explain why you're suggesting an action or how something works; they need to understand fully.

- Let them be right; if you don't agree on their approach, find another strategy to come to a consensus.
- Give them time to think about what you're saying, especially if they need to make a decision.
- Be precise and accurate; don't exaggerate.
- Know what you're talking about, and speak intelligently.
- Prepare for tough, probing questions.
- Encourage questions.
- Take time to think responses through and fully consider your answers.

THE TWENTY-FOUR BANKCODES

Although four primary BANKCODES exist, people are a combination of all four codes. The sequence of these codes—based on each person's set of values—determines their BANKCODE. Only twenty-four different sequences exist. They are:

BLUEPRINT	ACTION	NURTURING	KNOWLEDGE
• BAKN	• ABKN	• NABK	• KABN
• BANK	• ABNK	• NAKB	• KANB
• BKAN	• AKBN	• NBAK	• KBAN
• BKNA	• AKNB	• NBKA	• KBNA
• BNAK	• ANBK	• NKAB	• KNAB
• BNKA	• ANKB	• NKBA	• KNBA

CRACK THE CODE

Think of BANK as a language—the language of people. If people are important to you, then make an effort to crack their code and communicate with them based on the language of their code—instead of forcing them to engage with you strictly based on your code.

This idea infuses emotional intelligence into your communication style and will likely make you a much happier, more successful person in life and business.

> **"Language is the foundation of civilization. It is the glue that holds a people together. It is the first weapon drawn in a conflict."**
>
> — Jeremy Renner

The stories shared in this book reveal a series of powerful and impactful Make People Matter moments when the BANKCODES were used to communicate effectively to build, transform, or even save a relationship or life.

I am honored to share this journey with you. So, if you're ready to make people matter, let's get started!

"Think of an idea that can change the world and put it into action."

— *Pay It Forward*

INTRODUCTION

IS IT POSSIBLE FOR ONE IDEA TO CHANGE THE WORLD?

In the movie *Pay It Forward*, Kevin Spacey's character is a teacher who gives his seventh-grade class an extra credit school project: Think of an idea that can change the world, and put it into action.

The students are tasked with performing a kind act for someone else, with the expectation that the recipient will then "pay it forward" by doing a similar act of kindness for another person, creating a ripple effect of positive actions within the community; essentially, it encourages students to actively spread kindness beyond themselves.

I was moved deeply after watching this movie. What if it was indeed possible to think of an idea that could change the world? Could someone like me be bold enough and brave enough to come up with such an idea, and then actually put it into action?

The thought inspired me, but I had no idea what this idea could be—until I created BANK®. A simple four-letter word had the power not only to transform my life, but millions of lives around the world, and that is where my story begins.

THE IDEA THAT CHANGED MY WORLD

My journey with BANK didn't start with success—it started with struggle. When I first got into sales, I believed what everyone told me: "Sales is a numbers game." So, I played the game. I worked harder than ever, putting in long hours and following every piece of advice I could find. And my big reward that first year? I made $700.

That was a wake-up call. If I was going to make a living in sales, I had to get better—so I dove in. I studied everything I could learn about sales, took every training course I could find, and did my best to earn a living. After five years, my income climbed to $72,000 a year, which was a lot better than $700, but still far from where I wanted to be. I was buried in debt, frustrated, and on the edge of being burned out. I started to think: Maybe I'm just not cut out for this.

Then, one day, it hit me: What if the problem isn't me? What if it's the advice I've been given?

I realized the "sales is just a numbers game" approach was all wrong. It wasn't working for me, and it also wasn't working for a lot of other people. What if I flipped the script instead of focusing on getting more nos to get more yeses? What if sales wasn't a numbers game at all? What if it was a people game?

That idea changed everything.

THE SECRET THAT CHANGED MY LIFE

Immediately, I shifted my focus from studying sales to studying people—and everything changed. I dug in and started studying everything I could to understand people, and that's when I discovered personality science.

Personality science dates back thousands of years to Hippocrates, the Greek philosopher known as the Father of Medicine. He discovered the fact that people are fundamentally different, and he could categorize them into four specific groups, calling his idea the theory of the four temperaments. Using his philosophy, he was able to treat his patients differently, simply based on their personality temperament. This discovery was a game-changer for humanity.

Fast forward to our modern world. Many different types of assessments have been built to help people discover more about themselves. Some of the more popular models include DISC, MBTI, The Color Code, The Keirsey Temperament Sorter, Management Drives, Insights, and The Birkman Method.

I took a number of these assessments in my early career, and I was initially fascinated with what I learned about myself. But my fascination turned into frustration when I realized these assessments were great for self-awareness, but they didn't help me close more sales or connect with other people on a deeper level.

Ultimately, I was looking for an assessment that could tell me not who I was, but who they were—my buyers, clients, and team members, and what triggers the yes or no outcome. I wanted to know what mattered to them. I didn't want to use another assessment based in psychology, but instead based in BUYology, the science of buying (or buy-in) behavior.

It didn't exist—so I decided I would build my own model as an experiment, based on the art and science of influence, and I called it BANK—Blueprint, Action, Nurturing, and Knowledge. I discovered that my clients were not just one of these four types—but a combination of all four types. I called that combination their BANKCODE.

The challenge I had was trying to figure out what each person's BANKCODE was in a quick and accurate manner. Since twenty-four unique BANKCODES exist, that meant I had roughly a 4 percent chance of getting it right—but my theory was that I needed to know this code sequence in order to get the yes and avoid the no in my sales process.

The trick was finding a way to do it quickly and accurately. Really, only one way would work—I had to ask them to "crack their code." I devised a fun and interactive way of asking my clients to share their BANKCODE with me—a set of four plastic cards with different values on them, one for each personality type. I asked people to sort the BANKCARDS based on what was most important to least important to them. It was simple, but it worked!

As soon as I started using BANK, my income skyrocketed. In one year, I went from $72,000 to more than $500,000; within three years, I hit more than $1,000,000 per year. But it wasn't just the money that mattered. For the first time, I felt like I was connecting with people in a way that truly mattered.

THE MOMENT IT BECAME PERSONAL

What started as a sales experiment quickly turned into something much bigger. People began sharing how using BANK wasn't just helping them in business—it was changing their lives.

One woman told me BANK saved her marriage because she finally understood how to communicate with her husband after twenty years of marriage. A mother shared how learning her children's BANKCODES helped her see each of them as unique individuals and parent them in ways that brought more harmony to their family.

Teachers started telling me it was helping them connect better with their students in the classroom, and it even reduced bullying on the playground.

But I'll never forget the day one of our certified trainers told me that BANK had just helped to prevent a teenage suicide. Time stopped. I couldn't believe my BANK methodology was having so much positive impact on others and in ways I had never imagined. Not only was it saving marriages and families—it was saving lives!

These stories hit me on a deeply personal level. You see, my biggest "why" isn't about making more sales or building a massive business—it's my son, Kai. I gave birth to him at nearly forty-eight years young, and I've often thought about the effect I can have on his life and the legacy I will leave behind for him after I'm gone.

MY WHY—KAI
THE KEY AND THE CODE

Discovering *my why* was a process that went many layers deep. When I finally got to the core of my why, I discovered that if I could give my son Kai one thing before I passed on to the next life, it would be a key. This key was really a code. A code that could unlock every door he would want to walk through in life by knowing the code of the people he would interact with in his life. This code contains a secret power that would give him a super-power in life—the ability to communicate effectively in life, personally and professionally. The code is the BANKCODE.

That's what BANK is to me. It's not just a methodology—it's a way to empower people, to help them build stronger relationships, create connections in a disconnected world, and ultimately make people matter.

WHY I'M COMMITTED TO MAKING PEOPLE MATTER

For me, BANK isn't just about cracking codes—it's about connecting and empowering humanity. Today, the world is more disconnected than ever. Technology is advancing at lightning speed, but we've lost the art of real connection. People can text—but not talk. They can comment—but they don't know how to connect.

BANK is my way of countering that. It's a tool to help people see each other, hear each other, and value each other for who they really are. It's not just about making more sales; it's about building more meaningful relationships, personally and professionally.

And that's why I'm here—to help others crack their codes, transform their lives, and ultimately, make people matter. Because at the end of the day, life isn't about numbers—it's about people. And every single one of us has a code worth unlocking.

P.S. To learn more about our BANK system go to makepeoplematter.com.

"The need for self-transcendence is a fundamental human need."

— Abraham Maslow

SECTION 1: THE MISSION

Abraham Maslow was a pioneer in the realm of psychology who fundamentally altered our understanding of human behavior and motivation. Maslow believed that going beyond oneself and connecting with something greater was a universal human desire.

Maslow was more than just a psychologist; he was a visionary who saw humans not as they were, but as they could be. He developed the concept of a "hierarchy of needs"—a conceptualization of the needs (or goals) that motivate human behavior.

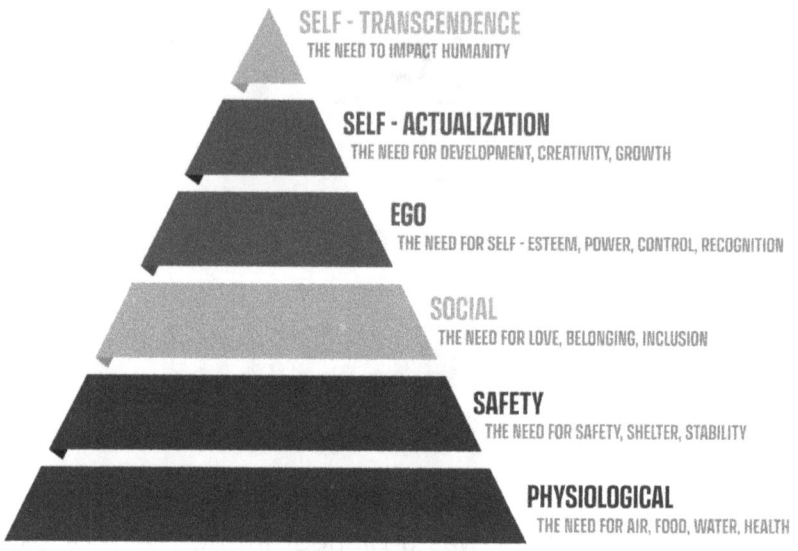

MASLOW'S HIERARCHY OF NEEDS AND SELF-TRANSCENDENCE

In the original model, self-actualization is at the top, with ego below it, then social, then safety, with physiological needs at the bottom. This order indicates that physiological needs are vital for survival, and they must be sated before one can move upward toward actualization and fulfillment. In his early work, Maslow considered self-actualization the pinnacle of human development and the highest human need: the realization of one's full potential. He later recognized the need for one more level of development.

Self-actualization is indeed a lofty (and worthy) goal of development and should not be cast aside in favor of the shiny new need, but self-transcendence is truly the "next level" of development; it is other-focused instead of self-focused, and it concerns higher goals than those that are self-serving.

Maslow explained, "Transcendence refers to the very highest and most inclusive or holistic levels of human consciousness, behaving and relating, as ends rather than means, to oneself, to significant others, to human beings in general, to other species, to nature, and to the cosmos."

Through his exploration of transcendence, Maslow provided a compelling vision of human potential that extends beyond self-fulfillment to embrace a holistic, interconnected existence, underscoring the depth of human consciousness and the possibility for continuous growth and harmony.

MY JOURNEY TO SELF-TRANCENDENCE

In my younger years, I was focused on self-actualization and achieving new pinnacles of success, which included earning millions of dollars. BANK helped me to "Take it to the BANK" and achieve my financial goals in ways I had only dreamed about prior to understanding the power of personality science.

As incredible as my success has been, it has paled in comparison to the happiness and joy I have experienced by hearing the stories of the lives that have been affected and transformed by this incredible methodology.

My focus has since expanded from the money to the mission, the mantra, and the movement behind BANK—and it can be summarized in three simple words…

MAKE PEOPLE MATTER.

CHAPTER 1

THE HUMAN FAMILY IS BROKEN

> "We are, without doubt, broken people living with other broken people in a broken world."
>
> — Tullian Tchividjian

In a rapidly changing world, where technological breakthroughs, societal upheavals, and shifting priorities redefine how we live and interact, the need for meaningful human connection has never been greater. The forces shaping our reality—technology, turmoil, transition, and transformation—can divide us or bring us closer together. We must equip ourselves with tools that foster understanding, adaptability, and growth to navigate these shifts.

The Make People Matter philosophy, powered by the BANK methodology, addresses this need by offering a roadmap to bridge the gaps created by modern challenges and inspire a collective transformation. Each of these foundational elements serves as a crucial steppingstone, setting the stage for how we can reconnect with ourselves, each other, and our shared purpose. Together, these principles form the backbone of a movement aimed at empowering humanity to thrive amid uncertainty.

Let's explore how these foundational elements create the context for making people matter and how BANK serves as a beacon of hope in these dynamic times.

1. Technology and Its Impact on Connection: Technology is advancing faster than we ever thought possible. Concepts like artificial intelligence, virtual reality, augmented reality, and 5G are changing how we interact and connect.

For example, by 2030, flying cars might be the primary mode of transportation (cool, I know!). Even more crazy, some experts are predicting that our children and grandchildren will be spending up to 50 percent of their lives in the metaverse—to the point that they won't even know the difference between virtual reality and actual reality. Yikes!

The challenge is that as connected as technology makes us, it can also disconnect and isolate us. People today text, but they often struggle to talk face-to-face, and they comment on posts, but they can't truly connect in a meaningful way. BANK can counterbalance the effects of technological disconnection.

BANK steps in by helping individuals understand each other on a deeper level, bridging the emotional and communicative gaps created by rapid technological advancement. Whether it's enhancing how teams collaborate in remote settings or ensuring that our interactions remain authentic amid virtual reality, BANK offers a framework to keep human connection at the forefront of progress.

2. Turmoil in Society: Today, we face an unprecedented level of turmoil. COVID-19, for example, greatly affected our emotional, physical, and psychological well-being. The isolation, lockdowns, and other disruptions created intense stress. Domestic violence, divorce rates, depression, and suicide attempts rose dramatically, highlighting the fragility of our social fabric. We can choose to let these pressures crush us—or transform us.

Amid such turmoil, BANK provides a toolkit for resilience and connection. At Codebreaker, our goal is to provide tools that support transformation, allowing people to flourish amid the challenges. By teaching people to understand themselves and others better, BANK turns challenges into opportunities for personal growth and stronger relationships. It equips individuals with the tools they need to navigate life's pressures with empathy, emotional intelligence, and effective communication.

3. Transition to a New Normal: A mass exodus from traditional work structures—a significant shift—is underway. Millions have left their jobs, yearning for freedom and control over their lives. The pandemic forced many to reevaluate their priorities, leaving behind toxic work environments and unfulfilling routines to embrace entrepreneurial pursuits, flexible lifestyles, or alternative career paths. This mass exodus is not just a rejection of old systems—it's a transition toward a future where people want to reclaim control over their time, values, and ambitions.

I see this as an opportunity to support people who are taking charge of their future by providing them with the mindsets, skillsets, and toolsets they need to succeed in business and life. BANK supports this transition by empowering individuals to thrive on their chosen paths. By providing the skills to communicate effectively, market authentically, and build lasting relationships, BANK becomes a guide for those stepping into new opportunities. Whether someone is starting a business, pivoting careers, or redefining success on their terms, BANK offers the practical solutions and mindset shifts needed to succeed.

4. Transformation for Humanity: Now, more than ever, humanity is ready for transformation. As a company, we at Codebreaker see ourselves as light-bearers here to help facilitate positive change, guiding individuals and communities through this transformation. Humanity stands at a crossroads. The choices we make today will determine whether we move toward self-destruction or collective transformation. As the pressures of modern life intensify, the demand for meaningful change grows stronger. Now, more than ever, people are ready for a shift—one that prioritizes connection, compassion, and understanding.

By leveraging the BANK methodology, we empower people to unlock their full potential and create lives of purpose, fulfillment, and connection. Transformation begins with self-awareness and extends outward, rippling through families, companies, communities, and societies, fostering a world where people truly matter.

CHAPTER 2

OUR VISION, MISSION, AND MANTRA

"Never doubt that a small group of thoughtful, committed citizens can change the world. Indeed, it is the only thing that ever has."

— Margaret Mead

OUR VISION—#8BILLIONCODES

Our vision is bold and audacious—to crack the code of every single human on the planet! More than 8 billion people live on earth—and every single one has a code locked inside of them. They will either go to their grave with this code still locked inside—or they will have the opportunity to meet a Codebreaker, who will help them unlock access to that code, empowering them to understand themselves better and optimize their success in life.

This code is so powerful that knowing it has the potential to transform every single relationship you will ever have in your lifetime. This code will help you communicate more effectively, build a successful business or career, strengthen your key relationships, increase your emotional intelligence, and even expand your influence as a leader.

Once you unlock your own code, you can help others unlock their codes—making you a Codebreaker.

Imagine how knowing the code of your spouse could make you a better partner with a stronger marriage. Imagine knowing the codes of your children and being empowered to parent each one of them uniquely, giving you a stronger family. Imagine knowing the codes of all your relatives, being able to communicate more meaningfully with the people you love, and as a result, having the power to create a lasting legacy.

Imagine knowing the codes of your neighbors, coworkers, colleagues, customers, and community and organizational leaders—anyone and everyone around you!

Can you think of anyone who doesn't deserve to know their own code and understand what makes them tick, or why they are wired a certain way? I can't. Life is already challenging—so why not make it easier for people to connect and communicate in meaningful ways?

For this reason, Codebreakers are on a mission to crack the code of every person in the world! And we're off to a good start—but we've got a long way to go—and we would love your help with our #8billioncodes initiative.

At the time of this writing, we have cracked the code of nearly 500,000 people—but that's not nearly the dent in the universe we are here to make. We've got a lot more codes to crack—so let's get cracking!

OUR MISSION—CONNECT AND EMPOWER HUMANITY

Our goal is to turn our vision into our mission—to connect and empower humanity with the BANK methodology. We are at a critical time in human history, and we want to reconnect the human family worldwide.

Imagine a world where we could all get along! Is the idea of world peace something championed only by Mahatma Gandhi, Martin Luther King, Jr., or the finalists in a beauty pageant? Or can it be something we can collectively strive to attain in our lifetimes?

Yes, our mission is bold and audacious. But just like Steve Jobs said, "The people who are crazy enough to think they can change the world, are the ones who do." The crazy ones disrupt the status quo and make a dent in the universe. So why not us—and why not now?

For our mission to be effective, we had to build a strategy and a framework to connect and empower humanity. We identified five key pillars where we could optimize the lives of human beings: communication, business, relationships, emotional intelligence, and leadership—all using the power of BANK and the BANK strategy to make people matter.

PILLAR 1: COMMUNICATION
THE FOUNDATION OF CONNECTION

The first pillar's objective is to improve your communication skills.

Language is the key that unites civilization. BANK is the language of people. Think about this: Every relationship, every transaction, every opportunity starts with communication. It's not just about what you say, but how you say it, and how the other person receives it.

Personally, learning to adapt my communication style to the BANKCODES of others was like discovering a universal translator. Suddenly, I wasn't just talking—I was connecting. Whether it was with a team member, a partner, or my own son, Kai, understanding their unique communication style changed everything. It wasn't just about getting my point across; it was about truly hearing, understanding, and valuing their perspective.

PILLAR 2: BUSINESS
TRANSFORMING RESULTS WITH PERSONALIZATION

The second pillar's objective is to increase your reach, revenue, and retention.

I'll admit it—early in my sales career, I was all about the numbers. I thought if I just worked harder, made more calls, and pushed through the nos, I'd eventually get the yeses I needed. But that approach was exhausting, and it didn't work. It wasn't until I applied BANK to my business that I saw a dramatic shift.

By understanding my clients' values and preferences, I could tailor my pitches in a way that resonated with them. The result? Not only did my revenue skyrocket, but I also built stronger, more meaningful relationships with my clients. I wasn't just selling—I was solving problems and meeting needs.

PILLAR 3: RELATIONSHIPS
STRENGTHENING BONDS THROUGH UNDERSTANDING

The third pillar's objective is to strengthen your relationships.

One of the most personal ways BANK has influenced my life is in my relationships. As a parent, understanding Kai's BANKCODE helps me see him as an individual with his own unique set of needs, values, and motivations. Because his code is NAKB, I am taking a much more nurturing approach to raising him and communicating with him, especially during some of his challenging toddler moments. This approach made a significant difference in our relationship, and he frequently hugs me, tells me he loves me, and that I'm his best friend!

The same applies to friendships, partnerships, and even casual interactions. When you try to understand someone's BANKCODE, you're not just building a relationship—you're strengthening it in ways that create trust, respect, and lasting connection.

PILLAR 4: EMOTIONAL INTELLIGENCE THE KEY TO MEANINGFUL IMPACT

The fourth pillar's objective is to raise your emotional intelligence.

In my experience, not enough people have a significant amount of emotional intelligence. I truly believe that kindness is a universal currency. The way to move us toward a much more connected and kind human family is to raise the emotional intelligence of humanity. BANK has been a game-changer for me in this area.

If I've learned anything on this journey, it's that emotional intelligence isn't a "nice-to-have"—it's a must. The ability to understand and manage your own emotions while empathizing with others is what makes all the difference. BANK took my emotional intelligence to the next level by giving me a framework to understand why people think, feel, and act the way they do. It's not just about managing relationships—it's about elevating them. When you show someone you genuinely understand them, you're not just communicating—you're connecting on a deeper level and in a much more meaningful way.

PILLAR 5: LEADERSHIP
INSPIRING AND GUIDING OTHERS

The fifth pillar's objective is to advance your leadership competency.

Leadership isn't just about having a title or being in charge—it's about influence. And influence starts with understanding the people you lead. Whether I'm guiding a team, mentoring someone, or even just having a heart-to-heart with a friend, BANK has taught me that leadership is about meeting people where they are. It's about inspiring them to reach their potential by showing them they matter.

Whether you're leading your family, company, or community, true leadership isn't about commanding respect—it's about earning it through empathy, understanding, and genuine care.

To be the ultimate leader, you need to be the ultimate influencer, and you can do that by learning how to make people matter.

OUR MANTRA—MAKE PEOPLE MATTER

Our original tagline for BANK is "Take it to the BANK®." It is appropriate for business owners and salespeople—and super-cool, I must admit! But it doesn't encapsulate the much bigger effect that BANK makes in the lives of our Codebreakers.

So, I began to contemplate what our vision and mission was and connect with my heart space. At that time, I was reading The Buddha and the Badass by Vishen Lakhiani, the Founder of Mindvalley. Lakhiani talks about his mission to "Make Work Matter" and how he used that mission to transform his business and drive it to more than $100,000,000 in revenue.

Suddenly, it hit me—our mission at Codebreaker was to "Make People Matter"! BOOM! This statement quickly became our company and community's mantra because of how effectively it described our mission and all the ways BANK worked for our clients.

What is a mantra? Derived from two Sanskrit words—manas (mind) and tra (tool)—the word mantra translates into being a tool or instrument of the mind; it's a powerful sound vibration through which we carefully focus our thoughts to transcend the mind to reach a deep state of meditation.

> "A mantra is not just something to chant. It is not chanting.

> *A mantra is something to let sink deep in your being, just as roots go deep into the earth. The deeper the roots go into the earth, the higher the tree will go into the sky."*
>
> — Osho

Our Make People Matter mantra has sunk deep into the core of our messaging and become an integral part of our Codebreaker community. It's the essence of our intent behind using the BANK methodology in every aspect of our communication, and it has become part of our Code of Honor.

THE BANK CODE OF HONOR

At Codebreaker, we live by a Code of Honor—the BANK Code of Honor, with a pledge to make people matter. We are here not only to help people achieve massive financial success, but to live the highest pinnacle of Maslow's Hierarchy of Needs—to self-transcend and dedicate our lives to the betterment of humanity.

Personally, taking the pledge to make people matter has completely changed me. I am far kinder, more patient, and more approachable—and much less judgmental. It allowed me to fall in love with people and truly appreciate them for who they are and how they show up in the world. Things that used to annoy me now amuse me. People are complicated and funny—but worth your time and effort to understand—and BANK has been the Holy Grail of communication for me.

TAKE OUR MAKE PEOPLE MATTER PLEDGE

Now that you understand our vision, our mission, and our mantra—I invite you to take our Make People Matter pledge. Pledge to truly understand the people you are communicating with. Know their codes. Be deliberate in your communication with them based on their codes.

Infuse yourself with emotional intelligence. Add a significant dose of kindness to your heart, your words, and your tone. As you do, you will find that building and fostering meaningful relationships becomes effortless and extremely rewarding, as you will see in the next section.

"We do not remember days—
we remember moments."

— Cesar Pavese

SECTION 2: THE MOMENTS

In Section 1, I shared with you the vision and mission behind our Make People Matter mantra, and why a small tribe of Codebreakers are gathering together to share our collective vision and mission with the people in our respective worlds.

In this section, you will read about special moments my co-authors experienced. These moments happened because they used BANK to make people matter. The moments they share are filled with profound insights and powerful lessons learned in the process.

These Make People Matter moments transpired in very diverse ways—from the classroom and the boardroom to even the bedroom. The joy of knowing how many lives have been touched and transformed by the power of BANK is priceless.

As you read each chapter, I invite you to look for ways you can apply the lessons shared, both personally and professionally. Whether you're simply looking for ways to optimize your key relationships, or you have strained relationships that are sitting in the crosshairs and at risk, these moments will guide and inspire you to make people matter.

BLUEPRINT

CHAPTER 3

BREAKING THROUGH: THE JOURNEY TO SUCCESS

BY JULIE STEPHENS

"Success usually comes to those who are too busy to be looking for it."

— Henry David Thoreau

I was born in 1966, the second daughter and last child to parents raised on Midwest farms. While both attended college, neither completed their degrees. Soon after my birth, my father's work brought us to Texas, where my earliest memories formed. Dad was frequently away for work, and my mother was home, dedicating her days to raising us. By the time I was four, my parents divorced. I was so young and didn't grasp what that meant, though I distinctly remember telling my friends, "My parents are getting a divorce—but we don't need presents for it."

In the years that followed, both my parents faced financial hardships. Despite his brilliant IQ, my father struggled with everyday tasks, like keeping the lights on and the rent paid. He never owned a home and tragically passed away at just age fifty-one from a heart attack. My mom had to find work to support my sister and me without any financial assistance from my dad. Our family often fell below the poverty line, and it became painfully clear that luxuries some other kids enjoyed were out of reach for us.

Eventually, Mom remarried a man twenty years her senior, bringing a semblance of middle-class stability to our lives for a short time. Unfortunately, their marriage lasted only five years, leaving us once again in rented apartments, struggling to make ends meet. When my sister and I were teenagers, my sister made the difficult choice to live with our father, drawn by the promise of fewer rules and more freedom. A few years later, I joined her.

Living with Dad was a learning experience. I was fifteen and discovering friendships, relationships, and the complexities of human nature. My sister and I, however, could not have been more different. I valued loyalty and honesty, while I perceived her as manipulative and self-serving. We clashed often and, during one heated argument, our conflict escalated to physicality. I gave her a black eye, and when she ran to Dad, I found myself on the outs. From that day forward, I was placed in foster care.

Being in foster care was one of the darkest periods of my life, but it is also where my resilience took root. This experience taught me to persevere, and when I was eventually back with my dad, I committed myself to success. In high school, I focused on academics and, later, in college, I felt my first surge of accomplishment. I was determined to prove myself, and attending college was my silent victory. My sister chose a different path, forgoing higher education, which, in my mind, placed me one step ahead of her.

During college, I met my future husband. We married young, and I became pregnant shortly after, putting my degree on hold—a goal I never accomplished. After thirteen years, our marriage ended, which felt like another failure. But I pressed on, eventually remarrying in 2001. By that time, I had spent years working for two different companies, but I found myself spinning in circles, financially stagnant, and still yearning for something more.

In 2005, I took a leap of faith and started my own business with no loans and only the income I was earning from my "job-job." I worked both roles tirelessly for the first two to three years, slowly building a client base to replace my regular income. That's when I learned a fundamental truth about business: Success hinges on relationships. My years as an employee hadn't exposed me to the nuances of relationship-building. I'd only done my job, but now, as an entrepreneur, everything was different. I had to do it all; nothing mattered more than building connections.

During my first five years, I relied heavily on relationships I'd nurtured over time, receiving many referrals. However, I struggled with getting referrals from those who didn't know me or, frankly, didn't like me. I joined networking groups, seeking guidance, but when I encountered BANK, my perspective changed entirely. After seeing Cheri Tree at a networking event, I felt compelled to join BANK, and the training transformed my approach. New habits replaced the old, and my business began to thrive.

My business success brought new challenges. Sales surged, but I struggled with staff retention, finding that hiring was only half the battle. I started using BANK principles to strengthen my team relationships, even training my staff to understand and celebrate each other's differences. Today, four of my fifteen employees are celebrating a decade with our firm.

BANK didn't just revolutionize my business; it impacted every aspect of my life. I got remarried in 2001, and BANK provided the tools to understand my husband on a deeper level. It has saved us from the potential strain of misunderstandings, bringing us closer together and allowing us to work toward shared goals. Fewer stresses at home mean more peace, better partnerships, and a stronger bond.

Businesses fail for countless reasons—lack of funding, poor partnerships, and weak marketing. Many consider success to be an annual revenue of $50,000, but I wanted more. Thanks to BANK, our company is on track to reach $5 million this year.

No other training has impacted my life like BANK, both personally and professionally. This journey has shown me that success, while never easy, is attainable. With BANK and unwavering determination, I'm proud to say I have far exceeded my expectations—and I am forever grateful.

JULIE STEPHENS | BKAN

Julie Stephens is a Real Estate Broker, CEO of Exclusive Association Management, a bestselling author, and a BANK Trainer and coach. Julie is a dual-licensed real estate broker in Georgia and Florida and serves as CEO of Exclusive Association Management, a firm specializing in HOA and condo management, property management, and traditional real estate services for both sellers and buyers. As a certified BANK trainer, Julie excels in personality-driven sales, enabling her to communicate effectively, resolve conflicts, and connect meaningfully with clients.

With a wealth of experience in project management, sales, and conflict resolution, Julie's leadership empowers her firm to deliver exceptional service and foster successful relationships within the communities they serve.

Author's Website: JulieAStephens.com

CHAPTER 4

TRANSFORMING EDUCATION THROUGH BANK

BY KELLEY TENNY

"The function of education is to teach one to think intensively and to think critically. Intelligence plus character—that is the goal of true education."

— Martin Luther King Jr.

How many teachers have struggled to connect with every student in their classroom? It's easy for them to feel overwhelmed by the diverse needs and behaviors of their students. Even if you have never taught, consider your own experience in education. Did you ever feel disconnected from your teachers? Did you feel like they didn't understand you or maybe, more accurately, misunderstood you? Perhaps there was a disconnect in the way they taught, leaving you to feel you were dumb or unable to learn.

How would your educational experience have changed if you had teachers throughout your years who made you feel seen, understood, and heard? Like you really mattered.

Imagine a classroom where every interaction is impactful, where every student feels understood and valued. This isn't just a dream; it's a reality made possible through the BANK methodology.

BEFORE BANK: UNDERSTANDING THE CHALLENGES OF DIVERSE STUDENT PERSONALITIES

Managing the broad spectrum of student personalities was often challenging in my fifteen years of teaching before discovering the BANK methodology. The diverse personalities made classroom management more demanding and significantly affected how I taught and how students learned.

Many people don't understand that in one classroom, a teacher deals with not only different learning styles and academic levels—what many educational systems focus on during teaching trainings—but they also deal with different personality types. I didn't truly understand personality types before BANK.

Let me share some examples. (Names have been changed to protect the privacy of my past students.)

Jamie the Nurturer: Jamie was always the last to leave the classroom. Whether it was tidying up the space without being asked or lingering behind to discuss the day's lessons, Jamie's nurturing nature meant she was always ready to assist and seek deeper connections. Her empathy was palpable, but this also meant she often needed more emotional support and affirmation than others, something I wasn't always prepared to give adequately. Jamie loved to come into class before school, wanted to eat lunch with me, or lingered after school, even though I was trying to get out the door. On days when I was tired (which was most), this was challenging and made me feel suffocated.

Marco the Action Taker: Marco was a whirlwind of energy. His hand shot up before questions were fully posed, and he often began tasks before instructions were completely given. His impatience led to frequent mistakes, and he struggled with projects requiring detailed attention or prolonged focus. Marco's drive for immediate results was commendable, but without the right direction, his efforts were often misdirected, leading to frustration on both ends.

Tomas the Inquisitive: Tomas' curiosity knew no bounds. He questioned everything, which, while intellectually stimulating, often derailed lesson plans and extended beyond the scope of the subject matter. His need to explore concepts in depth was a strength, but it sometimes exhausted his peers and posed a challenge in maintaining the flow of lessons. From a teacher's perspective, Tomas was always trying to steer the conversation into some tangent, ultimately wasting time.

Elisa the Perfectionist: Elisa was obsessed about details. She needed explicit instructions and clear expectations to feel secure. Any ambiguity in assignments caused her significant stress, and she was often overly concerned about her grades. Her perfectionism drove her to excel, but it also hindered her ability to adapt to flexible teaching methods or content that didn't follow a strict structure. Elisa was rigid and anxious. Her concern over minute details was exhausting and took time away from the other students.

Each day felt like navigating a minefield of competing needs. Jamie needed emotional validation, Marco sought constant engagement, Tomas required intellectual satisfaction, and Elisa sought structured clarity. My traditional teaching methods often fell short of addressing these needs effectively, leading to a classroom environment where not every student could find their footing. Without understanding the underlying causes of their behaviors, my responses sometimes veered toward frustration, affecting how I connected with and supported my students. I felt inadequate at times, and I know my students felt disconnected and misunderstood.

These challenges underscored a significant gap in my teaching approach—I lacked a systematic way to cater to each student's intrinsic motivations and personality. This lack impacted the students' learning experiences and my effectiveness as an educator. The realization that I was not reaching each student as effectively as I could deeply influenced my subsequent embrace of the BANK methodology, which promised a more tailored and empathetic approach to education.

DISCOVERING BANK: A TURNING POINT IN MY TEACHING CAREER

Discovering the BANK methodology fundamentally altered my understanding of student behaviors and revolutionized my teaching strategies. I gained insights into each student's intrinsic needs and motivations. For instance, I learned to channel Jamie's Blueprint and Nurturing traits into structured classroom roles and Marco's Action-oriented impulsivity into leadership tasks that require immediate engagement. I directed Tomas' Knowledge-driven curiosity toward research projects to satisfy his thirst for deep understanding, while providing Elliot, another Blueprint, with clear rubrics and explicit instructions to ease his anxiety over ambiguity. This personalized approach not only enhanced academic performance but also fostered a supportive and productive classroom environment. By applying BANK, I was able to truly connect with each student, making teaching not only more effective but also more fulfilling.

This deeper understanding through BANK transformed the classroom dynamics, allowing each student to thrive and helping me to become a more effective and empathetic educator. The methodology's focus on aligning educational strategies with individual personality types proved to be a powerful tool for enhancing both student engagement and educational outcomes.

Adopting the BANK methodology has not only revolutionized my teaching effectiveness but also deepened my relationships with my students. While I am no longer in the K-12 public school system, I have been able to use it at the university level with my college students. By understanding and applying the principles of BANK, I've been able to foster a learning environment where students are not just taught but are engaged in a manner that resonates deeply with their personal and emotional needs.

INTEGRATING BANK: STRATEGIES AND SUCCESSES

With BANK, my lesson planning evolved. I began to incorporate strategies that catered to each personality type:

- **Blueprints** needed structure and clarity, so I provided detailed rubrics and clear expectations.
- **Actions** were engaged through competitive games and active learning segments.
- **Nurturers** thrived in group discussions and peer collaborations.
- **Knowledges** delved into research projects and data analysis exercises.

This targeted approach not only reduced classroom friction but also elevated engagement and academic performance. Students felt seen and understood, and teaching became more joyful and effective.

Suddenly, I had a toolkit that allowed me to see beneath the surface of my students' actions and tailor my interactions to resonate with each type effectively. This approach has been instrumental in teaching them to think intensively and critically, as Martin Luther King Jr. envisioned as the goal of true education.

IMPACT AND OUTCOMES: ENHANCING TEACHING AND FOSTERING DEEPER CONNECTIONS

BUILDING TRUST AND CONFIDENCE

One of the most significant results of integrating the BANK methodology is the increased trust and confidence my students place in both the learning process and in me as an educator. By aligning my teaching strategies with their personality types, students are more responsive and engaged. For instance, Blueprint students appreciate clear expectations and detailed agendas, which help them focus and think critically about the content, while Action students thrive in dynamic, debate-driven environments that stimulate intensive thinking and quick decision-making.

PERSONALIZED SUPPORT

Furthermore, the BANK methodology has empowered me to offer more personalized support, enhancing each student's ability to develop both their intelligence and their character. Nurturing students, for example, are provided with a supportive and empathetic learning environment, allowing them to develop confidence and empathy—key aspects of character. Knowledge students who seek deep understanding are encouraged to engage in complex problem-solving tasks, boosting their critical thinking skills and academic prowess.

REFLECTING ON PAST TEACHING EXPERIENCES

Reflecting on my earlier years as a middle school teacher, I recognize countless moments where I could have made a significant difference in my students' educational journeys had I possessed the insights provided by BANK. This realization, though painful, has fueled my commitment to applying this methodology in my current role as a college professor. The pain of past missed opportunities drives me to ensure that my current students receive an education that truly balances the development of both intellect and character.

A NEW CHAPTER IN EDUCATION

Now, empowered with the tools provided by BANK, I am not just imparting knowledge but am actively participating in shaping well-rounded individuals who excel intellectually and possess strong character. It is incredibly rewarding to witness how personalized educational approaches foster not only academic success but also significant personal growth among my students.

The transformation extends beyond the classroom—students leave my courses not just better educated but also more self-aware and equipped to face the world with resilience and empathy. They carry this enriched character and enhanced intellectual capacity into their future endeavors, prepared to make thoughtful, informed decisions and to contribute meaningfully to society.

This benefit was evident in a recent humanitarian trip to South Africa, where I was privileged enough to go alongside the founders of Codebreaker Technologies and embark on the very first teaching event on behalf of the Codebreaker Foundation and their #MakeKidsMatter movement. Moving through three different schools, the students we taught came from underprivileged schools in the Cape Town area, facing adversities such as poverty and parentless homes. The students, from primary grades through high school, were introduced to this life-changing tool, BANK, which not only enhanced their learning but also their personal growth.

By learning and applying the BANK methodology, these students gained a deeper understanding of themselves and others. They will now be able to identify and communicate their feelings more effectively, recognize the perspectives of others, and build stronger relationships. This newfound knowledge will be especially crucial for students with hard challenges because it equips them with the tools to navigate their complex social environments with empathy and resilience.

The impact was visibly heartwarming and profoundly gratifying. These bright, hopeful students, filled with gratitude, demonstrated the unshakable potential within each young dreamer. As they integrated the BANK methodology, they also learned to apply these insights to understand their own behaviors and motivations better, and that of their peers and family members, which is critical in fostering self-awareness and emotional well-being.

This experience underscored the significant role educators play in supporting the holistic development of students. The smiles, love, and boundless dreams of these children reaffirmed my commitment to this journey. As an educator, it was a dream come true to witness their growth and know that the tools we shared will serve them for a lifetime.

Together, we are not just educating minds; we are nurturing hearts and empowering young individuals to face the world with confidence, resilience, and a profound sense of self.

Students will leave the classroom not only better educated but also better prepared to face life's challenges.

They carry forward the enriched character and enhanced intellectual capacity into their future endeavors, ready to make thoughtful, informed decisions and to contribute meaningfully to society. Moments like these, filled with genuine connections and transformative experiences, are what make the journey truly rewarding and a testament to the lasting impact of tailored education.

I've realized the profound truth in Martin Luther King Jr.'s words. True education is indeed about nurturing both intelligence and character, and through BANK, I am able to contribute to this noble goal more effectively than ever before.

YOUR TURN

As you reflect on this chapter, think about the diverse personalities you interact with daily. How could understanding and adapting to these personalities change your approach?

EXERCISE

1. Identify someone in your life who fits each BANK type. Consider how you might improve your interactions based on their personality.
2. Reflect on a situation where miscommunication occurred. How could BANK principles have altered the outcome?

SUMMARY AND CHALLENGE

Throughout this chapter, we've explored how the BANK. methodology not only transforms academic environments but also deeply enriches the lives of students, particularly those facing considerable socio-economic challenges. By integrating this powerful tool into education, we help students develop crucial skills such as empathy, resilience, and self-awareness, which are fundamental in navigating life's complexities.

As educators (which we all are), our mission extends beyond the classroom; it is about shaping the future one student at a time. We have seen how applying the BANK methodology can turn potential into excellence, helping students understand themselves better and communicate more effectively with the world around them.

CHALLENGE TO READERS

Now, I challenge you, the reader, to take the insights from this chapter and apply them in your own spheres of influence—whether you are a teacher, a parent, a mentor, or a community leader. I challenge you to apply one BANK principle this week in your interactions with those around you. Consider the next person who comes to you with a question or a problem and looks to you to share your wisdom and brilliance with them. Observe the changes and embrace the potential of truly personalized communication.

Remember that every small step we take to understand and communicate better can lead to significant changes in someone's life. By embracing the principles of BANK, we not only enhance our own lives but also empower others to build a more compassionate, understanding world. Let's continue to crack codes and build bridges, for it is through our concerted efforts that we can turn individual success stories into a collective victory for humanity.

KELLEY TENNY | BKAN

Kelley Tenny is a lifelong learner, educator, and curriculum expert course strategist. Kelley has been teaching for more than twenty years, empowering others through education. Her desire to empower even more led to the start of Kelley's company, Teach Your Brilliance™. She offers curriculum creation and micro-course strategy services to creators, influencers, and experts who are looking to turn their wisdom into wealth. Her newest love is teaching entrepreneurs about harnessing the power of AI. This passion for harnessing AI for greater positive impact brought her to Codebreaker Technologies, where she is currently Vice President.

Author's Website: TeachYourBrilliance.com

CHAPTER 5
DARING TO DO NURSING DIFFERENTLY

BY TERESA SANDERSON

> "If not me, then who? If not now, then when?"
>
> — Rabbi Hillel

Why are 33 percent of new nurses leaving the profession within their first two years? Why are seasoned nurses burning out and looking to leave the bedside? What would a stay in the hospital be like if there were no nurses?

My name is Teresa, and I've been a registered nurse for more than thirty years. There's a saying in nursing that

"Nurses eat their young." This saying describes the toxic culture pervasive in the nursing profession. It is not uncommon for new graduate nurses and nurses working in new areas to be met with disrespect, hostility, incivility, and even bullying. I experienced this incivility among nurses in the workplace for the very first time as a nursing student. Sadly, it continues even today.

As a new nurse, I had no training in emotionally intelligent communication; I don't think it was even a recognized term then. I had no knowledge of personality science and assessments, and no understanding of the value they bring to the workplace. All I knew was that being a new nurse was really hard.

Our nurse managers would call the nurses who showed up with hostility and incivility "strong personalities." This meant that leadership understood these behaviors were less than professional—and it was clear that nursing leaders were either unwilling or unable to do anything about it. The nurses eat their young culture has continued unchecked for decades because of staffing shortages and a lack of nursing leadership development.

WHY DO NURSES EAT THEIR YOUNG?

Asking this question is almost like asking: Which came first? The chicken or the egg?

Before I graduated from nursing school thirty years ago, we were talking about the nursing shortage. In my first job as a nurse, there were always ample opportunities to work overtime, get paid double time, and so on. Clearly, the nursing shortage is nothing new.

What happens with chronic nurse staffing shortages, though, is the working nurses get tired. Healthcare administration has long since solved the short-staffing problem by incentivizing overtime pay and other financial bonuses. This approach has consistently resulted in nurses burning themselves out by working too much.

So, experienced nurses are tired, stressed, and anxious. Working extra shifts to cover staffing needs leads to exhaustion, burnout, and less-than-optimal mental health. In this compromised state, seasoned nurses may meet new graduate nurses with an attitude of impatience and intolerance.

New nurses may be met with unprofessional behaviors like eye-rolling, heavy sighing, and apathy. They may feel they have no support or they are a burden. They may be unable to get their questions answered. And all the while, they are caring for patients.

Nurses get promoted to leadership roles simply because, within six months of being hired, they have the most tenure. New nursing leaders typically get no leadership training and have no understanding of how to lead a team.

Nursing leadership is also a paradox. In other professions, a promotion to leadership means perks, like a longer lunch, half-days on Friday, and so on. Nursing leaders are typically required to be available and accountable for all care delivered in their absence.

Clearly, no simple answer exists to the question: Why do nurses eat their young? Toxic nursing culture is a symptom of systemic healthcare issues that will require engagement, education, commitment, and tools to resolve.

THE DAY MY LIFE CHANGED

My career in nursing has taken many paths, including leadership and entrepreneurship. I started a home business in 2020 and struggled to create income. It seemed no matter what I did, I could not sell my products and services.

In September 2021, Cheri Tree presented a live webinar called "Why They Buy" for one of my business groups. I registered and was excited to attend. What attracted me the most about this webinar was that it mentioned a system that I could use to increase my income and impact by up to 300 percent. For a struggling nurse entrepreneur desperate to find answers and a proven method that would work, I was all in to learn about it.

That day my life changed. I learned about the BANK methodology and the simple ninety-second personality assessment that would allow me to influence my potential client's decision to buy from me. As Cheri Tree told her story and how she found massive success after living in a storage unit and overcoming some major business obstacles, I felt I could relate to her experience. But the biggest thing I learned was that sales is not an art—it is a science. As a nurse, I knew I could learn science.

As I learned more about BANK, I began to use it daily in my business. I incorporated the personality assessment into my appointment scheduling process. By doing this, my potential clients would be able to book an appointment with me and crack their personality code before we met. Each appointment would be based on the unique personality and values of the potential client in front of me. I began to run all email and text messages through the Codebreaker Decoder to determine the personality code of each sender. I practiced responding in code by using the Decoder as well so that I could learn to match my writing to the personality code of my contact.

Through the use of the BANK methodology, I was able to do far more than close sales. I was able to develop strong relationships with clients who became dear friends. Steady income began to flow into my business, and I was positively impacting my clients' lives.

THE NURSES FEED THEIR YOUNG MOVEMENT

In 2022, I decided to take another leap and go deeper into the BANK methodology. The more I understood it, the more I believed it would be helpful to nurses and nursing leaders. I saw enormous potential for using BANK to transform nursing culture.

I believed this ninety-second, values-based personality assessment could be a key to transforming nursing culture. I envisioned a transformation from Nurses Eat Their Young to Nurses Feed Their Young. I also started the Nurses Feed Their Young Movement, a global movement dedicated to transforming nursing culture and work environment. Our mission is to cultivate nursing leaders, innovate nursing continuing education, and develop nurse entrepreneurs.

I have a deep desire in my heart to leave the nursing profession better than I found it. Collectively, nurses are ready for change. And healthcare is changing. Right now. For better or worse. Nurses must be prepared to communicate clearly with emotional intelligence so we can advocate for ourselves and our profession.

The more I learned about the BANK methodology, the more I understood how transferable it could be to nursing. My mind began to race with ideas about how it could transform so many aspects of nursing, including hiring, recruitment, retention, employee satisfaction, patient experience, patient outcomes, nursing culture, nursing school curriculum, and so much more! These ideas drove me to start the Nurses Feed Their Young Movement and begin doing the work of creating positive change. The following is a brief summary of my personal ideas of how BANK can be applied in three areas of nursing. While many more applications are possible, I will confine this discussion to three.

APPLICATION OF BANK FOR NURSING LEADERS

Nursing leaders typically get little training in how to lead, influence, and motivate a team. They get no training on handling patient and family complaints or de-escalating emotionally volatile situations. The BANK methodology provides a simple framework for:

- Communicating to gain buy-in for change implementation
- Increasing engagement and participation in unit meetings
- Communicating with empathy
- Hiring the right nurse for the right role
- Fostering a culture of respect and kindness
- Communicating with intent to de-escalate emotionally volatile situations and complaints

APPLICATIONS OF BANK FOR NURSES

Nurses can make use of BANK to facilitate improved communication:

- Among nurses
- When onboarding new nurses
- With physicians and ancillary team members
- With patients and families
- With leadership to clearly make their needs known and advocate for themselves and the entire profession
- Communicating with intent to de-escalate emotionally volatile situations and complaints

As an experienced nursing leader, I believe it is every nurse's job to handle patient complaints and be able to de-escalate emotionally volatile situations. These tasks typically get immediately referred to the charge nurse or unit manager for resolution. For this reason, nursing leaders may feel their entire day is spent putting out fires with little time left over to plan and prepare for a better future on the unit.

In addition to training nursing leaders and seasoned nurses in BANK, I highly recommend that nursing students receive education in emotional intelligence and the BANK methodology as part of their curriculum. To create sustainable change for the future of the nursing profession, we must begin with our new nurses-in-training.

BANK FOR PATIENT EDUCATION AND THERAPEUTIC COMMUNICATION

Nurses who know me have heard me say that nothing new has happened in the field of therapeutic communication for decades. Nurses are tasked with educating patients about their disease process, treatment options, medications, risks, and benefits. As a nurse with more than thirty years of experience, I can attest that nurses provide patient education with a one-size-fits-all approach. We honestly have never had a clear understanding that each individual's unique personality and value set will cause their preferred educational approach to vary. Further, each will have different motivations for adhering to care and treatment.

With the BANK methodology, we can now easily customize patient education based on what the patient values most. This will allow us to develop an Individualized Communication Plan for each patient so we can elevate health-related communication. When we do this, we will have a better understanding of each patient's values and motivations so we can cater our messaging to their needs.

Simply put, we cannot deliver a message to a Spanish-speaking person in English and expect them to understand. The same is true for communication based on different personality types. When we communicate with and teach each patient according to their BANKCODE, they can easily understand what's in it for them when they adhere to care and treatment.

MY VISION FOR BANK IN HEALTHCARE

I envision a world where every electronic medical record contains the patient's BANKCODE. I see physicians entering patient rooms and communicating with them based on their code. I see patients feeling seen and heard.

I see the flow of healthcare working more smoothly because the culture is positive, caring, and kind within organizations. There is no more "Nurses eat their young." The toxic and tired culture of nursing's past has been left behind and replaced with a culture of Nurses Feed Their Young.

MAKING NURSES MATTER

As a nursing leader, I have a deep understanding of the issues surrounding the nurse staffing shortage. One of the most common comments made by nurses today is that they do not feel valued.

Other pressing issues among nurses include:

- Thirty-three percent of new graduate nurses leave the profession within their first two years
- Forty percent of nurses cite lack of leadership as a source of dissatisfaction
- Eight-six percent of nurses report they have left a position because of toxic nursing culture
- One-hundred percent staff turnover in hospitals in just five years
- Increased threat of litigation for errors
- Lack of support from employers

The BANK methodology is a powerful tool that can be used to enhance communication in healthcare. Profoundly simple and quick to use, it is the key to transforming nursing culture and making nurses matter.

In a time when nurse staffing shortages are peaking, it is time to put an end to "Nurses eat their young" and flip the script to "Nurses feed their young." The sustainability of the nursing workforce depends on it.

WHAT I LEARNED

Learning the BANK methodology opened my eyes to the beauty of each personality type. My main takeaway has been Cheri Tree's statement, "It's not personal. It's personality." I understand now that those nurses with "strong" personalities have never had access to a tool like BANK. The other key concept I learned was that because I have been trained, I am the one who should respond appropriately in all situations using BANK and emotional intelligence.

My view of the world and all of the people in it has changed. I have a heart of compassion for and a great appreciation for all of the codes. A strong nursing team benefits from full integration of all of the codes. No code is better than another; they are truly better together.

EXERCISE

These exercises can be used by readers from any profession. If you are not a nurse, simply remove the nursing terms.

1. Reflect on a time when you felt supported and valued in your nursing career. What were the specific actions or words that made you feel this way? How did this experience affect your work and relationships with your colleagues and patients?
2. Imagine a work environment where respect, empathy, and kindness are at the core of every interaction. How would this change your daily experience as a nurse? What steps can you take to contribute to creating this kind of environment in your own workplace?
3. Consider the challenges faced by new nurses entering the profession. What kind of mentorship or support

system would you like to see established to help them thrive? How can you personally take part in fostering a culture of growth and positivity for these new nurses?

THREE TIPS FOR NURSES TO DARE TO DO NURSING DIFFERENTLY

1. Invest in your personal development by enhancing your emotional intelligence. This investment includes understanding and managing your own emotions as well as recognizing and influencing the emotions of others. Building these skills can lead to more effective communication, improved team dynamics, and better leadership outcomes.

2. Use personality assessments to gain better insights into your colleagues and clients' values and motivations. By understanding different personality types, you can tailor your approach to communication, teamwork, and customer service, leading to more meaningful and effective interactions.

3. Advocate for a work environment where mutual respect and support are paramount. Encourage open dialogue, provide constructive feedback, and recognize the contributions of your team members. By creating a nurturing and inclusive culture, you can enhance job satisfaction and reduce turnover.

SUMMARY

I started using the BANK methodology as a means of increasing my sales and income. What I found was a system that is needed by nursing and all of healthcare. While nursing leaders may not be selling products, they are selling change, policies, procedures, and more to their teams and their patients. Nursing leaders must be able to lead and communicate with influence. When nursing leaders have an understanding of BANK, they can speak in the code of their team members so the team feels seen, heard, and valued. Nurses who feel valued are more likely to stay in their roles.

Nursing has been suffering from chronic staffing shortages for decades. It's time to clean up the culture and set the stage for a positive future for the profession. I challenge you to:

1. **Dare to buck the status quo.** Dare to question and disrupt the toxic cultural norms in your workplace. Advocate for systemic changes that foster a supportive and collaborative environment, ensuring that no new professional feels alone or unsupported.
2. **Lead with empathy.** Be the leader who leads with kindness and empathy. Show others how leadership rooted in understanding and compassion can dramatically transform workplace morale and performance.
3. **Dare to do nursing differently!** Commit to being an innovator. Experiment with new methodologies and strategies to revolutionize communication and teamwork. Dare to do nursing differently!

TERESA SANDERSON | BNKA

A veteran RN and nursing leader with three decades of experience, Teresa Sanderson leads with authenticity and the heart of a servant. She believes nursing leadership is responsible for creating a culture and environment where nurses can succeed and practice with excellence. Teresa founded the Nurses Feed Their Young Movement to eradicate the toxic "Nurses eat their young" culture.

A Certified and Licensed BANK Trainer and Coach, Teresa trains healthcare organizations, nursing leaders, and nurses on emotional intelligence, applications of personality science to nursing, and recruitment and retention strategies. Sanderson is an author, speaker, nurse entrepreneur, and homesteader. She resides on a homestead in rural Northeast Kansas with her husband, livestock, and honeybees.

Author's Website: Links.NursesFeedTheirYoung.com

ACTION

CHAPTER 6

YOUR KEY TO CONNECTION

BY ANNE LESPERANCE

"Get along"

— Dedicated to Anita Lesperance, my wise, loving, funny, and extremely kind Mom. (A Nurturing-Blueprint)

Do you experience deep communication struggles within your closest relationships and agonize over why that is? Perhaps you easily get frustrated and agitated with them. Or you feel they are repeatedly trying to annoy you or deliberately make your life difficult or impossible?

Do you yearn to finally achieve the financial success you've been working so hard for and that you deserve for yourself and your family?

Ever worry about one of your children not seeming to fit in with the rest of your family, and not knowing what to do about it?

Perhaps you end relationships due to too much conflict and wonder if you'll ever meet "The One," the love of your life.

THE LESSON I LEARNED FROM MY MOM

I didn't appreciate or register the wisdom and loving nature in my mom's words when I was young. When my (only) sister and I disagreed or fought, we would always hear a shout from my mom: "Get along!"

My sweet mama wanted us to *get along* because there was just the two of us, and she felt we should! She wanted us both to grow up and be financially okay, happy, and to get along with people, especially with each other. That's the precursor to what I'm about to share about becoming so passionate about improving my communication and connection with others, and then wanting to support the world in doing the same.

THE HARD DAYS, WHEN COMMUNICATION WENT SIDEWAYS

In a handful of years pre-2015, my life was a mess. I was barely getting by, working a few side gigs, doing part-time retail work, etc.

Life wasn't always like that.... Life had been *really good*, but my partner, the love of my life, began changing, behaving like someone I didn't know.

We had never argued, and we got along extremely well. I had felt deeply loved and connected with a partner I also loved deeply, and with whom there was very little friction; we were very compatible, and we had great friends and community. We had kayaked to a cabin in northern Ontario and exchanged rings and vows. Our relationship and connection was pure bliss.

Then, something completely unexpected began to unfold. My partner's sudden mood swings, erratic driving, car accidents, and general nastiness really took their toll. I was stressed to the edges of my breaking point; I didn't know what was happening, and my life no longer made any sense. I felt like I must be going mad.

I buried my head into researching everything I could online, with three clues for me to work with:

- a dragging foot
- handwriting that had shifted from great penmanship to scribbles
- mood swings—volatility demonstrated by suddenly being uncharacteristically angry, insulting, and demeaning toward others, everyone, and me especially.

This research provided the unthinkable! The pieces began to fit together like a well-designed and cut puzzle, clearly revealing the bigger picture: a spelled-out two-letter word and diagnosis: M.S.

Not the Public Relations version of Multiple Sclerosis, but the deeper, darker, buried little secret that one discovers only by digging: that this disease often affects the frontal lobe of its victims and wreaks havoc with their relationships.

At least I now had a reason for the feelings of madness! I wasn't actually going insane.

With the decline in physical ability and Tourette's-like outbursts at work, we soon went from two employed adults down to one. Then I was also laid off due to an economic downturn. This resulted in my plunge into full-blown entrepreneurship while also being an (untrained and ill-prepared) caregiver.

On a subconscious level, I believe that time created a very deep need to learn about everything communication-related, as our communication skills had spiraled down from incredibly easy and good to despairingly horrible. It set the stage for what was to come.

MY PHOENIX RISING YEAR

I call 2015 my "phoenix year" because I rose anew from the ashes. It marked a new beginning—and it was challenging, to say the least. Unfortunately, my partner had become a "former partner" at this point and was in a care facility.

I was heartbroken, lonely, and determined to rebuild my life the best I could and start a new career in real estate. I had so much to learn!

Thankfully, I was learning from the best—my sister, who had been running a successful team for more than twenty-five years at that point. Lorraine mentored me for just under a year before I took the scary leap to commission-only sales!

Around that time, I stumbled upon a tool while attending the Real Estate Expo in Toronto. This tool spoke to that subconscious desire to better understand communication and to better communicate with my fellow humans—to learn how to connect on a much deeper level.

I was planning to attend another real estate breakout session, but as luck (or the *Universe*) would better choose for me, that class was full.

So, I raced to my next choice and was the second-to-last person permitted into the room, the room I was *meant* to be in!

Cheri Tree blew me away! I had goosebumps as I learned about what she came to share with us, the BANK methodology, and the priceless four little *magical* BANKCARDS that not only determine someone's buying behavior in about a minute but is also groundbreaking in improving personal relationships! I was ALL IN!

AFTER THE BANK INTRODUCTION: THE STRESS RESPONSE

In residential real estate, we see it all—new beginnings and endings, from the excitement of moving in together, getting a puppy or kitten, and having babies, to separation, downsizing, and the loss of a beloved (or not-so-beloved) partner/spouse. My life experience and communication tools have pretty much equipped me to support it all. It's become my superpower, what I love most, supporting people in life's challenges and beautiful moments.

It's never just a transaction, another *deal*. It's usually the largest investment people make in their life; no matter the reason for a change, there will be stress. Guaranteed.

To best support that person, it's imperative I know how that stress will show up in their interactions with me as their safe person, the person who holds space for their emotions, their humanity, and as their professional REALTOR®.

I have to be prepared to support them in times when there are no offers, and they *have* to sell, or when they are selling the family home stacked to the ceiling with all their belongings, and they have health challenges or no family to assist them. Or perhaps the buyers insist on including one of the new prized possessions, like the chef-inspired BBQ, the big screen TV and surround sound, the riding lawn mower or snowblower that they require at their next place and has been intentionally excluded in the listing! Sparks can fly!

Stress can bring out the worst in people, as well as the inability to make a decision or to do what needs to be done, and as real estate professionals, it's part of our role to navigate and manage client stress. So, it's critical to know their stress response so we can fully serve them!

That is one of the greatest gifts of the BANK methodology that I was blessed to discover in that first full year of real estate! And this is how I approached prospective clients to unlock their values, and their stress position:

Early on in our meeting, I would pull out two sets of the magical BANK value cards, offer them to the clients, and speak the following magical words or script:

"I'm not your regular REALTOR®; I do things a little differently. Do me a favor, look over the information on these cards, and sort the cards in the order that is most like you, or most important to you, to least like you, or important to you. This will save us both some time, and will allow me to serve you better."

I would then smile, nod, and comment on some of the challenges that I saw the cards reveal for the couple. It would be like a mini-intuitive reading of who the couple were, and it would always intrigue them and build instant rapport. I learned so much about the couple's dynamics through this two-minute exercise! And it was fun! Getting instant insights into who people were and how they preferred me to treat them was absolutely priceless and made my work so much more satisfying. And, of course, they signed the paperwork to work with me! I had become the *Connection Magician!*

HOW BANK WORKED FOR ME IN MY WORK: THE PERSONALITY TYPES

Generally, we get along best and want to do business with people who are like us. We most easily get to work with people who like and trust us. People with similar codes (values) to our own. However, that is only about 25 percent of the people we meet. If we learn about the other personality types and communicate with them in a way that meets their needs, we can drastically improve our sales and serve more people at a much higher level.

Here are a few pointers on each Type:

The Blueprint Type: Be professional and on time, meaning about five minutes early. Clearly share your value, keep your paperwork organized, don't skip pages of your presentation, and include your credentials on email signatures, marketing material, etc.

The Action Type: Be fun, dress stylishly, have a sense of humor, and treat them like VIPs. They generally trust referrals from their people unless you give them a reason not to. They go with their gut about you; don't over-sell, over-explain, or generally over-talk. Let *them* talk, and give them the Coles Notes version of market conditions and what you will do for them. Read their body language and trial close. FOMO (Fear of Missing Out) is real for them.

The Nurturing Type: Kind and generous, and they love authentic connection and hugs, to chat, and to contribute to their community. Stay in touch with and involve them in your cause(s). You must demonstrate high morality and ethical behavior to stay in good standing. If crossed or disappointed, they can completely walk away.

The Knowledge Type: Smart, under-appreciated, often underpaid, have a lot to say, and don't like to be wrong, so don't challenge them. They want all the stats, comparisons, and pertinent info to make informed decisions, and they like to think it over.

Children can be the most vulnerable, feeling the most left out and misunderstood, and needing more support and connection with other intelligent children their age. If you deeply connect with this type, they will want to share all their fascinating expertise and research with you, often at the cost of being late for your next appointment.

The Reward

I have always had a certain intuition about people. Yet, in retrospect, I realize that before having this training, I could easily misread them, say something that didn't sit well, and lose the opportunity to work with them altogether. I was inadvertently affecting my conversion rate and ability to serve people by hitting what is known as tripwires—actions or words spoken that get you a NO!

So, I pretty much started to code all my clients so I would always know whom I was dealing with, how to best connect with them, what their behavior would be when they became stressed, and earn as much commission and referral business as I could.

And the reward? In a region where it is common for REALTORS® to complete an average of four deals in a given year, I completed eighty-four transactions in my first year without the aid of an assistant. That resulted from the power of BANK, my real estate mentoring, and my commitment to turning my life around.

I made a very sweet six-figure income for the first time in my life, and I spent the following years learning how to continue making a six-figure income and creating more balance, more time with my family, and some time to travel and replenish my soul.

THE LIFE BALANCE YEARS: COACHING AHA

Losing the love of my life was a very traumatic time. I eventually hired a life coach to help me work through what my new life could look like. My most transformational takeaway came when he asked me one simple question:

"Who says you only get one love of your life?"

Mic drop.... So simple and so profound, completely blowing open the doors of what I thought possible!

So, I mourned. I dared to hope.... In time, I decided to give it a go. But I was a busy REALTOR®, and I wasn't going to waste my time getting to know someone who would prove to be incompatible with me.

So, I used what I knew to be incredibly effective in my real estate career...my absolutely priceless and magical BANK-CARDS! And I knew I wanted compatibility. I wanted a partner who was kind, spontaneous, and fun, as well as someone who was an entrepreneur, authentic, into personal growth, ethical, and committed to contributing to the world. I also wanted someone who was flexible, stimulating, and exciting. No "opposites attract" business for me, thank you very much!

I pulled out the BANKCARDS early on to see if we'd have a long-lasting connection and compatibility if we pursued a relationship. I discovered we almost had identical codes! We were a great match! ANKB meets NAKB!

Many years later, we happily live in our home together, co-creating, constantly growing together, and learning how to communicate best and support each other and the world. We both speak the language of BANK; we code people in movies and people at the grocery store, always speaking the language that helped bring us together and that unifies all people once they invest in their relationships and learn what the codes represent.

It's so much *fun!*

THEN TO NOW

So, it began with me, with my desire to change my life, grow, increase my income, and get my life on track again. I had the best success of my business life. And now? It continues with a deep desire to help others positively impact their business and personal lives, to have great financial success resulting in freedom of choice, and to experience the best love and family life possible!

It all comes down to connection. How you connect with your clients, how you connect with your partner and your family.

WHAT I LEARNED THROUGH MY LIFE EXPERIENCES

If someone you care about has a sudden change in behavior, assess it ASAP. It may be medical.

We get a second chance if we take one. Be kind to yourself and live fully (at any age).

It's never too late to reinvent yourself and live your best life, unless you give up trying.

What I learned by becoming a Certified and Licensed BANK Trainer and Coach:

- *Only* the BANK methodology tells you someone's *buying* and *stress* behaviors and your *compatibility* within ninety seconds.
- Tripwires and Triggers are critical information to know.
- Don't guess! Code everyone you know and meet in person or virtually and learn to apply the methodology! (Carry the BANKCARDS everywhere you go). It's a language, a way to learn how people want to be treated.
- How to develop a deeper understanding and compassion for other codes; even opposite codes—especially in the workplace so that you can offset each other's challenges.

- How to better connect with your family and your love and *stay in love*.

EXERCISE

At Work:

- Whom do you most clash with at work?
- Why do you think that is?
- Do you know their code?
- Do you know *yours*?
- What does their unique personality type add to the work environment?

Your Financial Success:

- Are you where you'd like to be financially?
- Would you say you're in sales?
- How would your life change if you could significantly *increase* your conversion rate (By 10, 20, 30, 50+ percent)?
- What would be the benefit of coding all your co-workers, clients, service providers, and collaborators?

Personal Relationships:

- What personal relationship(s) would you like to improve?
- What would you say is the issue?
- What do you think *they* would say the issue is?
- Are you *committed to changing* this relationship?

- What are you *committed to doing and being* in order to *improve* this relationship? What would be the *benefit* of doing so?

The Love of Your Life:

- Are you searching for or open to finding the *Love of Your Life* (or the *next* Love of Your Life)?
- What *qualities and values* are you looking for in this partner?
- Would they have a *similar* code to you or the opposite?
- How would your *life look different/improve* if you found your ideal partner, the (next) *Love of Your Life*?

TIPS

- Get a set or half-a-dozen sets of the priceless BANKCARDS and keep them everywhere so you always have a set on hand.
- Supply your staff with BANKCARDS.
- Code everyone you meet in person or virtually; *never guess*! There's too much at stake.
- Memorize the script because it addresses all four codes. Make it a FUN game!
- Study what the codes mean; learn this methodology and about the Advanced BANKCODE Assessment.
- Involve your partner to enhance your relationship. Try coding people together playfully while watching movies, shopping, and waiting in line.

SUMMARY

I can't stress enough how fun and impactful this tool has been for me, and how I learned the hard way to code everyone you meet in person or virtually.

If you are looking for the Love of Your Life, don't waste your precious time with someone you ultimately will not be a fit with. Look for someone with the codes you are searching for. I recommend someone close to your code. If you try the "opposites attract" route, eventually, those things you found charming, exciting, and fun will annoy you to no end.

For example:

- Why do you always have to be late?
- You're so needy!
- I win! You lose!
- Why do you have to be such a know-it-all?
- I told you I love you; if anything changes, I'll let you know!

I challenge you to reach out to me, get some BANKCARDS, and invest in learning about yourself and your ideal partner. Then *Do the Thing: Use the BANKCARDS!*

If you are a professional salesperson looking to skyrocket your business results and experience the financial abundance and freedom you desire and deserve, I challenge you to embrace this tool and training throughout your office and invest in yourself to achieve the results you desire. You can impact your community and family in all the ways you've been only dreaming about. Or maybe you had given up on it because you weren't aware of this tool, *Your Key to Connection*.

Please don't keep struggling with any of your family members! I challenge you to learn their codes, learn about Tripwires and Trigger Points, and develop the skills to better *Get Along* now. Life is precious; relationships matter, and deep connection is the key to a fulfilling life.

ANNE LESPERANCE | ANKB

Anne Lesperance, a top 1 percent REALTOR and Certified and Licensed BANK Trainer and Coach, President's Club member, and author. She empowers real estate agents and other sales professionals with the BANK™ methodology, enabling authentic client connections and skyrocketing conversions through values-based engagement.

Anne strives to reduce the need to grind and hustle in the real estate industry by teaching REALTORS how to authentically connect with people according to their values.

Her work also strengthens team dynamics and connects real estate clients worldwide with professional agents who are true matches based on similar values.

Anne's passion extends beyond real estate—she advocates for deep interpersonal connections within couples and families, offering tools for real understanding and appreciation, and provides guidance in finding "the Love of Your Life." Through her work, Anne is dedicated to making people feel understood or "gotten," and like they truly matter.

Author's Website: YourKeyToConnection.com

CHAPTER 7

LOOK FOR THE OPPORTUNITY TO MAKE OTHERS MATTER

BY ERIK "MR. AWESOME" SWANSON

"The greatest gift that you can give to others is the gift of unconditional love and acceptance."

— Brian Tracy

Have you ever woken up and decided that today will be an awesome day? How would your life change if you embraced a positive attitude in every situation? Have you ever noticed how a single positive interaction can change the course of your day?

Imagine starting your morning with a smile, greeting the day with enthusiasm and gratitude. Your energy would be positively contagious, spreading joy to those around you. The barista at your favorite coffee shop might share an extra kind word, or a colleague might feel inspired by your optimism and, in turn, lift the mood of the entire office.

A positive outlook can positively influence your experiences, interactions, and environments. Challenges might still arise, but with a positive mindset, you approach them as opportunities for growth rather than setbacks. You might find yourself more resilient, creative in problem-solving, and connected to others.

Embracing positivity doesn't mean ignoring difficulties; it means choosing to find the good amid the bad, focusing on solutions rather than problems, and spreading kindness even when it's easier not to. It even means changing how you talk to yourself and others. Using positive language and intentional words with positive meanings can go a long way.

Positivity helps build a resilient mindset to weather life's storms with grace and optimism. By consistently practicing positivity, you cultivate a habit of looking for silver linings and opportunities for growth, no matter the circumstances. This approach enhances your well-being and influences those around you, creating a more supportive and uplifting environment.

Remember, positivity is a powerful tool that can transform your perspective and, ultimately, your life. It encourages you to celebrate small victories, appreciate the present moment, and remain hopeful for the future. So, take a deep breath, smile, and embrace the positive energy within and around you.

Over time, this shift in perspective can lead to a more fulfilling, enriched life filled with meaningful connections and a more profound sense of purpose.

MY STORY

Before I discovered the power of understanding people at a deeper level, I was navigating life and business with enthusiasm and eagerness to learn. I spent more than ten years learning from the best sales professional in the world, Brian Tracy. Brian served as my main mentor in life and business, and I call him my second father. Through his mentorship and guidance, I learned invaluable skills that reshaped my approach to both personal and professional relationships. One of the most profound lessons was the art of active listening. Brian emphasized that truly hearing and understanding another person is the cornerstone of meaningful connections and successful negotiations.

Brian taught me the importance of empathy and the ability to put myself in someone else's shoes and see the world from their perspective. This skill transformed my interactions, allowing me to build trust and rapport effortlessly. I began to see my clients, colleagues, and even strangers as people to connect more deeply with and saw them as individuals with their own stories, challenges, and aspirations.

Another crucial lesson was the power of clear and honest communication. Brian showed me that clarity in expressing our thoughts and intentions eliminates misunderstandings and fosters an environment of mutual respect and cooperation. He also stressed the importance of integrity, teaching me that being true to my word and values is the foundation of lasting success and fulfillment.

Brian's mentorship also taught me the significance of continuous learning and personal growth. He instilled in me a passion for self-improvement, encouraging me to read, attend seminars, and always seek ways to enhance my skills and knowledge. This relentless pursuit of excellence has driven my career, enabling me to adapt to changing circumstances and seize new opportunities.

In essence, Brian Tracy didn't just teach me how to sell; he taught me how to connect, communicate, and grow as a person. His influence has guided my journey and shaped me into who I am today.

As a speaker, coach, and the creator of Habitude Warrior, I pride myself on my ability to inspire and lead. But I've always had that nagging feeling that I could do more, connect more profoundly, and influence stronger. I often pondered how I could elevate my message and impact. One day, I learned that vulnerability and authenticity were the keys to unlocking this potential. It was then I decided to share not just my successes but also my struggles and failures.

I began incorporating personal stories into my speeches, stories of times when I had stumbled, made mistakes, and learned valuable lessons. My audience responded more passionately than ever before. They saw a reflection of their own challenges and found hope in my perseverance. Additionally, I made it a point to actively listen to those I coached, creating an environment where they felt truly heard and valued. This shift fostered deeper connections and allowed me to tailor my guidance to their unique needs.

As I continued to embrace this approach, my influence grew in depth. People began reaching out to share how my words had profoundly touched their lives. Being genuine and open could foster a powerful sense of community and support.

In the end, I learned the true essence of leadership lies in our ability to be real and relatable. By breaking down the walls of perfection, we allow others to see they can overcome obstacles and achieve greatness. In doing so, we create a ripple effect of inspiration and empowerment that extends far beyond our immediate reach.

Moreover, my role as a speaker and coach took on new dimensions. I began tailoring my messages to resonate more personally with my audience, leading to more impactful and transformative experiences. The feedback I received was overwhelmingly positive; people felt seen, heard, and understood in ways they hadn't before.

This journey of understanding wasn't without its challenges. It required a significant amount of introspection and a willingness to confront my own biases and preconceptions. But the rewards were immeasurable. I learned that true leadership and influence come not from asserting control but from fostering empathy and connection.

As I continue to grow and evolve, I remain committed to this path of understanding. It has enriched every aspect of my life and has become the cornerstone of my mission with all of my companies, including Habitude Warrior International and Speaker Hearts International. Through this journey, I've realized we unlock the potential for extraordinary relationships and unparalleled success when we truly understand one another.

I continued to use my experiences and teachings to pass on to my fellow members in my masterminds, which have members worldwide.

WHAT I LEARNED

From my experiences, I learned that understanding and adapting to different personality types isn't just a skill; it's a superpower. It allowed me to connect more deeply with everyone I interacted with. I learned that my natural tendency to take action and be nurturing could be balanced with structure and information.

One of the most significant lessons I learned was that making people matter begins with recognizing and honoring their unique values. When you speak their language, you create trust, respect, and a profound sense of understanding. This isn't just about improving sales or business relationships; it's about enriching every aspect of life. By appreciating diverse perspectives and approaches, I saw personal growth and strengthened my relationships. Empathy and active listening became my tools for navigating complex interactions, thereby transforming potential conflicts into opportunities for collaboration.

Moreover, I discovered that continuous self-reflection and learning are essential. By remaining open to feedback and willing to adjust my strategies, I improved my effectiveness and inspired others to embrace growth and change. This journey taught me the value of resilience and the importance of adapting to challenges.

Ultimately, these lessons have shaped me into a more compassionate, understanding, and effective individual, capable of positively impacting my personal and professional life.

All of that being said, I would be leaving out one of the most critical and crucial trainings I have gone through in my life if I didn't share this. Years back, I ended up meeting a super-dynamic individual one of my clients introduced me to. At that time, I had branched off from working under Brian Tracy and received his blessing to expand my wings into the world. That's what a true leader does—help others spread their wings and grow to new heights.

I created the super-popular and rewarding Habitude Warrior Conferences, which quickly grew to have a two-year waiting list for speakers to grace my stages. We are an all-

TED Talk event that still runs strong today across the nation and the world.

My client introduced me to someone she felt would be a great speaker on my platform and stages. She kept saying things like, "I'm not sure why, but I have a funny feeling the two of you are going to get along so well!"

My client was referring to the one and only Cheri Tree!

We set up a time to meet, and well, can I just say that Cheri is like a sister to me? We felt an instant connection and enthusiasm. Have you ever met someone you feel you have known for years and years yet have just met? Well, that was my and Cheri's experience.

Why do I mention this to you?

Because it wasn't just a coincidence that Cheri and I felt so comfortable with one another. It was our training in how to *make people matter*! It was a culmination of all of the teachings Cheri and I had learned from the past twenty-plus years to that point.

We have all heard that people love to work with people they know, like, and trust. Cheri and I knew this before we met. We had both learned the secrets and strategies for truly adopting these attributes into our daily habits. I call them "habitudes!" Habitudes are a cross between your habits and your attitudes.

When I found out Cheri had created the amazing BANK-CODE to truly learn how to identify other's true values and understand their emotional intelligence, I was hooked! I was so incredibly excited to find out a structured system existed to use not only in my personal experiences and relationships but also in my business relationships and agreements; I knew I needed this right away. Right then and there, a magical friendship for life was born. Thank you, Cheri, for creating this system to change the world for the better. I literally use my BANK methodology and training every single day to create, foster, and maintain amazing relationships throughout my life.

Today, I am one of the most well-known individuals in the world, and I have the most meaningful and long-lasting relationships in the speaking industry and publishing industry as a number-one bestseller. I owe a lot of this success to Cheri and the BANK methodology!

EXERCISES

High-Five Challenge: For the next week, commit to giving at least five high-fives to strangers daily. Observe how this simple gesture affects your mood and the mood of those around you. Reflect on any changes you notice in your interactions and overall energy levels. You may be surprised at the results! High-fiving strangers can break down social barriers, create moments of spontaneous joy, and foster a sense of community. As you extend your hand for a high-five, you might see smiles light up faces, feel an instant connection, and even spark conversations you wouldn't have had otherwise.

By the end of the week, you might find yourself feeling more positive, energized, and connected to the people around you. This simple act of kindness can make both your day and the days of others a little bit brighter. So, go ahead and start the High-Five Challenge—you might make someone's day and, in turn, make your own.

Compliment Campaign: Each day, give a genuine compliment to at least three different people, whether they are friends, family, colleagues, or strangers. Take note of their reactions and how these interactions make you feel. Consider how spreading positivity influences your environment and relationships. You might be surprised by the impact such a simple gesture can have. A heartfelt compliment can brighten someone's day, boost their confidence, and even strengthen your bond with them. People respond with smiles and gratitude; they may often pay the kindness forward, creating positivity.

As you continue with this campaign, reflect on your own feelings. You may find that offering compliments lifts others' spirits and enhances your mood and outlook. It fosters a sense of connection and empathy, reminding you of the good in those around you and yourself.

By consciously nurturing a culture of appreciation and kindness, you contribute to a more supportive and joyful environment. Over time, your relationships become more prosperous and meaningful, and your community becomes a more vibrant, positive place.

Sixty-Second Morning Mirror: Start your day with the sixty-second morning mirror exercise. Look in the mirror and affirm positive statements about yourself, such as "I am the best," "I am focused," and "I will succeed." Do this for a week, and journal any changes in your confidence and attitude. By consistently practicing this morning ritual, you may notice subtle yet profound shifts in your mindset. Speaking kindly to yourself can help rewire your brain to focus on your strengths and potential. Over time, these affirmations can become self-fulfilling prophecies, guiding you toward a more confident and positive outlook.

To enhance this practice further, consider combining it with deep breathing exercises or a short meditation session. This can help ground you and set a calm, intentional tone for the rest of your day. Reading your journal entries at the end of the week can provide valuable insights into your progress and highlight areas where you've grown.

Remember, everyone's journey to self-improvement is unique. Celebrate your small victories and be patient with yourself as you cultivate a habit of self-love and positivity. Embrace the power of your words, and watch how they transform your life, one morning at a time.

Thank You Notes: Begin or end each day by writing a thank you note to yourself. They can be minor or significant notes of gratitude for both personal and professional reasons. Reflect on how focusing on gratitude affects your mindset and interactions with others over time. Additionally, consider expanding this practice by writing thank you notes to others. They can be family members, friends, colleagues, or even strangers who have positively impacted your day. Expressing gratitude nurtures a positive mindset within yourself, strengthens your relationships, and fosters a supportive community around you.

As the days turn into weeks, you'll likely notice a shift in your overall outlook. Challenges may seem less daunting, and you might be more resilient and optimistic. Gratitude highlights the good in every situation, making it easier to navigate challenging times with grace and patience.

Furthermore, your interactions with others will likely become more harmonious and empathetic. When you consistently focus on the positives and make it a habit to express appreciation, you create an environment where others feel valued and understood. This can lead to deeper connections and a more fulfilling, joyful life.

So, take a moment each day to acknowledge the good in yourself and the world around you. Let gratitude be the lens through which you view your life, and watch as it transforms your days into a tapestry of cherished moments and meaningful connections.

PEA Every Day: You have to PEA (Have a Positive, Energetic, and Awesome Mindset) every day. Consciously choose to be positive, energetic, and awesome in your interactions. At the end of the week, reflect on how this approach has influenced your personal and professional life.

Take note of the subtle changes in your mood, productivity, and relationships. Did you find yourself more motivated and resilient in the face of challenges? Did your positive energy inspire and uplift those around you? You may have noticed increased collaboration and support from colleagues or a deeper connection with loved ones. Remember, cultivating a PEA mindset is not just about temporary changes; it's about building a sustainable habit that enhances overall well-being and success. Keep practicing, and soon, Positive, Energetic, and Awesome will become second nature.

Random Acts of Kindness: Perform at least one random act of kindness daily. It could be helping a colleague with a task, paying for someone's coffee, or simply holding the door open for someone. Reflect on how these acts of kindness make you feel and impact the recipients. Consider keeping a journal or writing notes to document your experiences with random acts of kindness.

Over time, you may notice patterns in your feelings and the reactions of those you help. This practice fosters a mindfulness habit and serves as a beautiful reminder of the positive impact you can have on the world around you.

Additionally, sharing your stories with friends or family can inspire them to engage in their acts of kindness. Creating a ripple effect, where one small act leads to another, helps build a more compassionate and connected community. Kindness is a powerful tool that can brighten someone's day and contribute to a more harmonious world.

STAYING AWESOME WITH THESE TIPS

Identify Your Values: Take time to understand your primary values. This self-awareness is the first step in making meaningful connections and making people matter and feel awesome. Knowing what you stand for will guide your interactions and decisions, whether integrity, compassion, creativity, or perseverance. Reflect on past experiences and consider what made you feel most fulfilled and aligned with your true self. Write these values down and revisit them often to ensure they remain at the forefront of your consciousness.

Practice Active Listening: Engage fully in conversations by listening more than you speak. Show genuine interest in others' thoughts and feelings, and respond thoughtfully. This will make the other person feel valued and help you build more profound, more authentic connections.

Be Authentic: Authenticity fosters trust and openness. Share your true self with others, including your strengths, weaknesses, dreams, and fears. People are more likely to connect with you on a meaningful level when they see the real you rather than a curated facade.

Show Empathy: Empathy is understanding and sharing another person's feelings. Put yourself in others' shoes and try to see the world from their perspective. This understanding can bridge gaps and build strong, compassionate relationships.

Communicate Clearly: Effective communication is key to any successful relationship. Be clear and concise in your messages, whether verbal or written. Avoid ambiguity and strive to express your thoughts and feelings honestly and respectfully.

Be Open to Feedback: Accepting constructive criticism and feedback can help you grow and improve your relationships. It shows that you value others' opinions and are committed to personal development.

Invest Time and Effort: Building meaningful connections requires time and effort. Make a conscious effort to nurture your relationships through regular communication, shared experiences, and acts of kindness. The more you invest in your relationships, the stronger and more meaningful they will become.

Continuous Learning: Keep learning about different communication styles and how they manifest in behavior and interactions.

Feedback Loop: Ask for feedback on your communication and be open to adjusting your approach.

By applying any of these techniques and steps, you can create a network of meaningful connections that enrich your life and the lives of those around you.

In a world where connections can feel fleeting and superficial, making people matter is more important than ever.

I challenge you to understand your values and apply this knowledge in your interactions. Doing so will enhance your relationships and empower others to feel seen and valued. Let's make people matter, one meaningful connection at a time. Remember to decide to be awesome!

ERIK SWANSON | ANKB

As an award-winning international keynote speaker and multiple-time number-one international best-selling author, Erik "Mr. Awesome" Swanson is in great demand worldwide! He speaks on average to more than one million people per year. Mr. Swanson has the honor of being invited to speak to many schools and universities around the world, including Harvard University. He is a recurring Faculty Member of CEO Space International and an Alumni Keynoter at Vistage Executive Coaching. Erik also received 2024's International Book Impact Award and the United States Presidential Lifetime Achievement Award presented by the White House in 2024 for his ongoing community service and philanthropy work. Erik's speeches can be found on Amazon Prime TV, and he joined the Ted Talk Family with his latest speech, "A Dose of Awesome."

Erik has created and developed the super-popular Habitude Warrior Conferences and Speaker Hearts Mastermind & Retreats. He is the Creator, Founder, and CEO of the Habitude Warrior Mastermind, Global Speakers Mastermind, and Cafe Mastermind.

Author's Website: FollowMrAwesome.com

CHAPTER 8
THE TIME IS NOW TO EMPOWER WOMEN
BY ESTHER WILDENBERG

> "The real voyage of discovery consists not in seeking new landscapes, but in having new eyes."
>
> — Marcel Proust

Have you ever felt misunderstood or different? What's holding you back from living your best life? Are you ready for an iconic life?

MY STORY

I know I was messed up by my parents, teachers, and community members during the first eighteen years of my life.

I'm a spiritual being having a human experience. Like everyone else, I was in my purest state when I was born—in my childlike state, I was so clear on my life purpose and connected to the Higher Power and the source of the Divine. I believe my soul chose my parents and the lessons I needed to learn as a child to become the adult I am today. This journey has not been an easy ride. And yours hasn't been easy either. That's the point of life! You learn, fail, grow, and then it's your turn to share it with others.

My ninety-one-year-old grandmother shared a wise lesson with me before passing away. She said: "Don't be mad at life and lessons you must learn. The lessons will be there every day until your last day and breath. I'm still learning every day. Embrace it and be happy you have another day alive."

The world needs you; your story must be told. Even if you only impact one heart and one person at a time.

I grew up in a middle-class family with my dad, mom, identical twin sister, and younger sister. We lived in a small city on the West Coast of the Netherlands. I remember feeling not seen, heard, or loved by my dad. He was a very strict person with many (unspoken) rules—good was never good enough. He didn't inspire me to become anything I wanted; he didn't encourage me to live a great life and think outside the box. He wanted me to study, get a well-paid job, and have insurance and a pension plan in place. He shared many times that I had to save money and prepare for the future. My mom was always there as a stay-at-home mom. She loved me deeply, but she was not a strong person, had low self-esteem, and was dependent on my dad.

I grew up with parents who were always fighting, and it was an emotionally abusive environment. It shaped me as a child and young adult. The positive impact as a child came mostly from my loving grandparents, my only uncle, aunt, and three cousins. I spent a lot of time with them. I felt safe, loved, and seen with them. My best childhood memories are with them. I was committed to healing my childhood and having a better life! But how?

The whole journey has been a rough road. As a child, I had very low self-esteem, no confidence, and I really didn't talk a lot. I had a few friends, but not that many. People were always confused; they had difficulty seeing the difference between me and my twin sister. I fought for my identity and personality for eighteen years and beyond. My twin sister and I have always been different, almost opposites, our entire lives. We were both more masculine compared to my feminine younger sister, who always had to stand up against her two big sisters. My family environment was unhappy and abusive at times. At my high school, I was sexually and emotionally abused by one of my teachers, and that three-year experience shut me down spiritually. I was ashamed and felt lonely because I couldn't talk to anyone about it. I never really talked or spoke out, but I learned to become a great listener and observer. That served me well later in life.

Life only shifts when big things happen. I remember attending a university different from my twin sister in another city. It was difficult and a relief at the same time. I could be me without being compared to my twin sister. I asked myself, "Who am I?" I couldn't answer that question. I felt lost for a long time. Between the ages of fifteen and twenty-three, I had many life questions, and I thought about suicide many times. When I was twenty-three, I was in an accident and ended up in the ICU for two weeks. I had two near-death experiences. I spent weeks at the hospital to recover. My rehab took me close to three years. It shifted everything: my occupation, my friends, my partner choice, my life, and my self-awareness. And now, going back in time, it changed my BANKCODE. As a child, teenager, and young adult, I was a NABK (Nurturing-Action-Blueprint-Knowledge) type. Since my accident and becoming an entrepreneur, my BANK-CODE has shifted to an ANKB (Action-Nurturing-Blueprint-Knowledge) type.

Looking back and connecting the dots, I realize two major near-death experiences completely changed my perspective. Both experiences were totally different and magical. They were beautiful, and when they happened, I didn't want to come back from them. The first near-death experience was something many of us have heard about in stories or tales of people seeing the light of death. I saw this beautiful white light and white angels. It was peaceful and a feeling of coming home. The message was clear: "You have a big task in this lifetime, and we're here to support and guide you. Listen to your intuition and the signs we give you. You're wanted. You're loved. You have a message!" This experience is unforgettable and undeniable.

The second near-death experience was totally different, although the message was also clear and loud. Almost like a dream or a vision, I saw myself floating above my own body. This tall Native American Tribal Leader with a beautiful headpiece with feathers showed me why I was on the planet. He smiled and had a key with a feather attached to it in his big hands. He gave it to me, and the symbol was the key to my life purpose, heart, wisdom, and creativity. The feather symbolized faith, following my intuition, angel protection, power, strength, freedom, and connection to the great creator.

The second near-death experience was associated with the time in my life when I met Cheri Tree and learned about the BANK methodology. Suddenly, my whole life flashed before me in a vision, and I could identify each person's personality type: a huge "aha" moment and a feeling of healing simultaneously. Going through the BANK training allowed me to heal, forgive, and love the people who hurt me throughout my life. I could finally forgive myself for hurting others as well. I have learned that just knowing the BANKCODE is not an excuse or reason for existence; it's a tool to understand better, communicate, and connect with other humans—something I realize is the angel shared with me. BANK can transform lives, relationships, businesses, and organizations, such as education and non-profits. Once you know the code, you can't unlearn or unknow it. You will see it everywhere and in everyone—that's the beauty of it. The best way to make people matter is by healing your heart and seeing people by looking through the lens of other people's personality types with compassion and empathy. That's where the real connection happens. BANK is the world's universal language of EQ (Emotional Quotient).

With all of my life experiences, I feel like I can understand you, like I can be in your shoes, and I want to help you achieve your dreams and goals and discover your true self amid struggles, much like I have. Most importantly, I'd love for you to reconnect with your life purpose and start living an iconic life.

The first step is learning to understand yourself by knowing your own personality type via the BANK system.

The next step is understanding others, learning their values, and altering how you communicate with others based on their BANKCODES.

Then, align with your true self, heart desires, passion, and gift! What are you committed to achieving in this lifetime?

WHAT I LEARNED

Here are my three main commitments in this lifetime.

1. **Raising my son Kai as a young man with people skills, living the BANKCODE, learning high emotional intelligence, developing spiritual intelligence, and learning kindness, resilience, and humility.**

In today's world, sexuality is fluid, and masculinity and femininity are blended into a new way of living and loving. I want my son Kai to love all people worldwide, their differences, languages, cultures, food, architecture, and nature. I want to raise him in his masculine energy and not emasculate him. I want to help him develop his natural charismatic confidence and show his feminine side at the same time. I dream of traveling the world with him—all the above will be the best gift I can give him.

Becoming a mom changed my view of life. Looking through Kai's eyes, I see the innocence, the unknown, the curiosity, and the excitement for exploring life. Life is short, and I'm committed to living full-out every day so he will remember me as an inspiration and I will have a positive impact on the person he will become! Life is all about creating lasting memories and impacting as many lives around the world as possible. I hope to teach and instill in him the value principle that money is the energy you receive back as a reflection of that.

2. Being the first person in our family to become wealthy and financially free.

I desire financial freedom to show the next generation what's possible when you work hard and are committed to impacting humanity. As a child, I loved riding my bike through the neighborhoods with big homes, villas, and mansions. It inspired me, and I wanted that lifestyle. I grew up in a poor money mindset environment, so I had to learn and train myself through personal development to rewire my brain and hire mentors and coaches to heal my childhood traumas and belief systems.

Today, I have accomplished many of my dreams and lived a wealthy lifestyle in Laguna Beach, California. The BANK methodology has helped me in so many ways to understand people, their choices, their behavior, their excuses, their objections, and their fears. I have been using BANK for the past ten years, and I learn new things every single day about myself and how to help others. You can accomplish anything in life you want if you do the work.

3. **Empowering (young) women to rise up, step into their power and independence, and live a joyful life while balancing femininity and masculinity.**

I urge all young women everywhere not to wait until a life-changing event occurs to take care of themselves, such as the loss of a loved one, divorce, bankruptcy, illness, or accident. This was the message I received during my near-death experience, and I have been sharing this message for two decades now. When you heal your heart, you will shift your mindset. All choices in life we make follow the same path. Our soul—intuition—knows; we feel it with our heart, and with our mind, we choose either to listen to it or talk ourselves into going in the opposite direction. I advocate for young women everywhere to embrace their heart's intuition and listen to it daily.

EXERCISE

Write down what you're committed to in this lifetime. Create a vision board and journal your wins and the things you're grateful for daily.

Make a list of people you'd like to connect with from the past, crack their BANKCODE, and have an authentic, vulnerable conversation with each of them. And look through the lens of their personality type and perspective with compassion.

Identify one additional area of your life where you can grow and become a better version of yourself. (For example, a better leader in business, a more present life partner, traveling more, joining a sports club, eating healthier, etc.)

TIPS

BANK helped me evolve, empathize, and be less judgmental. It helped me to heal my past relationships and have amazing relationships with my family and friends today. Together, we can heal, grow, and rise. It's time to scale up and reclaim your authority and power to live in love, joy, overflowing wealth, and prosperity to leave a legacy while alive. I believe BANK can connect and empower humanity. The world needs a simple tool and system like this more than ever. Our world has never been more disconnected or lonely!

The world needs you to be connected to the highest form of self, live your life purposefully, and succeed in every way possible. Many women feel abused, bullied, undervalued, and mistreated. Many successful women end up divorced because they out-earn their partner, have no support from their partner, are jealous, or lack personal growth as a couple. The main reasons for this are unclear, as well as the roles can balance feminine and masculine energy.

Let's include men in our transforming journeys to collaborate at the highest vibration possible. It's all about finding the Yin and Yang in all of us.

SUMMARY

To "Make People Matter," you must start with yourself. Heal your heart pain, improve your mindset, and connect with your soul purpose. Understand people and put on "new eyes" or colored glasses to see with a different view through the lens of BANK. Discover a new world by looking through the eyes of the other person in all your relationships. "Beauty is in the eye of the beholder," and "How you love yourself is how you teach others to love you." Find your tribe and join our Codebreaker global community. Be kind!

ESTHER WILDENBERG | ANKB

Esther Wildenberg is a visionary leader, coach, and international speaker dedicated to empowering individuals and organizations to unlock their full potential. As the Co-Founder and President of Codebreaker Technologies, LLC, the global leader in personality coding technology, Esther has revolutionized how people understand and connect with one another. With more than twenty years of executive experience across multiple industries and continents, she has held numerous C-Suite positions and built a reputation as a dynamic, results-driven professional. By age thirty-three, Esther was the CEO of a European consulting company, leading a team of more than 800 employees. She later founded her own consulting and coaching business in the Netherlands.

Esther is also an accomplished retreat host, mastermind facilitator, and influencer. Her transformative events and workshops focus on fostering self-discovery, resilience, and growth. A leader's leader, she inspires teams and individuals to achieve sustainable success and lasting change, leaving an indelible legacy of empowerment for future generations.

Author's Website: EstherWildenberg.com

CHAPTER 9
YOU MATTER! YOU ARE SIGNIFICANT!

BY JON KOVACH JR.

"You can make more friends in two months by becoming interested in other people than you can in two years by trying to get other people interested in you."

— Dale Carnegie

Have you ever felt that people were drawn to you, not because of what you could offer, but because of who you are? Have you wondered how certain individuals seem to influence effortlessly, leaving a positive impact on those around them? Making people matter is not just about popularity; it's about creating genuine, lasting connections that honor the value each person brings.

Learning how to make people feel seen, appreciated, and understood is essential in a world filled with fast-paced connections and surface-level interactions. Through my business, leadership, and personal journey, I've seen how powerful authentic relationships can be and how they transform lives. With my ANKB personality—Action, Nurturing, Knowledge, and Blueprint—I've built connections that go beyond the surface. This chapter invites you to explore these principles, drawn from years of experience, and discover how you can make others feel valued and inspired.

THE POWER OF AUTHENTIC CONNECTIONS

One of my most transformative experiences occurred during a mission trip to the Philippines. Walking through neighborhoods in the Cavite province of Luzon, I stood out like a sore thumb, being a foreigner. Many locals had experienced hardship and held onto resentment from broken promises made during wartime by foreigners who had visited or been stationed in their area before me. As I knocked on door after door to connect with people and share a positive message, I encountered harsh words, slammed doors, and even disrespectful insults. Yet I didn't let that stop me.

One day, when I approached a home, a man saw me coming and rushed inside to hush and hide his family. Undeterred, I knocked and asked if I could meet him. After a few hesitant moments, he finally cracked the door open, and we shared an unexpected laugh over his murmur of, "Nobody home!" That laughter dissolved his defenses, and we connected over our shared humanity. Over time, we worked together to clean up his neighborhood, repair homes, and rebuild the community's spirit. That experience taught me that people are often just waiting for someone to see them—truly see them.

Like Dale Carnegie's principles in *How to Win Friends and Influence People*, authenticity unlocks doors that might otherwise remain closed. You become magnetic when genuinely caring and connecting without expecting anything in return. It's not about "winning friends" in the transactional sense but about making others feel valued. Through laughter, empathy, and genuine interest, I saw the power of human connection that transcended language and history.

ALIGNING WITH PURPOSE AND PEOPLE

Alignment is more than simply agreeing with others; it's about harmonizing with the people, values, and goals that resonate with your core purpose. In my work, whether leading a team or speaking to an audience, I've found that creating alignment is a powerful way to foster meaningful connections. Alignment isn't just a principle but a natural law governing human attraction. I call this the "Law of Magnetism."

When I campaigned for a national executive board position with the Public Relations Student Society of America, I knew my competitor was highly qualified, even more so than I was. However, rather than trying to outshine her with qualifications, I focused on aligning with the needs of society. I dedicated myself to getting to know people, learning their names, and understanding their goals. By the time I gave my speech, they weren't voting for a candidate; they were voting for someone who had aligned with them and understood their vision.

Creating alignment means connecting on a personal level and understanding the dreams, values, and aspirations of those you engage with. People want to feel you're working alongside them, not just for your own goals. This level of alignment fosters a deeper relationship and, ultimately, makes them feel valued.

TRANSFORMING CHALLENGES INTO CONNECTIONS

If approached with the right mindset, challenges can become opportunities for connection. When I participated in a speaking competition in Salt Lake City, I arrived late due to prior commitments and missed the entire first day of coaching. My competitors had an edge, having bonded with the judges and the audience. Despite this, I stayed true to myself, sharing a story from my childhood that reflected my authentic personality. Instead of worrying about the competition, I focused on connecting with the audience in a meaningful way.

I created a powerful connection with the audience and judges by being open and relatable and allowing my personality to shine through. I received a standing ovation not because I had prepared better than the others but because I was fully present and made an effort to reach people at a human level. When challenges arise, embrace them as chances to make an impact. Sometimes, the best connections are formed when people see you handle difficult moments gracefully and with resilience.

LEADING WITH EMPATHY AND INFLUENCE

As a leader, my goal has always been to make others feel like champions, to see them not just as members of a team but as essential contributors. Leadership isn't about accumulating power but empowering those around you. By applying empathy and understanding through the lens of my BANKCODE, I can build trust, show appreciation, and cultivate an environment where people feel heard and valued.

Empathy means listening without an agenda and showing up for people in a way that meets their unique needs. As an ANKB personality, I'm Action-oriented and thrive in high-energy environments. Yet I understand that not everyone shares my pace. Some people need more time to process information, while others respond better to a more nurturing approach. Knowing my own personality type helps me adapt my approach to make those around me feel comfortable and valued.

Dale Carnegie once said, "People don't care how much you know until they know how much you care." That has been a guiding principle in my leadership journey. Whether it's a one-on-one conversation or a large group meeting, I make it a priority to show genuine care for those I work with, recognizing their contributions and giving them room to shine.

WHAT I LEARNED

Knowing my personal BANKCODE has been an awesome experience for me—not only in understanding others but in helping me become a more effective and compassionate communicator. I have always had drive, ambition, and a passion for leadership, yet I often felt frustrated when I couldn't connect with people on the level I wanted. I thought that pouring my enthusiasm into my interactions was enough to make an impact. I didn't realize that while my energy and motivation resonated with some, it left others feeling overwhelmed or disconnected. BANK has been a great resource and has shown me that to influence and serve others truly, I need to meet them where they are—listening and adapting my approach to speak their language and honor their values.

Before BANK, I thrived on action. My natural approach was to dive into new projects with excitement, assuming others would match my pace and enthusiasm. Through my journey, though, I learned that effective leadership isn't just about energy or vision; it's also about alignment. The BANK approach helped me see that people value different aspects of connection. As someone with a strong Action and Nurturing profile, I realized my strengths could be amplified by understanding, serving, and respecting the Blueprint and Knowledge-oriented people in my life.

For example, in my work as a public speaker and mentor, I used to believe my role was to inspire, speak with high energy, and drive action. However, BANK revealed that while inspiration is powerful, influence requires a personal connection. I started using BANK principles to listen deeply to others' values and saw incredible results. When speaking to audiences, I could connect with those who shared my Action-oriented personality and those who valued structure, detailed explanations, or a nurturing environment. This understanding transformed my approach to leadership and public speaking; I became less focused on impressing people and more focused on genuinely connecting with them.

One of the most profound lessons BANK taught me was the importance of nurturing. In the beginning, I often pushed forward without giving others enough space to contribute or share their ideas. But with BANK, I learned that nurturing can be as powerful as taking action. I saw the value in encouraging others to step up, to share their insights, and to feel truly seen. This change in mindset allowed me to build stronger teams, cultivate meaningful relationships, and create an environment where everyone feels they matter.

BANK has also deepened my understanding of adaptability. I used to see myself as someone who could adjust easily, but BANK taught me that adaptability is more than just changing tactics. It's about recognizing the unique needs of each individual and adjusting my approach to create a win-win situation. I became more attentive to the different personalities around me and used this awareness to improve my communication. Whether it's coaching someone who needs structure, nurturing someone seeking encouragement, or engaging someone with a thirst for knowledge, BANK has empowered me to tailor my interactions, resulting in stronger connections and greater impact.

Since incorporating BANK into my life, I've seen a shift in my relationships, both professionally and personally. I now approach each interaction with the intent to understand and honor the other person's values. This shift has not only increased my influence but allowed me to create deeper, more fulfilling connections.

EXERCISES FOR APPLICATION AND REFLECTION

To make these principles actionable, here are some reflective questions to help you connect with others at a deeper level:

1. How can you authentically show interest in others? Reflect on a recent interaction and consider how you could have shown more genuine interest. Practice this with someone new each week.
2. What shared goals or values can you align with? Consider a relationship you want to improve and think about what common ground you can build on.
3. When have you turned a challenge into a connection? Recall a moment when you faced a challenge and used it to connect with someone. What did you learn from that experience?

TIPS FOR ENHANCING YOUR CONNECTIONS

Based on my experiences and the BANK methodology, here are five practical tips to make others feel valued:

1. **Listen Actively:** People want to be heard. Show you're listening by asking open-ended questions and giving them your full attention.

2. **Celebrate Small Wins:** Acknowledge others' successes, no matter how small. This shows that you value their progress and efforts.
3. **Express Sincere Gratitude:** Thank people genuinely and often. Small acts of appreciation go a long way in strengthening connections.
4. **Personalize Your Communication:** Tailor your approach to fit the other person's personality type. Knowing their preferences makes them feel understood and respected.
5. **Share the Spotlight:** Make it a habit to uplift others and share recognition. People remember those who helped them feel like heroes.

CALL TO ACTION

I challenge you to apply one of these principles in a meaningful way. Show genuine interest, find alignment, embrace challenges, and lead with empathy. The more you make others feel valued, the richer your own life will become. Remember, true influence is not about making people follow you; it's about inspiring them to feel valued and empowered. Together, let's create a world where everyone feels they matter.

JON KOVACH JR. | ANKB

Jon is an award-winning international motivational speaker and global mastermind leader. Jon has helped multi-billion-dollar corporations exceed their annual sales goals. In addition, in his work as an accountability coach and mastermind facilitator, Jon has helped thousands of professionals overcome their challenges and achieve their goals by implementing his accountability strategies and Irrefutable Laws of High Performance. Jon is the Mastermind Facilitator and Team Lead of the Habitude Warrior Mastermind and the Global Speakers Mastermind & Masterclass founded by Speaker Erik "Mr. Awesome" Swanson.

Jon speaks on topics including accountability and the mastermind methodologies. He is a multiple times number-one national bestselling author and TEDx speaker and a featured keynote speaker on Amazon Prime TV's series Speak-Up. Jon's motivational messages have been viewed by more than 750,000 people online. His positive messages have trended and been used by global brands on TikTok and Instagram, such as: Red Bull, Michael Bublé, NHL, Powell Books, GoDaddy Studio, Canada's Wonderland Amusement Park, and the LSU Cheer Team.

Author's Website: JonKovachJr.com

CHAPTER 10
INCREASING YOUR INCOME INTELLIGENCE WITH BANK

BY KATHLEEN VICENZOTTI

> "Every problem is a gift—without problems we would not grow."
>
> — Tony Robbins

What if the secret to scaling your business lies not just in understanding your customer and their values but in applying these principles to enhance your ability to connect and communicate more effectively, generating more income in less time?

Imagine a system that decodes each decision a client makes, while equipping you with the skills, strategies, and insights needed to maximize your income in any profession—a goal especially important for those in commission-based and performance-driven roles.

That's Income intelligence—the level of smarts you must have to find and make money in your business and life. Let's face it—nothing we do today can be done without money or income. The ability to earn income allows us the freedom to spend time with loved ones, experience things that set our soul on fire, and afford us the necessities of life. Yes, life itself.

> **"They say money can't buy happiness... not true. Money allows you to do things for others, and that leads to happiness."**
>
> ~ Cheri Tree

Let's discuss the BANK methodology and how it can help you increase your income so you can work less, earn more, and have a more fulfilling life doing the things you love with the people you love.

This is the story of how I gained powerful insights into myself and my business and how applying the principles of BANK can unlock revenue and income in your business. When implemented, these strategies will empower you to create a business that works for you—so you can earn the income you desire and deserve.

A JOURNEY OF DISCOVERY

Let's rewind to the beginning: How did I even discover BANK, the system that would forever change the way I approach both business and life? It all started when my friend and colleague Tiffany traveled from Minnesota to California for a BANK conference. She was diving into the methodology to strengthen her direct sales business, improve her leadership, and grow her customer base. I saw on Facebook that she was in town, and I reached out immediately. My intentions were purely social—catch up, share some laughs over dinner—but, as fate would have it, our dinner conversation took an incredible turn that changed everything.

It was January, the heart of a challenging winter, and our concrete coating business was struggling. When my husband, Joe, and I started our business, getting leads was a breeze; a few posts on Facebook would keep the phone ringing. But times had changed, and we found ourselves in a tight spot, unsure how to get our business back on track. Little did I know that casual dinner would set us on a path to discovery, equipping us with the tools to revive our business, transform the way we operated, and generate close to an additional $500,000 in revenue.

HOW BANK TURNED OUR STRUGGLING SALES INTO A $500K SUCCESS STORY

My husband Joe and I own JAK Concrete Coatings Inc., a small family business that makes ugly concrete beautiful. When we first started our business, things were awesome;

we recruited a sales team, leads were plentiful and inexpensive, we could post a few before and after images on Facebook, and opportunities came our way. Only a few competitors were advertising on the platform, and we were getting dozens of appointments a week, crews were booked, and we were making money.

My BANKCODE is ANKB. I am all about ACTION—taking action. I'm a "shoot now, ask questions later" kinda girl, and with B, Blueprint as my last code, I didn't have the necessary systems in place monitoring the details of the business at hand. I was just enjoying the windfalls of our success and didn't see the trends of what was really going on in our business. After eighteen months or so, things started to change; revenue dropped, and the bank account reflected it. Competition on Facebook increased, the algorithms changed, and our cost of leads nearly tripled as our competitors started to copy our system and hijack our leads.

Things were not good. We were spending more money, but the quantity and quality of leads were down, our win rate (closing rate) was decreasing, and we started discounting our price to win deals, which led to a decline in revenue and profitability. We needed to get more leads and increase our closing rate while maintaining our profit margins. Rather than having systems in place and structure around our sales process, I felt like I was throwing spaghetti at the wall to see what stuck. How could we improve our efficiency, capture interest, cut through the noise on Facebook, and be more effective in closing the opportunities we did have?

Is there an area in your business that needs improvement? Something that you should be tracking that you aren't? Where it seems to be going well but is deteriorating or lagging? Pressure or changing conditions can often expose areas of opportunity or weakness. The competitive environment I was experiencing exposed areas of weakness (and opportunities) in our sales process, specifically monitoring and tracking business operations and metrics. Learning that, although painful at the time, allowed us to scale and grow.

THE TURNING POINT: EMBRACING BANK

When Tiffany and I met, she told me about BANK, the book *Why They Buy*, and the accompanying on-demand Sales Master Class. Immediately, I realized this was exactly what I needed. If we could increase the win rate and percentage of closed sales and maintain or increase our average sales, we could immediately increase income and revenue. BANK was the quickest and most impactful way to regain control of my business and our sales process. As I listened to the BANK Sales Master Class I kept thinking, *Yep, yep, yep, this makes sense and is exactly what we need for our business.* It was so simple, yet so profound. BANK was a game-changer that allowed me to regain control of our business.

I learned one of my biggest mistakes was training and teaching our sales team to deliver one singular presentation. With "A" Action as my primary BANKCODE, brand image was very important to me. Our salespeople represented my company, and I wanted brand consistency. I thought the best way to achieve that was to train them to run their appointments the same way, using the same presentation with every customer.

Huge mistake. As a student of BANK, I quickly realized that in an effort to control the message, I was holding my sales reps back and limiting their ability to let the customer determine the presentation. As you learn in BANK, every customer has a unique buying code—a specific set of values that drives their purchasing decision. Yet, here we were, delivering the same one-size-fits-all presentation to every customer, completely missing the mark for 75 percent of them. No wonder our closing rate was stuck at a frustrating 25 percent! Without allowing my team to tailor their pitch to each prospect's BANKCODE, I was essentially asking them to throw darts blindfolded and hoping for a bullseye.

Although I knew we weren't performing as we should, I couldn't crack the code to move the needle. One rep was doing her own thing, touting, "My way works; I am closing more than the others." My other rep said, "I am presenting the information you've given me, so I don't know why they aren't buying." As the sales manager, this was frustrating. We were having inconsistent results, burning 70-75 percent of our leads, and I felt overwhelmed.

> **"Insanity is doing the same thing over and over again and expecting different results."**
>
> — Albert Einstein.

It was time to do something different. After clarifying how the BANK system could improve our business, I decided our entire team needed to be introduced to and trained in the methodology. We went through the twelve-week BANK IOS coaching program, studied the personality types, learned about their idiosyncrasies, and learned how to speak their language and sell to them.

THE INSIGHTS WE GAINED

The program gave me a framework for deconstructing our sales process and coaching and mentoring my team more effectively. It also helped me understand who our customers were, how to connect with them and speak with them in a way that honored their values and what they expected from our company, and the tools I needed to optimize our business systemically and democratically.

Learning my sales team's BANKCODES and their primary personalities helped me understand what was happening while they were running appointments, why they were effective, where there was an opportunity for improvement, and how to coach them according to who they were. It explained a lot about what motivated them, frustrated them, and gave me the insights I needed to increase their productivity and, ultimately, job satisfaction.

My Action-Nurturing sales rep was a whirlwind: constantly shifting appointments, running late, a little disorganized, and full of animated energy and emotion. Can you guess who she was turning off—and who wasn't buying from her? Yep, Blueprints and Knowledge types! And can you guess who loved her style? Right again—Action types and Nurturers. Although she was one of our best closers, she was costing us a fortune by unknowingly alienating nearly half of her prospects. And the stress didn't stop there. My Nurturing-Blueprint office manager felt frazzled when Ms. Action ran late, leaving customers calling the office at 2:15, wondering if she'd make it to her 2 p.m. appointment. Some even asked if we could send someone else, saying she didn't seem prepared. Recognizing this dynamic was a game-changer, and once we made adjustments, both our clients and our team felt the difference.

On the flip side, we had my Blueprint-Knowledge sales rep. He was the model of punctuality, organized to a T, incredibly knowledgeable about the product, and always professional and patient with prospects. But there was one snag—he didn't have that fire to push the close. When we sent out a limited-time offer or a "get it now" install date, his clients would be the first to call...imagine how much sooner we could have booked those jobs if he had recognized that at the time of sale. As a true Blueprint, he struggled to connect with Action types, who sometimes need a bit more enthusiasm, follow-up, or incentive to buy right now. The gap was clear, and it was time to shake things up for him too.

BANK gave me the solution to the problem. Hindsight really does offer clarity, and I am excited that you are reading this so you don't make the same mistakes I made. The cost of failure on my part was huge. Not only financially but emotionally and mentally. Understanding BANK not only improved our sales performance but also improved our team culture.

Once we integrated BANK into our organization, things transformed. Suddenly, we were connecting with clients on a deeper level, building that like-know-trust factor, and shortening the sales cycle. Our presentations became sharper and more on-target, and our "yes" rates and average deal values increased. Now, we weren't just guessing; we were hitting the bullseye by speaking directly to what mattered most to our prospects. And team dynamics—those improved, too. I recognized that some of our team needed more structure, consistency, tracking, and feedback; others needed recognition and acknowledgment. It helped us all be more understanding and accountable for what each of us needed. The business became a lot more enjoyable and fun.

Beyond just boosting our closing rates and deal values, BANK transformed how we set appointments and fine-tuned nearly every operational system in our business. When scheduling appointments, we've learned to align the right sales rep to each lead based on a few telltale cues from them. For instance, if a caller says they're "researching the product," we know we've got a Knowledge personality on the line; if they're looking for a local company, they probably lean toward being a Nurturer. Someone who needs a quick turnaround? That's our Action type. And those calling to discuss budgets or planning ideas? They're likely a Blueprint. With this additional information, we schedule appointments with the rep best suited to their suspected BANKCODE; we're no longer just hoping for a match; we are using the BANK methodology to strategically run our business with a focus on efficiency.

The year following our indoctrination of the BANK into all our operations and sales processes, we are now closing 44 percent of our deals, a 76 percent increase, and our average deal value increased by 12 percent, resulting in close to an additional $500,000 of annual revenue. Now that's income you can take to the BANK.

Can you see how implementing BANK into your business could reveal some insights and opportunities for improvement? It's about implementing high-income building skill sets so you can earn more and work less.

UNLOCKING YOUR INCOME INTELLIGENCE

When maximizing your income and truly enhancing your life, the BANK methodology has been nothing short of revolutionary for me. It reshaped our business and profoundly impacted everyone relying on its success. The extra revenue we generated didn't just keep our crews busy; it provided them with the financial stability their families depended on. Our sales reps saw their earnings soar, and ultimately, I was able to break free from the structure of a 9-to-5 job. I was working to embrace my true passion: focusing full-time on building our family business and allowing me time to coach and mentor others in launching their own businesses, fulfilling their dreams, and unlocking their income intelligence so they could live the life they desired and deserved.

BANK did more than keep my business afloat; it completely shifted my perspective on how I approach my business and life. It taught me to look at sales and business success differently, focusing not just on closing deals but also on ways to maximize income from those successes. Not all sales are created equal! A high closing rate doesn't guarantee a bigger paycheck; it hinges on so many more things: average deal values, commission structures, lead generation, activity, and team dynamics. BANK, which increases emotional intelligence, combined with business intelligence, is crucial for unlocking your earning potential. Once BANK helped me with our sales process, I started looking at ways to optimize all areas of my business.

Adding the emotional intelligence component—leading a team, fostering a positive culture, and creating an environment that encourages synergy—further enhances your bottom line. Multiply that by scalable, increased activity, and you have a powerful formula for continually maximizing your income. It's about mastering high-income skill sets and uncovering the financial opportunities within your business to support the life and lifestyle you desire and deserve.

ARE YOU READY FOR MORE?

Implementing BANK into our operations was transformational and profitable. It had such an impact on our business that I felt called to share it with you and the world. As a Certified and Licensed BANK Trainer and Coach, I am now sharing this methodology with other small business owners, sales professionals, coaches, and entrepreneurs, teaching them how to increase their sales and maximize their income and profitability.

Are there dynamics within your business and team that you'd like to improve? Start by cracking your staff's codes.

Have them read their personality report and corresponding sales playbook and share their BANKCODE with you and each other.

After everyone reviews their BANKCODE, ask if they can think of a situation in which they may have lost a sale or caused internal conflict because they communicated using the wrong code with a prospect or team member.

When you understand BANK, everyone can feel more confident working together and more confident in serving clients and customers in a manner that will allow your business to be more efficient and generate more income.

KATHLEEN VICENZOTTI | ANKB

With more than thirty-five years of sales, marketing, and leadership expertise, Kathleen Vicenzotti has dedicated her career to empowering individuals in commission-based, results-driven fields. She has held executive roles at Ford Motor Company, excelled as a top-producing State Farm Insurance Agent, and led high-achieving teams within the Direct Selling industry.

Currently, Kathleen is the co-owner of JAK Concrete Coatings in Long Beach, California, and co-owner of the Selling Edge, a sales training and development company. Her passion lies in equipping professionals with the skills they need to generate consistent income, build strong client bases, achieve financial security, and create the life they envision.

Author's Website: KathleenVicenzotti.com

CHAPTER 11

THEY WEREN'T WHO I THOUGHT THEY WERE

BY MARTHA KREJCI

> "I see you."
> — Jake Sully, Avatar

MY HUSBAND WASN'T WHO I THOUGHT HE WAS AND NEITHER WAS MY DAUGHTER

What would change in your life if you found out people weren't trying to push your buttons…but filling their own needs? What if people are rarely trying to trigger you? What if you just don't understand what they need? How would your relationships change?

Well, that's exactly what happened to me after learning the BANK methodology. My entire life changed, and my hope is yours will, too, because that's how we really shift this world, in my opinion—through understanding.

I can't talk about BANK without mentioning how it's revolutionized my business, so let's address that quickly before we discuss how it changed my entire life and how I live it.

I run a huge coaching/implementation business to the tune of seven figures a month, so I serve a lot of people. Before I learned about BANK, I coached everyone the same. The way I saw things, there were sound business strategies and things you shouldn't do. Now, there were nuances to the things that worked, but as I was teaching, coaching, and mentoring, I worked within the business nuance. What I was totally missing was the interpersonal nuance, and when I nailed that…it was over.

I learned the methodology and immediately implemented it (because I'm an Action). When people join my program, the first step is to identify their code. Now, when I coach them on a call or one of my strategists works with them via email, we know their code, so we know exactly how to work with them, what matters to them, and ultimately, how to help them implement their program according to their BANKCODE.

It has been an absolute game-changer. People went from accomplishing goals to absolutely crushing them! There's something so special about being able to know someone really even better than they know themselves and to coach them in a way that makes them feel seen and heard. I believe that's what the world is really missing right now. People feel visible and like they matter. BANK has changed the game for us business owners in that capacity.

Now, let's move on. Don't get me wrong; business is important to me, but something else will supersede it any day of the week—my family.

It's time to circle back to my first question, "What would change in your life if you found out people weren't trying to push your buttons…but rather filling their own needs?"

When I first started learning the BANK methodology, I learned it to increase sales and impact. What I didn't realize is that it would save my marriage, which I didn't even know was struggling, and create an incredible relationship with my daughter—not to mention eliminate her need for therapy.

Here's how everything went down. I learned about BANK, and like you, I got super-excited to see how it related to everyone in my life. I asked my husband and daughter to take the tests. My daughter did…but my husband wouldn't. You'll understand why when you find out his code.

We'll talk about my daughter first, since she actually took the test. She's a Blueprint, through and through, but I had no idea! I figured she must also be an Action because she was just like me. I always thought she was just being a kid and pushing my buttons when she constantly asked things like, "What time are we leaving?" and wouldn't accept "In a few minutes" as an answer…she needed to know the actual time. She also needed other sources of structure within her day, which is totally foreign to me as an ANBK. It's not only foreign to me because Blueprint is my third letter, but it's actually my trigger. EEK!

So, all those times she begged for structure and defined times, I was triggered and thought she was doing it on purpose, but through BANK, I realized she actually needed these things to feel *safe and secure*. I mean, holy smokes!

My daughter, whom I thought was exactly like me, is exactly the opposite of my BANKCODE. She needs structure to thrive, and quite frankly, I thrive in what looks like chaos because I live inside of inspired moments and jump from one inspired moment to the next as an Action.

The way this knowledge has changed our world is almost incalculable. If I had gone through life thinking she was trying to trigger me, I would have assumed her intentions were to always upset me. That would have led to her not caring about me or just wanting to see me upset, which, of course, would have led to distance between us.

Now that I know that's not at all what she was or is doing, she's just asking for literally what she needs to soothe and satisfy her own mind; I can look at that and happily give her the details and structure she needs because I love her more than anything!

What does this do for *her*? It helps her, as a seven-year-old, feel seen, heard, and understood for her needs and intentions. Do you have any idea what that does for a little girl? I mean, if this was the only thing BANK ever did in my life, it would be enough. But it's not the only thing. Now, let's get to my husband.

We had been married for about nine years when I learned this methodology. Were there some rough years? Yes, for sure, but we went to therapy, and both of us got sober and calmed everything down by the time our girl was born. I thought everything was good. We didn't really argue much, loved each other, and didn't have any visible issues.

Until I learned about BANK. When I immersed myself in it, and he didn't want to take the test, I made my best guess about what his code was because I wanted to be able to give him what he needed in the relationship, too. BANK is one of those things that when you know it, you have to implement it. Know better and do better, right?

I started to decode what I believed he was, and it went something like BKAN. Yes, I thought he was a bacon. So, based on that, I started playing into his "B." At that time, we lived in Orlando and were going to have another Disney day, so I thought this would be an amazing time to let his "B" shine! What happened next floored me and changed us forever.

I remember it clearly. We were sitting in our bedroom, and I was so excited to ask him to plan the whole thing because, as a "B," this would have been totally in his wheelhouse. When I brought it up, he immediately got stressed out, his face changed, and he absolutely did *not* want to do it.

I was confused because this was not making sense to me at all. He's a "B," so why is he freaking out? He always does stuff like this. So, when I explained why I asked and how I thought he would respond based on the definition of a Blueprint, that's when it happened—a release I could not have seen coming.

He said, "I don't do that stuff because I want to; I do it because someone *has* to."

At that moment, I realized he wasn't a Blueprint. Blueprint was *actually* the code he goes to when he's under *duress*.

This man, whom I have loved and been married to for nine years, has lived under duress the *entire time*. Can you imagine? Maybe you do know how he felt—needing to live in a code that is problematic for you out of necessity and not knowing any different.

That night, our worlds broke open and healed together all at the same time. I saw him for who he really was. And he saw me caring enough to find the real him in there and make sure he never ever had to pop into Blueprint again. (I mean, he had already done his time, right?)

That night, as I looked back on all of the times that made me think he was a Blueprint, it was clear to me he was never happy in that role. It was always frustrating. It was always stressful. And it was always unhappy. As I'm writing this right now, my heart is breaking again for putting him in that position for nine years. But thank God for BANK because had I never learned this methodology, he would still be in that space, and frankly, we may not have made it as a couple. And it wouldn't have been because we didn't love each other. It would have been because we didn't understand each other.

You may be curious (as I was) to know what he really is.

Remember when I said he wouldn't take the test? What's the code that is most likely not to take the test? (If you know, you know....)

He's a Knowledge. He's a KNBA. Makes sense, right? I was more or less pushing him into B and A and driving him nuts in the process, not to mention making him feel less than because he wasn't being understood.

Now that I know he's a Knowledge, I ask him for things like research, or I ask "how to" things, and he gets back to me when he's exhausted all of his research and has his best conclusion. I'm smiling as I write this because he is now the "happy kid" version of himself. The trouble these days is to get him to stop talking about his research. Honestly, I'd happily let him talk all day long because he spent nine years in sacrifice for us. I just love him so much.

BANK did this. BANK saved my family. BANK brought my daughter and me together. BANK completely changed my husband's life. And I'm certain it will 100 percent change your life as well as the lives of the people around you.

All in all, what I hope you took away from this discussion are some ideas of how to use BANK in your business so people feel seen, heard, and understood in a world that has its blinders on and is only concerned with itself.

But more than that, bring it home. Change your world. Love your family. Love your people. Love your life. Make people matter.

MARTHA KREJCI | ANKB

Do you know anyone who has gone from being an exhausted and undervalued mom in the corporate 9-5 world to a multi-million dollar thought leadership brand in the blink of an eye? Now let's add without a college degree and without ads.... Well, now you do!

Martha Krejci is a high-vibin' mama, wife, business coach, growth strategist, and social media marketing powerhouse who has taken the internet by storm. She turns business owners into thought leaders in their communities. She even has her own bi-weekly segment on Tampa's WFLA TV News Station, where she expands on building a personal brand from the ground up. Martha is featured in Fox, ABC, and CBS News, Oprah Magazine, Fast Company, Cosmopolitan, Shape, and Huffington Post, among other places; her intuitive marketing expertise has helped her change the trajectory of her family's life in no time using a strategy she teaches openly through courses, group coaching, and other tried-and-true resources. She now writes for Entrepreneur and Forbes Magazine and is on the Forbes Business Council. From finding your passion to building a personal brand from nothing, she teaches it all to anyone ready.

Author's Website: WithMartha.com

CHAPTER 12
THE ASSIGNMENT: UNDERSTANDING YOUR MOTHER

BY MICHELLE LAFRANCE

> "My request is that you remember me as a kind person, forgive me for the times that I was unkind, as there were many. Forgive yourself for the times you've been unkind. I ask that you treat others with kindness and be good to one another."
>
> — Ruth Dean, My Mother

Have you ever noticed how your family dynamics impact your life? Perhaps a difficult relationship with your mother (or father) shaped your self-perceptions and the way you interact with others. Maybe this issue has even crept into your professional life. Is there a certain type of person who annoys or frustrates you?

THE TRIGGERING PERSON

Oh, I could recognize "that" person a mile away. They were everywhere: in my dating life and my family; they were heavily represented in my client base.

Do you know who I'm talking about? The nitpicker. The control freak. The buzz kill. In business, they seemed to exist solely to derail my sales efforts. They scrutinized me as if I were a specimen under a microscope.

Why are they staring at me like that? Why the seriousness? For God's sake, lighten up! What's with the endless, seemingly irrelevant questions?

Although I could easily identify this person, I had no solution. My natural exuberance felt out of place, prompting me to tone down my energy and speak slower, but honestly, I had no idea how to handle this person.

On the surface, I smiled, but under my breath, I was quoting the Serenity Prayer.

THE ASSIGNMENT THAT CHANGED EVERYTHING

The pivotal moment came during an advanced training called Level 5: Communication Mastery led by Cheri Tree.

"Pick a traumatizing experience and look at it through the lens of personality science," she instructed.

Boom! I was there in a nanosecond. My seven-year-old self with my mom screaming at me. "I wish you were never born," my mom said. "Why don't you go play in the road? I hope a truck runs you over." Those were words I heard frequently in my childhood.

Oh crap! I thought I had resolved my feelings, but the scene popped up as if in full living color. My heart ached in having to reveal this. Despite all the work I'd done, I still had a scar on my heart that didn't seem to heal.

Who would say such things to their child? Mothers are supposed to love their daughters, right? I felt humiliated and defective, believing my mother's words reflected my worth. It was as if I ingested those words.

I got paired with another trainer but was unable to complete the exercise. Overwhelmed, the weight of my family's dysfunction felt insurmountable. Tears flowed, and I doubted that personality science could even begin to unravel it.

NAVIGATING DYSFUNCTION

I grew up in what I call a blizzard of dysfunction. My hometown was an hour south of the Canadian border, so I know about blizzards. And if there was ever an Emmy given for family dysfunction, I can hear it now; the Emmy goes to, yeah, it would be my family.

My family was characterized by alcoholism, codependency, narcissism, abandonment, neglect, and abuse. Just like a blizzard, it was hard to see clearly, and honestly, I wondered how personality science could possibly have anything to do with it.

Weeks turned into months, and this incomplete assignment haunted me. I knew I'd find a pearl by completing this exercise. I knew I needed to persevere.

To further complicate things, my mother passed away before I became a BANKCODE Trainer. The BANK tools work wonderfully for the living...but could they be applied to someone who had passed away? I was trying so hard to figure it out. Seriously, my brain hurt. I kept looking at the values of the BANKCARDS: Blueprint, Action, Nurturing, and Knowledge. Who would say those things to their daughter?

I was frustrated. Every attempt to solve this mystery felt like hitting a brick wall. I threw my hands up in the air. "This is stupid!" I declared. I was swearing like a sailor, and one time, I even threw the cards across the room. Clearly, I was not going to figure this out in my mind.

But then a breakthrough: "Values drive behavior." It was the heart of the training.

> "Every person has a hidden set of values that drives their behavior and their buying decisions."

Aha...a lightbulb. Since my mother was gone, what if I were to make a list of behaviors and see if I could backtrack the behaviors to reveal her values? Is it possible I could reveal her four-part personality code? It was a brilliant problem-solving moment!

DISCOVERING MY MOTHER'S VALUES

I immediately got to work recollecting her behaviors. The first memory came back instantly. It was the daily commentary on the mailman's punctuality. One minute late, and she'd announce, "The mailman is late!" A few minutes later... "He's supposed to be here at eleven." Followed by "What do you think happened to him?" She'd sit in front of the picture window until he arrived, and then, with a big sigh of relief, she'd announced, "Oh, here comes the mailman." It was as if order had been restored to her day. Okay, got it. The mailman *must* be on time. Mom likes predictability. This was a good first clue.

Next, I recalled her love of gardening; she transformed the entire front yard into a flower garden with her tomato plants alongside the house. She cherished her gardens. One day, my brother and I overheard her excitedly talking to the neighbor about her "new tomato plants" that were "*growing like a weed.*" I looked at him and said, "You did not plant your pot plants in her garden," and he said, "Yes, I did. Look at how well she takes care of them. She even fertilizes them! My mother found joy in nurturing life, sharing flowers and the fruits of her garden. Her caring nature is clear.

After she passed, I discovered boxes of journals. Who knew? I was hoping for something juicy and exciting, but instead, I found a documented life. Each day was labeled with the date, time, and information on who called, who stopped by for coffee, and a few thoughts on what was on her mind. *Hmm, this is very revealing. A detailed description of each day.* Another important clue.

Thirty years before she passed, my mother started planning her funeral. I got a letter one day with instructions. "Wait. Isn't this a little premature?" I asked. "No," she was going to donate her body to the University of Minnesota and was proud of it, too. "I've decided I'm going to recycle myself. That way, nobody needs to spend a dime on my funeral." She liked to plan ahead and was frugal. Clarity set in.

CRACKING HER CODE

I'll never forget. It was as if it was slow-motion; I took the Blueprint card and placed it in the first place of the four-part sequence. She valued predictability and planning; she was budget-conscious, detail-oriented, and a rule follower. All of a sudden, I realized my mother was "that person," a Blueprint personality. Whoa! But what about the rest of the sequence?

My father drank. He was never around; he'd rather be at the bar than at home with his family. I caught him in bed with another woman when I was thirteen. It prompted my mom to kick him out. He neither protected nor provided for the family while he was in the house, and once kicked out, it was even worse. No food in the fridge. Electricity would go out. And apparently, the mortgage wasn't being paid. I discovered our house for sale in the daily want ads. It was grim. We were about to lose it all.

Desperate, my mother and I went to the courthouse each week to plead our case before a judge. We needed help, and we needed it fast. Anything would have helped—alimony, child support, food stamps. Week after week, we'd go to the courthouse, yet nothing changed. Wasn't there a system to support situations like this?

My mother was depressed. Sometimes, she didn't get out of bed for days. I'd get myself up in the morning, along with my younger brother, make us Cheerios, and head off to school. It was a sad time. Despite our weekly appearances at the courthouse, nothing changed. Time was running out.

About this time, a state law passed allowing the Iron Ore Mines of Northern Minnesota to hire women. A beloved aunt and uncle encouraged my mom to pursue it. And then one day...it was like a switch flipped in my mother. All of a sudden, she had a fire in her belly. She got up and drove to the mine to apply for a job. Standing five-foot-two and 110 pounds, she was not equipped for labor.

She did this every day only to come home and report that there weren't any jobs. "That's okay. I'll just go back tomorrow." One day, she came home, somewhat hopeful. "Michelle, the guy said he didn't have any jobs, but as I walked away, I heard the guy next to him say, "You know she's just going to come back tomorrow, right?"

My mother became one of the first women hired in the mines of Northern Minnesota. She got hired as a janitor. It saved us from losing our house. This story is portrayed in the movie *North Country*, a true story about women like my mother who could not rely on the men in their lives to provide for them.

It all became crystal clear to me. It was as if I could see my mother's life playing like a movie right before my very eyes—the dynamics of her life. For the first time, I saw her as a human being doing the best she could managing the trials and tribulations of her life.

That's when I took the next card, the Nurturing card, and put it in the second place. Despite the start of this story, my Mother was a very kind person. She liked simple things like growing flowers and feeding the birds. She volunteered at the Humane Society and had a heart for all animals. She was truly a caring and kindhearted woman.

Next, I put the Action card in its proper place, the third spot in the sequence, the stress code. I saw how, as a Blueprint, she wanted to follow the rules and get the courts to do something, but it wasn't until the eleventh hour, when we were about homeless, that her stress code kicked in. Later in life, I asked her about the mining job. She told me how defeated and humiliated she felt to have a drunk, cheating husband. One day, she decided she was not going to lose her house because of that SOB. A tiger came out, a persistent one who drove to the mines daily until she got hired.

I then placed the Knowledge card in the fourth position because she held few of its values.

A NEW NARRATIVE

For the longest time, I just stared at the BANKCARDS. In cracking my mother's personality code, I gained a completely new perspective. It was cracking the code on forgiveness. I was liberated from the story that my mother didn't love me. All the harsh words that scarred my heart just melted away.

I could finally see my mother as a person. This woman was desperately trying to find some happiness in her life. The story I'd been carrying, the hurt, the resentment disappeared. In its place, a fresh perspective.

Instead of seeing my mother as the angry person who lashed out at me, I saw a human doing the best she could. She'd had a horrible childhood, and she so wanted a happy family, something that eluded her. I don't think she knew how to be a mother.

This, indeed, was the assignment of a lifetime. It liberated me from the story of my childhood. It became clear that the hurtful words were never about me. Regarding my father, she was trying to get a square peg to fit in a round hole, and he wasn't having it.

I fell in love with my mother that day. I spoke the words out loud. My heart filled with compassion and appreciation for her. My hope for you reading this is that you find freedom from whatever story you may be stuck in and find freedom to see your life from a new perspective.

BEING ENLIGHTENED TO PERSONALITY TYPES

They're gone. The stories are gone. They don't exist anymore. The story about the difficult client who killed my business deals? Gone!

Today, I do business with the once dreaded Blueprint personality and enjoy it. I understand now they require different things from me. And you know what? It's no skin off my nose to give them what they need, show up early, and report more frequently. In fact, it has helped me grow a part of myself that needed development. Thank you, Blueprint!

The story about my angry mother who didn't love me? Gone. In its place, a more empowering and life-giving story. She was a resilient woman in a challenging situation, doing her best to raise kids. Did she lash out with hurtful words? Yes. Did she mean them? No.

The exercise set me free. Today, I have nothing but love in my heart for my mother. The resentment has been replaced with compassion. In its place is a beautiful remembrance of her.

By the way, my mother spent most of her life apologizing and taking responsibility for her hurtful words. Taking responsibility is one of the hallmark traits of the Blueprint personality.

Today, when I think of my mother, I smile. I am at peace. My only regret is that I wish I would have known about these tools while she was still alive. I'm a happier person, and I'm a better person with more kindness and patience toward others.

The stories that hinder you can shift, too. Your relationships will improve; you'll let go of stories that don't serve you and find creative solutions to people's problems. And you'll make more money as a result.

LESSONS LEARNED

The personality types I was most critical of were the ones least like me. Their biggest crime was that they were simply different than me.

Judging people gets in the way of doing business with them. The Blueprint's personality needs to make safe decisions; it's why they are so thorough. Now, instead of judging them, I help them feel safe in doing business with me. Paradigm shift!

When you shift your perspective, you free not only yourself but the person you've been judging. Both of you get released from the story.

People have personalities, and personalities have preferences. It's well worth the time to learn about other people's hidden set of values.

EXERCISE

1. **Identify Your Triggers:** Is there a type of person you resist, ignore, or criticize? Is it a specific person, or is it a group of people?
2. **Reframe Your Perspective:** Write down the labels you have assigned to this person or group. What are they doing that upsets you?
3. **Explore The BANKCODE:** What is your BANKCODE? What is their BANKCODE? Are they similar or different? Are you able to find a more compassionate view of them?

FIVE TIPS TO BETTER UNDERSTAND OTHERS

1. If you're lucky enough to have parents who are alive, don't waste a second in cracking their code! Do this with your partner and children, too.
2. People treat you the way they do because of who they are, not because of who you are.
3. Don't allow yourself to be a victim of any person, situation, or story. Use the tool of looking through the lens of personality science to free yourself.

4. Catch yourself when you judge another; you'll feel better to find a kinder thought about them.

5. When you notice someone judging you, don't take it personally; smile and realize they're just different than you.

SUMMARY

If you're ready to change your story with the person you've been frustrated with, then by completing this assignment, you can experience an increased sense of personal freedom.

This healing process will free you from the stories that keep you stuck. It will help you shift your perspective from that of a victim to one of a victor.

I have one more important piece of advice. It has to do with you. When you get down on yourself, what do you say to yourself? One of the great benefits of the BANKCODE methodology is you'll also learn empathy for yourself.

The first part of your code is who you are; you don't have to try to be this way. You'll notice that sometimes it is a strength, and other times, it can be a weakness. Celebrate your wins and acknowledge yourself for the things that come easily for you. Make sure to find acceptance and be gentle with yourself when you see your weakness.

BANK has helped me heal my relationship with my deceased mother, giving me peace of mind and greater acceptance for both me and her. With this new peace of mind,

I have been able to create a life of greater impact, income, and influence.

Your assignment, should you choose to accept it, is to take action toward healing your relationships. I encourage you to apply the great wisdom of the BANKCODE methodology to set yourself free.

My final challenge to you is to become the best version of yourself. To achieve this, stay focused on healing your relationships and living your life with passion and purpose so you can create your best life now.

MICHELLE LAFRANCE | ANKB

Michelle LaFrance is the founder, and visionary behind an innovative marketing program that is transforming the HVAC industry. Her powerful approach is disrupting traditional marketing models while providing exceptional results to her clients.

Michelle also offers *Winning At The Kitchen Table*, a program designed to increase people's understanding of others. This skill can be used in business to increase closing ratios and resolve conflict and is especially helpful in healing personal relationships.

Today, you'll find Michelle featured in prominent industry outlets such as *ACHR News, Service Mastery Podcast, The HVAC Jerks,* and *Smart HVAC Podcast.*

A passionate advocate for personal growth and transformation, she also draws on her own inspiring journey of overcoming personal challenges to help others resolve deep-seated issues and move forward with renewed purpose.

Author's Website: HeySmartyPants.com

CHAPTER 13
MASTERING COMMUNICATION FOR YOUR ULTIMATE SUCCESS

BY MICHELLE LEE MYRTER

> "To effectively communicate, we must realize that we are all different in the way we perceive the world and use this understanding as a guide to our communication with others."
>
> — Tony Robbins

How effective is your communication? Have you ever had a breakdown of communication with someone you love? Have you ever lost an opportunity or relationship because you didn't get your message across the way you wanted to? Have you ever lost a relationship because you just didn't understand each other?

SALES AND RELATIONSHIPS ARE HARD

Relationships and sales are hard, and I was failing miserably at both.

Have you ever had to rebuild your life or start over?

I did when I lost my job of more than twenty-eight years, had to rebuild my life in my forties with two young children, and had no idea what I was going to do or how I was going to get there. I decided to start a company in the only industry I knew: the food industry. It was not what I would have chosen, but it was all I knew.

Trying to grow a business is hard enough; then add in being a parent raising two kids. I felt like I was failing miserably at both. Plus, I thought my oldest son couldn't stand me, and we couldn't communicate with each other at all. This was not what I signed up for and definitely not how I thought my life would turn out. I was doing the best I could, trying to juggle everything, but I did not spend nearly enough time with either one of my children, causing us to grow further and further apart.

My life was spiraling out of control. I had no money, and all my relationships were suffering. I was tired, frustrated, and completely done with life at this point. The only thing that kept me going were my kids and my amazing husband.

As I was trying to grow my business, I met someone who introduced me to network marketing, something I was unfamiliar with. She told me she had an opportunity, but at the time, I wanted nothing to do with it. Even though the products completely changed my son's and my life, I already had enough on my plate.

That woman never gave up, and because of my dear friend Holly, I joined a different network marketing company. This put me in the exact place I needed to find my purpose: a conference where I met Cheri Tree, the Founder and CEO of Codebreaker Technologies. By the end of her presentation, I thought I understood everything in my life: my kids, my husband, my parents, the sales I lost, and why I struggled so much with past relationships. For the first time in my life, *everything* made sense! I finally knew who I was and that I wasn't broken! I needed to know more because Cheri Tree had reverse-engineered personality science and unlocked the secret to not only sales but also people!

CRACKING THE PEOPLE CODE

After leaving the conference, I was cracking everyone's code. Cracking the code is so much fun and so easy; Cheri Tree created a set of four plastic cards that have values listed on them. All you have to do is sort the BANKCARDS in order of importance, and BOOM, that's it! Once the code is cracked, you have unlocked that person's operating system, core values, and what is most important to them. I was *on fire*. I felt free for once in my life. Cheri lit this magical light inside of me, which gave me hope and a vision for having the life I always wanted.

As soon as I got home, I read her book *Why They Buy*. I also carried my set of BANKCARDS everywhere I went, and of course, I cracked the codes of my family and friends.

I started to see the world in a whole new way. I found out there was a coaching and training program as part of this system, and I really wanted to participate. I had to learn more! This was what would allow me to grow my business fast and finally be free.

The day I started the BANK Intelligence Operating System (IOS) Coaching program, I had no idea what I had signed up for other than I wanted to increase my sales and grow my business in half the time.

After the first session, I completely broke down, but in a good way. Sometimes, you need to have a breakdown before you can experience a breakthrough. Before the session, I thought I knew everything about my son. Now, I understood I was treating my son not as he wanted to be treated, but how I wanted to be treated. It was very surface-level, with no communication; it was unemotional. I realized, for the first time, "who" my child was. When my son walked in the door, I said, "I am so sorry. I have done it wrong for eighteen years." That day, everything permanently shifted in our relationship.

For the first time *ever*, we understood each other. We truly understood why we had such a hard time communicating and getting along. We were wired completely differently, and now we knew how to get along and why we were so different. It wasn't personal; it was just *personality*! We were able to find common ground, learn a way to connect, and understand what we each needed to feel loved.

From that day on, I implemented this in every area of my life and every relationship. I immersed myself in training to master the skills of communication and people.

Because of BANK, I was able to have a relationship with my son, was able to grow my business, and sell it in less than three years, and then focus all my energy on building a coaching and training business where I get to help people become the best versions of themselves.

TAKING IT TO THE BANK

Have you ever had something change your life so dramatically that you knew you had finally found your purpose?

This one presentation by Cheri Tree answered all the questions: Who are you? Why are you struggling with all the relationships in your life? Why is growing your business so hard?

Everything came down to one thing—being able to truly understand people and how they are wired with a simple system that anyone can learn and implement. Cheri created a way to understand this in less than ninety seconds!

The secret was finally unlocked, which changed my life and business forever!

In less than ninety seconds, I understood my son's operating system, something I had been trying to figure out for eighteen years. Our core values were opposite, and now I understood how he needed me to show up for him.

It's crazy how life works. If you are open to it, you will find what you need at just the right time.

EXERCISE

1. Which people in your life do you miscommunicate with the most?
2. Describe how your personality is different than those of the people mentioned above.
3. What do you need to do to change your mindset so you start speaking in the personality of your mother, son, boss, etc.?

THE CHALLENGE

I challenge you to crack the code of every person in your life and see how you can truly *make people matter*, build stronger relationships, and become the best version of yourself. When preparing for any communication with the above three most challenging people (son, mother, boss), I challenge you to mentally prepare to change your personality and language only for that conversation.

THINGS TO REMEMBER

Communication is not personal; it's personality! From this perspective, communication can become more personal and effective.

To truly change your life and the world, crack the code, read the report, speak the code, and live the code.

If you make people matter, you can take that to the BANK!

SUMMARY

Everything you do in life is about people and relationships. The way to succeed in life and business is to master an understanding of people and communication skills. BANK gives you the tools, training, and state-of-the-art technology to easily master these skills, becoming the best version of yourself and living the life you have always dreamed of having.

MICHELLE LEE MYRTER | ANKB

Michelle Lee Myrter is an award-winning Certified and Licensed BANK Trainer and Coach, Keynote Speaker, and Networking Ninja. She has more than thirty years of experience in corporate sales and many years in network marketing and direct sales. Implementing BANK, she took her start-up company from 0 to more than $2 million in less than three years.

BANK saved her relationship with her son. Seeing the power of BANK, Michelle knew she had found her purpose and passion. Her mission is to empower the lives of every person she touches and have a ripple effect so others can learn to live their best life ever, having financial and time freedom and the best relationships possible.

Author's Website: https://artandscienceofinfluence.now.site/home

CHAPTER 14
LIVING YOUR BEST LIFE WITH CONNECTION

BY MONICA RITCHEY

"It's not personal; it's personality."

— Cheri Tree

Have you ever wondered why some relationships feel effortless while others are riddled with challenges? Why do you click with some people instantly and struggle to connect with others? These questions have intrigued me for years, weaving their way into my professional endeavors, personal relationships, and even how I interact with strangers. What is it about certain connections that spark like fireworks while others fizzle out before they even begin?

I've always been fascinated by people—their behaviors, their decisions, and the way they communicate. From a young age, I noticed patterns in relationships, both within my family and with the people I met. Growing up, my family dynamics were a myriad of contrasts, filled with moments that taught me resilience and adaptability. I witnessed how relationships could shape a life—for better or for worse.

In my early years, I tried to make sense of these dynamics. Why did some conversations flow effortlessly while others felt like trying to climb a mountain in heels? Why did some people naturally gravitate toward me while others seemed indifferent? Not until years later, when I began exploring personality science, did I realize the answers lay not in some flaw within myself but in the beautiful, complex differences that define us all.

I learned that connection isn't about changing who you are to fit someone else's mold. It's about understanding the language they speak—their personality code—and meeting them where they are. This revelation became the foundation of my personal and professional transformation. It gave me permission to embrace my unique qualities while finding ways to genuinely connect with others.

These questions didn't just shape my relationships; they became the cornerstone of my growth as a mom, spouse, businesswoman, and leader. Whether effortless or challenging, each connection held a lesson that guided me toward a deeper understanding of myself and the people around me. Over time, I realized that understanding these dynamics wasn't just about fostering better relationships—it was about empowering myself to live a life of authenticity, purpose, and joy.

This journey is the messy, beautiful, and transformative power of connection—whether you want to improve your professional interactions, deepen your family and friend bonds, or simply understand yourself better.

MY JOURNEY TO SELF-DISCOVERY

I grew up in Pittsburgh, Pennsylvania, surrounded by a world of contrasts. One side of my family came from wealth, and the other lived a more modest life. This duality gave me a unique perspective on the world from a young age. Some weekends were spent shopping with my grandmother at Saks Fifth Avenue, where she encouraged me to "get whatever I wanted," followed by lunches at the most elegant restaurants downtown. Other times, I was with my mom at thrift stores doing back-to-school shopping, carefully searching for brand-name labels that caught my eye amid the racks. Finding a designer piece at a bargain felt like winning a small victory. These experiences, though drastically different, shaped my understanding of resourcefulness, gratitude, and the value of hard work.

Hard work also defines me. I started teaching kids how to swim at a young age; I was a lifeguard for several years, I babysat my cousins on summer break, and I was a waitress for well over a decade. Whether it was waiting tables at Denny's or a five-star fine dining establishment while I was in college, I have been working with people of all ages in many forms and facets since I was an early teen.

Swimming was the centerpiece of my childhood. For thirteen years, the sport defined my schedule, relationships, and identity. Starting with age-group club swimming, I worked my way up to one of the country's most successful high school teams. We dominated every single meet, winning state championships twice during my four years on the team. My dedication paid off when I joined a Division I college swim program, where the challenges grew tougher, but so did my determination. I even had the chance to train at the Olympic Training Center, an experience that taught me the importance of aiming high and striving for excellence, even in the face of pressure. Swimming instilled in me qualities like discipline, loyalty, perseverance, and focus—traits that would later serve me well in the business world.

But not all lessons came from victories. My parents' divorce marked a significant turning point in my life. They separated when I was twelve and finalized the divorce when I was eighteen, after years of courtroom battles and emotional strain. Their divorce taught me about the fragility of relationships and the deep complexities of human interaction. On the one hand, I had the privilege of seeing what financial abundance could provide; on the other, I learned how to thrive without it. These life lessons planted the seeds of my fascination with people—their motivations, decisions, and how they navigate life.

After college, I transitioned into what I thought would be the next logical step: the corporate world. I worked in healthcare client management at Blue Cross Blue Shield, commuting daily to the city, clocking in long hours, and spending evenings tethered to my laptop. Despite my hard work, I quickly realized my salary was capped, my creativity was stifled, and my time was no longer my own. I craved freedom—freedom to set my own hours, pursue my passions, and create a life that aligned with my values. But how?

That answer came in 2004 when I tagged along with my mom to a home party. It was my first introduction to direct sales, and I was captivated. Watching the distributor effortlessly sell gourmet food while chatting with guests, I realized this could be a way out of the cubicle. The flexibility, the control, and the potential to earn beyond a fixed salary intrigued me. I joined the business immediately and began building my future.

Initially, direct sales was a side hustle, but I started to see the bigger picture as I became more immersed. I was inspired by the stories of others who had turned this business model into thriving careers. In 2011, the universe gave me a nudge, and I took the leap into direct sales full-time. It was both exhilarating and daunting, but I knew I had found my calling. I was no longer working to fulfill someone else's vision but building my own. After six years of being in direct sales, I transitioned to apparel. There, my inner fashionista tendencies shined brightly. My passion for dressing for success allowed me to help women take the stress out of dressing and become more confident in their skin. There I built two multi-million-dollar businesses.

The journey wasn't without its challenges, but each obstacle taught me resilience and reinforced my belief in the power of forging one's own path. The foundation laid during these formative years—through swimming, family struggles, and my corporate detour—prepared me to take control of my destiny. Little did I know the lessons I learned then would become the bedrock of my approach to life, business, and relationships today.

DISCOVERING BANK AND ITS IMPACT

Years into my direct sales career, a dear friend and savvy businesswoman—introduced me to the BANK methodology. I vividly remember our first conversation about it. She spoke with such conviction and enthusiasm that I couldn't help but be intrigued. At first, I was skeptical. Could a personality system really unlock better relationships and professional success? I had dabbled with personality assessments before, but they felt more like labels than tools for transformation. Still, her passion was infectious, and my curiosity eventually led me to explore BANK further.

What I discovered was a refreshingly different methodology. It wasn't just about categorizing people; it was about understanding them on a deeper level. BANK taught me the phrase, "It's not personal; it's personality." Those five words became a mantra that reshaped how I viewed every relationship in my life.

Before BANK, I often internalized failed connections, thinking they reflected something I lacked. I questioned whether

I was doing enough if a team member didn't thrive under my leadership. If a potential client didn't respond to my pitch, I assumed I'd chosen the wrong words. BANK helped me see these moments differently. They weren't about my shortcomings—they were about communication gaps. With this new perspective, I began adapting my approach to fit the personalities of the people I interacted with. When I spoke to someone who valued facts and structure, I leaned into logic and detailed plans. For someone driven by excitement and spontaneity, I focused on energy and possibility.

This methodology didn't just improve my professional interactions; it revolutionized my family life. One of the most poignant applications of BANK has been with my spouse. We are polar opposites—he's a high Knowledge, while I'm more Action-oriented. Before understanding our personalities, we often found ourselves at odds (getting frustrated). His love for logic, research, and development clashed with my spontaneous, let's-jump-in approach. Small disagreements with our personal communication styles quickly escalated into misunderstandings.

BANK changed all of that. I began to see his Knowledge nature not as rigid, but as a source of accuracy and security. I learned to appreciate his need for competence and intelligence as primary values, and I started communicating with him in ways that aligned with these preferences. Instead of jumping into the next endeavor, I began discussing projects ahead of time, giving him the big picture and the universal truths he needed to feel aligned with the end goal in mind. He began to understand my need for excitement and flexibility, meeting me halfway by embracing spontaneity when it mattered most.

The insights from BANK have definitely enhanced my primary role as a mom. My oldest daughter is a miniature Blueprint, thriving on order, predictability, and well-laid plans. She loves knowing what's coming next and feels secure when her environment is structured. On Sunday nights, we organize her outfits for the week, carefully laying them out on her closet valet bar. Each morning, she can confidently grab her clothes in an organized fashion without the stress of deciding what to wear at the last minute. Similarly, we keep her school calendar visible, marking art, physical education, music days, and other activities to ease her anxieties about the unknown.

In contrast, my youngest daughter is a mirror of my Action-oriented personality. She's spontaneous, playful, and full of boundless energy. Her joy comes from unstructured playtime, colorful adventures, and moments of creative freedom. Recognizing these differences has allowed me to parent both girls authentically, meeting each of them where they are rather than trying to mold them into something they're not.

BANK has also helped me better understand myself. As an Action-Nurturing-Knowledge-Blueprint (ANKB) personality type, I thrive on excitement, connection, and learning, but I had often dimmed my light to fit into spaces where I felt I didn't belong. Learning about my code gave me permission to unapologetically embrace who I am. It also helped me recognize when I needed to tap into my lesser strengths, like my Blueprint side, to bridge the gap in business as well as in my connection with others.

One of the most profound lessons from BANK is: Connection isn't about changing who you are. It's about learning the "language" of others and finding common ground. Whether in business or family life, adapting to someone else's personality doesn't mean losing your authenticity—it means enhancing the relationship through mutual understanding. The clarity and confidence I gained through BANK continue to impact every corner of my life, proving that the right tools can truly change how we show up in the world.

LIVING WITH PURPOSE AND CONNECTION

BANK didn't just change how I interact with others; it transformed how I view myself. As an Action-Nurturing-Knowledge-Blueprint (ANKB) personality type, I thrive on freedom, fun, teamwork, personal growth, nurturing relationships, and seeking the big picture. But for years, I held back, afraid of the brilliance within me and the power it might unleash, choosing instead to shrink into spaces where I felt safer. I often adjusted my energy to match the room's dynamics, suppressing my vibrant, action-driven nature in favor of being "appropriate" or "acceptable." It wasn't until BANK came into my life that I truly gave myself permission to embrace my strengths unapologetically. Understanding my personality code showed me that my qualities weren't liabilities to be muted—they were assets to be amplified. This shift in perspective not only changed how I navigated relationships, but it allowed me to align my actions with my core values.

Amid these experiences, life threw me a series of big curveballs. In early 2015, I had just completed the most successful month in my career at the time. My second direct sales company, which I had poured my heart and soul into, abruptly closed its doors. It was a devastating blow, one that echoed the emotional upheaval I felt during my parents' divorce. It was a sharp reminder of how quickly stability can be pulled out from under us. My business had been more than a job; it was a part of my identity as a single woman building her future. It was a source of pride, and a testament to my hard work. Losing it felt like losing a part of myself. The closure left me feeling caught off guard, questioning what would come next. Yet, in that uncertainty, I leaned on the resilience honed through years of setbacks and triumphs, reminding myself that every setback can be a setup for a comeback. I quickly pivoted, aligning with a new company and embarking on a fresh chapter, determined to rebuild what I had lost.

In 2021, I experienced the most profound loss of my life. My mother, the blueprint of my early world, passed away unexpectedly at age sixty-five. That summer, I drove to her house and discovered she had died in her home. The pain of that moment is something I will carry with me forever. My mom and I had a close bond. She was my best friend and my biggest cheerleader. During my teenage years, we had not always seen eye to eye—we were, in many ways, opposites in personality. Her Blueprint nature was rooted in structure, caution, and safety, while my Action-driven approach embraced risk and spontaneity. As a teenager, I often found myself frustrated with her protective instincts, particularly when she said no to fun things I desperately wanted to do. It wasn't until much later, with the clarity BANK brought into my life, that I fully understood her choices came from love and her deep need to ensure my safety. Losing her taught me to treasure my life's relationships and approach them with empathy and understanding. Time is fleeting, and the connections we nurture today are what matter most.

By late 2024, another seismic shift occurred. My alignment with a company I had worked with as a legacy leader for nearly a decade ended. This wasn't just a professional loss—it felt personal. After years of dedication, success, and growth, I found myself at another crossroads. But just as I had done before, I leaned into life's lessons: resilience, adaptability, and the importance of relationships. I clung to the mantra that setbacks are setups for comebacks, choosing to see the opportunity within the challenge. Setbacks are not reflections of failure—they're opportunities to pivot and grow. They are most often setups for our future!

With this mindset, I turned toward a new chapter. My pivot wasn't just a professional business decision based on more than twenty years of experience, but a personal commitment to myself and my family. I chose to build something that aligned even deeper with my life purpose and values. This time, I approached my new venture with a different lens, focusing on empowering people to easily navigate the journey of healthy non-toxic living, clean and clinical wellness, and beauty, style, and entrepreneurial success. BANK became my secret weapon, allowing me to communicate with my clients, colleagues, and team members in a way that resonated deeply with their unique needs and motivations.

As I opened my next chapter in 2025, adding health and beauty into the mix, I carried with me the words of the late Kobe Bryant: "Turn every setback into a comeback." This pivot isn't just about professional success; it's about living in alignment with my purpose and using my experiences to build connections that matter. I now approach relationships—whether personal or professional—with a renewed sense of purpose, understanding that every connection has the power to shape our lives.

Through all these challenges, I've come to realize that people matter more than anything. Family, friends, clients, team members, and colleagues aren't just part of the journey—they are the journey. They give us the strength to rise again after a fall, the wisdom to see beyond our current struggles, and the love that reminds us why we keep moving forward. Today, I choose to make people matter, not just because it enriches their lives but because it transforms mine.

One of the most empowering aspects of this journey was realizing the extent to which understanding personalities could influence not just professional success but also personal fulfillment. When I began applying the principles of BANK in my new business, I noticed how easily relationships flowed. Conversations felt less transactional and more authentic. Clients trusted me because I spoke their "language," tailoring my communication to what mattered most to them. This alignment wasn't just beneficial for my business—it was deeply fulfilling for me.

The lessons of BANK also seeped into my everyday life, helping me create a home environment rooted in understanding and connection. As a mom, I now see my daughters as unique individuals with distinct needs. My oldest daughter's Blueprint tendencies mean she thrives on structure and predictability, so I've made it a priority to maintain routines and clear expectations. My youngest daughter, who mirrors my Action/Nurturing-oriented personality, finds joy in spontaneity, relationships, harmony and creative freedom. Recognizing these differences has allowed me to meet each of them where they are, celebrating their individuality rather than trying to impose a one-size-fits-all approach.

Even my romantic life has been transformed by these principles. My spouse and I have navigated our differences with greater compassion and understanding. His Knowledge nature complements my Action tendencies, creating a partnership that balances opportunity and spontaneity with expertise and logic. Our ability to appreciate and adapt to each other's personalities has deepened our connection, turning potential friction points into opportunities for growth.

Looking back, I realize every challenge I faced—whether losing a business, navigating family and spousal dynamics, or adapting to motherhood—has been imperative toward living a life of deeper purpose and connection. BANK gave me the tools to see these experiences not as obstacles but as lessons, each shaping me into who I am today.

WHAT I LEARNED

I've learned that connection is the heart of success through setbacks and triumphs. Whether building a business, nurturing a family, or navigating friendships, understanding people unlocks potential. BANK taught me we are all wired differently, and adapting to others' codes isn't just beneficial—it's transformative.

1. **Adaptability is key:** The ability to tailor your communication to resonate with others opens doors you didn't know existed.
2. **Self-awareness fuels growth:** Knowing your strengths and embracing them unapologetically is the foundation of confidence.
3. **Resilience is non-negotiable:** Setbacks aren't failures but lessons that prepare you for your next breakthrough.

EXERCISE: REFLECT AND CONNECT

- Think about a recent conflict or miscommunication. How might different personality styles have influenced the outcome?
- Identify one relationship in your life where understanding the other person's code could deepen your connection.

TIPS FOR LIVING YOUR BEST STYLED LIFE BY LEADING WITH CONNECTION

1. **Embrace your unique strengths:** Stop dimming your light and own your unique personality.

2. **Learn the BANK methodology:** Understanding others' codes is a game-changer in all aspects of life. LIVE THE CODE. It's one thing to learn something; it's another to adapt it into every conversation, both oral and written to truly enhance your life.
3. **Prioritize relationships:** Whether in business or family, meaningful connections are the foundation of success.
4. **Adapt your communication style:** Meet people where they are, not where you want them to be.
5. **Stay resilient:** Challenges are opportunities in disguise. Turn your setback into a setup.

CONCLUSION AND CALL TO ACTION

My passion for people has empowered me to live my truth and create the best life possible for me and my family. This personality tool allows me to show up authentically and share that gift with others. It has touched me to my core; it has changed my life for the better, and I want to encourage you not only to crack your code but to have anyone you are connected to, whether it's family, workplace, or community, do the same. I encourage you not to stop there; take it a step further. Learn the methodology and then live it every single day in every single conversation you have. That is where the magic happens.

Every relationship, every business endeavor, and every moment of growth begins with understanding. BANK taught me that connection isn't just about communicating—it's about truly seeing and valuing people for who they are.

This insight changed how I approached relationships and gave me the courage to embrace my own unique strengths unapologetically.

I challenge you to explore how to build more authentic connections. Start by considering the people you interact with daily. How well do you understand their needs, motivations, and personalities? What simple adjustments could you make to connect more effectively? Tools like BANK offer a roadmap for this kind of transformation, but even small steps—like listening more intently or asking thoughtful questions—can make a profound difference.

This journey isn't just about making others feel seen. It's about realizing how much you matter. When you live authentically and align your actions with your values, you inspire those around you. So start today. Identify one relationship you'd like to nurture, reflect on how you can approach it with empathy, and take that first step.

> **"Yesterday is history, tomorrow is a mystery, and today is a gift. That is why it is called the present."**
>
> — Eleanor Roosevelt

Connection isn't a destination—it's a daily practice. And the beauty of that practice is that as you make others feel valued, you'll discover the power of living a life that aligns with your purpose. Take action today and make the most of your connections and relationships.

MONICA RITCHEY | ANKB

Monica Ritchey is a dynamic entrepreneur, business mentor, network marketing leader, Certified and Licensed BANK Trainer and Coach, wellness advocate, and personal stylist with a mission to empower women to achieve holistic success through health, beauty, style, and entrepreneurship. As the Founder and CEO of Your Styled Life, Monica has dedicated her career to helping women enhance their lifestyle and embrace their individuality through innovative fashion solutions and balanced clean living. With twenty-plus years of proven experience in direct sales and business development, she is a recognized leader, top seller, and industry veteran.

A Pittsburgh native, Monica holds an MBA from Waynesburg University and a degree from the University of Kentucky, where she honed the resilience and discipline that fuel her entrepreneurial journey. As a former Olympic-trained, Division I swimmer, Monica understands the value of dedication, teamwork, and personal growth. These qualities now influence her role as a mother to two daughters, a friend to many, a trusted mentor and legacy leader in the direct sales industry.

Author's Website: www.YourStyledLife.net

CHAPTER 15
THE ENTREPENEUR'S PATH TO SUCCESS

BY PATRICK SNOW

"To inspire people, don't show them your superpower. Show them theirs."

— Alexander den Heijer

Have you ever wondered why some people are successful in life, business, and relationships while many others are not? Have you ever wondered what knowledge these successful people have that you and others may be missing? If you were to master this "missing" knowledge, how would your life improve? I will attempt to answer these questions in this short chapter by offering four proven strategies that will forever put your life on a path to success while also making people matter!

MY STORY

For as long as I can remember, I have been an entrepreneur. When I was a kid growing up in Michigan, my loving parents always taught me that I could have anything in life I wanted as long as I was willing to work hard for it and pay for it myself. So, I was busy working when I was not playing sports or riding my bike. I earned my own money starting around ten years old by mowing grass and shoveling snow, and by age thirteen, I was selling *Detroit Free Press* subscriptions door-to-door and earning $80-120 per night. This pay rate was much better than working at Burger Ranch and earning $3.35 per hour.

Moving forward, after a back injury ended my college football pursuits, I transferred to the University of Montana. I graduated three-and-a-half years later with a political science degree while also studying entrepreneurship. Soon after, I moved to Seattle and started my adult career as an author, speaker, and coach in corporate sales and entrepreneurship. Prior to quitting my job at thirty-four years old, I achieved modest success in my corporate sales career in the travel industry, air freight industry, car rental industry, and finally, the printed circuit industry. All the while, I wrote my books and moonlighted as a speaker. Then, I transitioned to being full-time out on my own and successfully building my business.

During my first dozen years or so in corporate sales, I made all the mistakes that many young sales professionals make. In an effort to build rapport, I once asked a female prospect during a sales presentation, "How many months pregnant are you?" She replied, "I am not pregnant; my stomach just looks this way!" From that day forward, a woman's water might have broken, and she could be on her way to the hospital to give birth, yet I would never again ask about her pregnancy until the baby was in hand.

Another mistake I made was during a sales presentation. I somehow ripped the seat of my pants completely wide open from front to back. As I finished up, I shook hands and slowly walked backward out of the office in an attempt to hide my skivvies, which were completely visible through the seat of my slacks.

And, of course, in my early days, there were many sales calls where I would "show up and throw up" by talking so much that I would talk myself right out of a sale rather than letting my prospect clearly express their wants and needs. That was a sure way to starve rather than make it in the sales industry. Certainly, it was a mistake that the young, passionate, loud, and energetic Patrick Snow would make. After learning the hard way, the middle-aged Patrick Snow has wised up and not made such mistakes now for many, many years!

After retiring from my corporate sales career at age thirty-four, I became a full-time entrepreneur, earning income solely by my own efforts. That has been my path now for almost twenty-five years. Thankfully, I have learned from all the mistakes of my youth, and I have become much better at not showing my superpowers and, instead, helping my clients recognize theirs.

WHAT I LEARNED

Thankfully, while learning from these tough mistakes, I was on a payroll with my employer, so it was possible to earn an income. However, since 2001, I have been a full-time entrepreneur, a bestselling author, a professional keynote speaker, and a writing, publishing, and book-marketing coach. During my years of building my business, The Snow Group, I have applied the following four foundational principles I learned from making so many mistakes early in my career:

1. **Provide Massive Value to Your Clients:** One of my all-time favorite authors and speakers is Zig Ziglar. He always said: "You can have everything you want, as long as you help enough other people get what they want." To me, this means your quickest path to success in life and business as an entrepreneur is to help all the people you come across by assisting them in achieving their goals. As a result, you will achieve your goals with the income earned in serving others.

2. **Listen Your Way to Making More Sales:** My friend and publishing client Christine Miles has written what I believe to be the world's greatest book on listening. She titled her book *What Is It Costing You Not to Listen?* because she thinks that is one of life's most important questions. She argues that the ability to listen is one of the most important skills you need to develop. Whether you realize it or not, listening—or the lack thereof—affects every aspect of your life. It can cut and leave deep wounds while also having the power to transform your relationships, business, and personal growth in ways you

never imagined. For more information on this book, visit TheListeningPath.com.

3. **Let Your Prospects Determine Your Presentation:** World-renowned author, speaker, coach, and mega-best-selling author Tony Robbins has taught this principle for many years. Early in my career, I adopted his exact approach to life and business with great success. At the core, this principle means that instead of coming up with a sales pitch or presentation and giving the same dog-and-pony show to all of your prospects, you simply ask them, "What are your needs? What do you want? What are your goals and objectives? What is important to you?"

4. Once you have gathered the answers to these questions, you can create a *customized* presentation, a unique offering, or a strategic approach that completely addresses all *their* concerns and delivers it in a way that meets their style, level of comfort, and personal needs. This will improve your close ratio massively and grow your income.

5. **Learn Your Prospects' Codes and Market Yourself Accordingly:** When Cheri Tree, Founder and CEO of Codebreaker Technologies, launched her business several years ago, she set out on a mission to prove that succeeding in sales was not a numbers game but a people game. After thousands of hours of research and development, she identified four different "buying personalities" in people: Action, Nurturing, Knowledge, and Blueprint. She also clearly defined people's personality coding technology.

Since then, she has taught more than half-a-million people worldwide learn their personality codes and quickly identify and crack their prospects' personality codes. Once you know a prospect's personality type, you can customize your approach to match their buying personality type and achieve far greater success. Understanding Cheri Tree's teachings has completely changed the way I market my business.

EXERCISE

1. How can you add more value to your prospects and clients?
2. What is it costing you not to listen to your prospects and clients?
3. What would your results be if you let your prospect determine your presentation?
4. How could identifying others' personality codes improve your life?

FIVE ENTREPRENEURIAL TIPS TO SUCCEED IN LIFE AND WORK

1. Take the leadership role in your life by launching and building your own business.
2. Treat others exactly how you want to be treated.
3. Always listen to and observe your prospects and clients' needs.
4. Learn from your past failures and try the above new proven principles.
5. Know that people are the product, so make them matter.

SUMMARY

When you follow the strategies in this chapter, you will do an even better job of making people matter! As a result, you can and will experience, realize, and create your own destiny! The best part about these principles is that they will not only work in your life as an entrepreneur, but they will also work in your relationships with your professional colleagues, children, and partners. These principles will literally work in all areas of your life.

CALL TO ACTION

I invite you to apply these principles to your life and business. Furthermore, I challenge you to provide massive value to your clients, listen your way to the sale, and let your prospects determine your presentation. Finally, I challenge you to learn your prospects' personality codes and adjust your approach accordingly.

When you do all this, you will not only make people matter but also help your prospects and clients find their superpowers. As a result, you will help others achieve their life's karma and truly experience self-worth, self-love, and self-acceptance. If we can all do this, not just entrepreneurs but all of humanity will evolve on the path to success!

PATRICK SNOW | ANKB

Patrick Snow is an international bestselling author of multiple books, a professional speaker, and a publishing, speaking, and book marketing coach. He has delivered 3,500 speeches on four continents. For twenty-five years, Patrick has mentored more than 1,500 clients worldwide to successfully publish their books.

Patrick's "destiny" message has been featured in The New York Times and Forbes Magazine. His book, story, and family photo made the cover page of USA TODAY. Patrick's first book, Creating Your Own Destiny, has sold upwards of one million copies in five languages and 108 countries.

Originally from Michigan, Patrick graduated from the University of Montana and lived in the Seattle area for more than twenty years. Then, in 2013, he achieved his lifelong dream of moving to Maui, Hawaii, where he currently resides with his lovely wife, Amy.

Author's Website: BecomingABestSellingAuthor.com

CHAPTER 16

A JOURNEY TOWARD YOUR PURPOSE AND PASSION

BY TERESA RYAN

"Success is something you attract by the person you become."

— Jim Rohn

Have you tried everything to improve sales and relationships yet don't see results? As a team leader, are you challenged with developing your team? Have you missed opportunities to connect with others because you didn't know how to communicate effectively?

THE GRIDLOCK

Improving sales and nurturing my relationships was challenging, no matter what I tried.

From 2001 to 2017, I owned the brokerage Ryan Hill Realty in Naperville, Illinois, before taking my team to Century 21. Ryan Hill Realty had fifty-plus sales agents who were significant breadwinners for their families.

As an owner—and now as a team leader—I have always been keenly aware of my responsibility to ensure every person on my team succeeds. This requires coaching and mentoring each agent continually. Our mission is to deliver impeccable customer service and results and build lifelong relationships with our clients. My vision was to be among the best brokerages, and now the best team, with top agents for our buyers and sellers who would refer their family and friends.

Because I am committed to and have a personal obligation to support my agents and staff, I have participated in several real estate training systems and coaching programs throughout my career. I attend ten to twelve seminars annually and read dozens of inspirational and motivational books.

My goal is to continuously improve my skills and those of my team. I have been coached by experts like Mike Ferry, Brian Buffini, Craig Proctor, and Tony Robbins. I attended Tony's Platinum Partners trip to India to get more clarity and direction and to tap into a deeper sense of meaning and purpose in my life, to make meaningful contributions to humanity and our planet, and to help save animals. I've always strived to learn and improve myself in every role to continue to be "the best I can be." I believe investing in my education and development helps me become a better and wiser person. My five favorite personal development books are:

1. *The Miracle Morning* by Hal Elrod
2. *The 5 AM Club* by Robin Sharma
3. *The Power of Positive Thinking* by Norman Vincent Peale
4. *The Power of Now* by Eckhart Tolle
5. *The Greatest Secret in the World* by Og Mandino

THE KEY

In 2017, I attended the Real Estate Wealth Expo, which featured Tony Robbins as the keynote speaker and an incredible panel of speakers that included Suze Orman, Daymond John, Pitbull, and Cheri Tree. A lightbulb went off for me. I was hooked within the first ten minutes when Cheri took the stage and introduced us to the science of BANK.

Cheri, similarly, had extensive sales training but hadn't seen dramatic results. She shared how standard personality tests showed her about herself but didn't result in a substantial increase in sales. She saw the change when she studied Hippocrates' theory of the Four Temperaments. Hippocrates had tremendous success treating each individual patient according to their temperament and preferred communication style. This insight helped Cheri better communicate with people in their preferred styles, dramatically improving her sales, influence, impact, and income.

That was the key! Cheri's insight was what I needed to increase my sales and impact. I already knew about myself and what I wanted, but what about what my clients wanted, and how I could best serve them? What did they want? What were their preferred styles? What about my husband, Nick, our kids, family, and friends? Understanding the person in front of me and focusing on their needs and style inspired me. I could better connect by listening to my clients, how they spoke, and what they wanted, rather than thinking about my response based on what I wanted.

Cheri states four basic personality codes make up BANK: Blueprint, Action, Nurturing, Knowledge. As Cheri explains, everybody has a combination of all four codes, but they have a primary one that is dominant. Speaking in someone's primary code is the key to building rapport, connection, and trust.

My primary code is Action, followed by Nurturing and Knowledge. Blueprint is my last code. I learned that if I communicate using someone's last code, I'll likely turn them off. They will not be interested in what I have to say, probably won't trust me, and they may not want to work with me or be friends.

I asked myself, "Is understanding these styles the key to building rapport and trust with clients? Could this really transform my sales, income, influence, and impact?"

THE SCIENCE OF BANK

After Cheri's presentation, I ran (as an Action would) to sign up for her two-day training. I became a Level IV trainer so I could train my team and "give them an edge" in their career and relationships. While I initially joined for business growth, Codebreaker Technologies has immensely impacted my personal relationships—even more than business.

As an Action fast-paced person, it has always been easier for me to quickly connect with other Actions. I understand their fast pace, brainstorming, vision, spontaneity, and fun. My wild Irish husband Nick is an Action!

On the other hand, I used to be so frustrated by Blueprints needing all the information before they could make a decision. This drove me crazy. I'd think, "Why can't you just decide?" I had family members I loved dearly (including my late mom) constantly asking questions and not committing. This frustrated me so much. I'd be agitated, argue, and maybe not listen to them as I should have. I'm sure this made them feel "devalued."

I wish I had better understood the Blueprints' true need for as much information as possible before deciding on anything to avoid loss or mistakes. If I had understood Mom's BANKCODE, I would have understood her more, been more patient, and when I had the chance, listened to my late mother more and showed more love. I regret I didn't have this wisdom while she was alive.

I'm grateful to understand now how Blueprints are wired, their thought process, and the value they bring. I've developed patience and appreciated their care for details and accuracy. In my business, I love having agents and staff that have high Blueprint as I know they are careful and detailed and don't make decisions without careful consideration. This is a benefit to our clients and to me.

Every code has strengths and challenges. Over the years, I've learned to appreciate each code's value, so I've worked to raise my scores in all areas. This builds Emotional Intelligence (EQ)—more important than IQ, in my opinion. High EQ requires listening to and caring for the other person without judgment. Even if I don't fully agree with another person's perspective, it's okay; I still respect and care about them.

I have used the BANKCARDS to crack the codes of my agents, staff team members, and family. My husband and I have even cracked our grandkids' codes with the kids' version that has pictures instead of words.

APPLYING BANK IN MY BUSINESS

So, back to bringing Codebreaker to my real estate business. Training agents to understand clients' codes helped transform their personal relationships, too. When we improve our relationships, we can transform our lives and the lives of others.

One Codebreaker tool is a set of BANKCARDS showing each code's values. Meeting clients, I'd hand them the set of values cards, saying:

"Thank you for the opportunity to meet with you to discuss the sale of your home. Before I share our market analysis and sales strategy for your home, would you take a minute and sort these cards in order of most like you to least like you? This will help me better understand your preferred communication style and what's important to you, and it will help me deliver my information in the way that's most valuable to you. This will help me to better serve you today."

All my clients loved it. And often, spouses were fascinated by insights into their different codes. They smiled, relaxed, and enjoyed the process. Now with this "connection," our meeting was more "at ease" and our communication more open. I also encouraged using the BANKCARDS with their family by giving them a set to keep. It is a great icebreaker that intrigues them. It also delivers the message that I want to learn about them and am focused on serving them and their unique needs. Understanding their codes helped me specifically tailor my presentation for each client. As Tony Robbins says, "Let your prospect determine your presentation." Genius!

I've always been a sponge to learn and grow since my early twenties. I've strived to be a better person in every area of my life, from business to being kinder, smarter, a better listener, and improving health through diet, exercise, rest, cleansing, juicing, and meditation. I've also deepened my faith and spiritual connection to our Creator, God, the Divine.

I've been to India twice on self-improvement journeys, where I ask myself life's bigger questions: What am I here on Earth for? What is God's purpose for me? How can I do God's work and be my best every day?

> **"An extraordinary life is all about daily, continuous improvements in the areas that matter most."**
>
> — Robin Sharma

Real estate coach Brian Buffini has a "Win the Day" philosophy:

Do the most important things daily and be your very best.

- Win four days in a week—you win the week.
- Win three weeks in the month—you win the month.
- Win eight months—you win the year.

None of us are perfect, but I do my best. I love this philosophy—I win each day by not stopping until I do. Therefore, I win each year!

EVOLVING MY LIFE'S PASSION

So that "all-important question" needed an answer—what is my ultimate purpose?

Here is a little bit of background on my life—I was raised in Independence, Missouri, by Billy and Virginia Hill. My parents had very tough childhoods and shared many stories of survival and loss. Dad was part Cherokee Indian and was very connected to nature. He planted a beautiful garden every year that he lovingly cared for and prayed over. That garden had the most tasty and beautiful vegetables ever! (God heard his prayers!) Both of my parents had a love of all plants and animals. I've always felt a deep love and connection to all nature and animals because of how my parents raised me. Mom and Dad believed in God, teaching respect for people, animals, and our Earth. This love is core to who I am.

In my twenties and thirties, I wanted to be married with kids. I got my wish and was blessed with two beautiful children, a son, Jeremy (a brilliant Knowledge/Nurturing), and a daughter, Natalie (a loving Nurturing/Action). Of course, raising and loving my children became my top priorities.

In 1991, I married my wonderful husband, Nick, and we became a blended family. I was blessed with three amazing bonus kids: Jayla, Trevor, and Tara. Today, our lives are rich with love and laughter from our kids, their spouses, and eleven grandkids, all with different personalities. Using the BANK methodology, we cracked each other's codes to understand and appreciate one another even more.

Now, with the power of BANK in the present day and more relevant than ever, real estate connects me to our clients, our community, people, and my purpose. I'm blessed to fulfill my mission of making a difference for other people and saving animals; to "Being a Force for Good." Nick and I have long supported charities worldwide in areas such as food scarcity, shelter, child enrichment and education, animals, and our environment.

APPLYING BANK IN DOG RESCUE

It's interesting how you eventually land on your path of purpose in life. In August 2023, I discovered that two Illinois-based rescues had abandoned several dogs and stopped paying for their boarding, care, and veterinary bills. These dogs had been rescued from euthanasia in Georgia and Texas. They were brought to Illinois for safety, only to be abandoned and sent to another shelter to possibly face the same fate again. I couldn't let that happen!

Nick and I decided I'd take over all expenses and care. Instead of simply donating funds, I took on the responsibility for these sweet dogs' ongoing care and safety and finding loving foster and, ultimately, forever homes. Not just any home, but the perfect fit for the dog where the dog would be safe, loved, and a part of the family. As an Action, I committed to figuring it out—and did! I started Angel Dog Alliance, NFP (an Illinois Department of Agriculture licensed rescue), allocating my real estate staff to manage details and medical records. Dear friends have volunteered at our adoption events since November 2023. Adoptive families now volunteer, too. Our mission grows, and we're saving more dogs.

These dogs come from the highest kill rate US shelters in Southern California, Florida, Tennessee, Texas, Georgia, Missouri, and Kentucky. Truth is, all shelters nationwide (and worldwide) are overcrowded. More than one million healthy dogs are euthanized yearly—quite often strays and owner surrenders.

This work is so difficult because I can't save all the beautiful animals, though I want to. I am fulfilled by focusing on these sweet dogs we do save. The beauty is seeing our impact on the dogs and their adopting families.

As I've said, BANK has impacted every area of my life. Call me crazy, but I use BANK for the dogs, too! Each dog has a primary code. BANK helps me understand and relate differently to build trust and rapport and find the best family fit for each dog's needs and past experiences. With every dog, we initially need to "go slow," respect their space, and let the dog take their time to come to you to show you they are comfortable to be petted. Never "rush in" or hover over their head because it can make them nervous.

MY OBSERVATIONS ON DOG BANKCODES:

Blueprint: These dogs are reserved, shy, and take time to trust. They are slower to come out of their shells. They are curious about the new home and family members but cautious at first.

Action: High energy and fast-paced, these dogs want to jump, run, play, and be happy. They are outgoing and may want to be the Alpha. They love walks, car rides, and meeting new people.

Nurturing: These dogs are lovers, cuddly, snugglers, and sensitive. They want to be with their owners and be petted all the time.

Knowledge: These dogs are curious, slow to come out of their shells until they trust, and need to get to know the people and environment. They are observant.

When meeting with potential adopters, we first have them fill out an application, then make a follow-up call, and then schedule a "meet and greet" with the dog they are interested in adopting and their current pets. BANK helps me understand the family and our dogs. I watch the dog's comfort level to ensure a good fit, matching their needs, energy, and temperament.

TAKING IT TO THE BANK

Codebreaker Technologies' BANK science, systems, training, and tools have tremendously impacted my life—in business, connecting with clients, family, and friends, and quickly taking action in dog rescue. It has also influenced others to join my vision of making a difference for these animals and families.

THE CHALLENGE

We each have only so much time here on Earth and need to make the most of each day, each opportunity, and each relationship. And so, I ask you, where could Codebreaker and BANK help you achieve your dreams?

EXERCISE

Do you allocate your time effectively?

How self-aware are you? Describe your traits, quirks, impact on others, etc. Remember the adage that "People remember how you make them feel." How do you think you make them feel?

What do you need to change in your approach to communication and relationships?

What is your life's purpose, and what are you doing to make it happen?

TERESA RYAN | ANKB

Teresa Ryan is an accomplished real estate professional and dedicated philanthropist based in Naperville, Illinois. As the Team Lead and Managing Broker of the award-winning Ryan Hill Group at Century 21 Circle, she leads a team of top-producing agents, serving buyers and sellers in the Chicagoland area's luxury and traditional home markets since 2001. Ryan Hill Group has been consistently ranked among the nation's top real estate teams by RealTrends and *The Wall Street Journal*.

In addition to her real estate success, Teresa is the Founder of Angel Dog Alliance, a nonprofit committed to rescuing dogs from high-kill shelters across the United States and finding them forever homes. Through fundraising, strategic partnerships, and hands-on rescue efforts, Angel Dog Alliance provides critical funding and support to give at-risk dogs a second chance at life.

Teresa's passion for serving others extends to numerous local and global philanthropic causes focused on aiding the homeless, supporting children and families, animal welfare, environmental conservation, and more. She and her husband actively contribute to more than eighty charitable organizations through their family trust.

Author's Website: AngelDogAlliance.com and RyanHillGroup.com

NURTURING

CHAPTER 17
ENHANCING YOUR SUPERPOWERS USING BANK

BY DEB CASH

"The ultimate test of a moral society is the kind of world that it leaves to its children."

— Dietrich Bonhoeffer

Did you or someone you love have difficulties in school? Did you feel as if no one understood you or this loved one? Was it frustrating to find the answers? Do you feel as though you were heard?

MY STORY

My name is Deb, and I am a closet Action personality mixed with tons of Nurturing and Knowledge; I'm also a stress-filled Blueprint. My upbringing was with a German, Marine Corps trained, BKAN father who grew up as the second of twelve children. He was a college graduate wannabe and a Catholic priest wannabe who married the love of his life.

My mom was a phenomenal NABK middle child of fourteen, born into a German/Irish household. She slept in one bed with six other sisters and seemed to be their Cinderella, doing many chores for them while putting aside her dreams of becoming a registered nurse. She again set aside her dreams to raise three girls and two boys during the 1950s through 1970s.

My parents were married for sixty-five years. I was the oldest of those five children. As you can imagine, our extended family was huge! I grew up with forty-four aunts and uncles, with almost two hundred first cousins. There was always family and many kids to play with, fight with, and get into mischief with. I babysat my younger siblings and neighbor kids starting at the ripe old age of eleven. The money I made from my "job" was spent on Barbie clothes and once on an outfit from the Spiegel catalog.

With this limited background knowledge, I have given you a snapshot of my upbringing to help you understand where my superpowers were nurtured.

If you were to guess:

What would you say is your father's BANKCODE?

What would you say is your mother's BANKCODE?

What is your BANKCODE?

SUPERPOWERS AT AN EARLY AGE

Knowing how to read by the age of four and going to first grade at the age of five, Debbie, as I was called then, quickly became the favorite of her teachers, who were nuns. The nuns managed a class of first to fourth-grade students in one classroom and then fifth through eighth in another (yes, a two-room schoolhouse).

Debbie helped others learn their alphabet and how to count. She took little groups of children to the corner of the classroom and read Dick and Jane books with them. As she advanced through the grades, she was the teacher's favorite who helped with bulletin boards, graded papers, and conducted small group tutoring in subjects such as social studies and science because the teacher didn't have time. Another thing Debbie did was watch and observe all the children in the classroom when she had nothing to do.

As you can imagine, she grew up wanting to be a nun and a teacher. From her classroom observations, she was always intrigued by the kids who were having a hard time in school, the kids the nuns were disciplining, and those kids the other kids didn't like. Why did observing others appeal to Debbie? I have no idea.

After grade school, graduating from a class of seven, Debbie went to a private Catholic convent boarding school for high school with the intention of becoming a nun and a teacher. Much was learned living away from home at such a young age.

Debbie's environment was very scheduled, which suited the Blueprint that had been fostered in her first thirteen years, along with hours of study and preparation for college (so Knowledge, don't you think?). Debbie's nurturing spirit was fostered by the community and dormitory life for those four years.

Her imagination and spirit were fostered by the global thinking of the women she lived with, who introduced her to world religions, world political issues, civil rights issues, yoga, and meditation. During her senior year, Debbie wrote a term paper on mental retardation after visiting a home where, at that time, people with all kinds of disabilities lived.

While deciding on a college, Debbie found that some universities in Ohio had started a four-year program in special education. Since she was still very curious about people with different behaviors and abilities, she enrolled in a program at Kent State University. She was accepted on December 13, 1969, for the fall of 1970.

STOP AND REFLECT

What do you recall as your strengths and superpowers during your school years? What do you recall as your failures during your school years?

DEVELOPING AND RECOGNIZING MY OWN SUPERPOWERS

Let's switch to the first person for the rest of this chapter. After transferring and graduating from Bowling Green State University in 1974, I taught in various school systems and types of schools for forty-two years.

Most of my classroom work was done with students with learning disabilities and/or behavior problems. This area of higher-than-average IQs has always intrigued me, and yet, I believe they are the hardest to teach because they are, for the most part, those everyday kids you see with seemingly nothing wrong with them. They don't look different. They don't talk differently. So, why are they in "special education"? That in and of itself is another whole chapter.

Part of my job description as an intervention specialist was to sit on committees that followed federal, state, and local guidelines to determine a student's eligibility. The eligibility process is long and arduous. It was not always like that when I started in 1974. At first, we went by IQ testing done by the school psychologist. Whatever that school psychologist determined was enough to label someone.

In Ohio, if your IQ was under seventy, you were considered educable mentally retarded (now intellectually or developmentally delayed). The processes for eligibility have changed over the years and have been brought into a fairer compliance regiment that allows for much more input from teachers, parents, administrators, school psychologists, and teams.

WHO DO YOU KNOW WHO...?

Were you or any of your siblings or your children in a special education program? What was the diagnosis? Did this person have an IEP (Individual Education Program)?

MAKING KIDS AND ALL PEOPLE MATTER

Over many years of observation and study, I have seen behaviors as ways of communicating rather than just being defiant or disobedient. I recognized that each child has their own unique blend of behavioral traits—some were highly sociable and extroverted, or they needed more time to process information before responding.

When teachers came to me wanting them to be given an IEP and out of their classrooms, we sat down and looked at the evidence. We wrote a list of "good" traits as opposed to the "bad" traits. We looked at trauma, home life, sleep patterns, diet, allergies, and so forth. When we looked at these behaviors many times, we were able to see they were not necessarily problems to be solved but clues to help us understand and adjust.

A child's behavior pattern, as seen through the lens of parents, teachers, administrators, and, yes, even the child, helped me help them manage whatever behavior was causing the interruption in the learning process. Certain children were often labeled problematic or difficult, but I sensed there was more to behavior than overt acting out.

As teachers approached me with their frustrations about certain children, I saw a common thread: Those children did not fit into the traditional mold of what the teacher expected for classroom behavior and individual learning styles. Common complaints were that they talked too much, fidgeted, resisted instruction, challenged authority, were messy, didn't complete work, or withdrew into themselves. Instead of viewing these behaviors as disruptions, I realized they were manifestations of deeper underlying needs and tendencies within each child's personality.

CAN YOU RECALL?

Can you recall children in your classes whom you thought shouldn't be in your class?

Why did you feel they shouldn't be in your class?

MY SUPERPOWERS PUT TO THE TEST

In 1978, my son Christopher was born. Chris was born deaf and with Down syndrome. He has been, and still is, an incredible gift to my life, teaching me lessons in patience, tolerance, and acceptance. He has certainly increased my superpowers and put them to the test. Through his unique perspective on the world, Chris has showed me the beauty of simple joys and the strength found in overcoming challenges like learning to walk, using the bathroom, and putting on clothes. Chris's presence in my life has been a continual source of inspiration and frustration, reminding me every single day of the power that unconditional love brings and the importance of embracing differences.

Since being trained with Codebreaker, I can now reflect on raising Chris through the lens of my new knowledge of BANK. This journey has been deeply enriched by understanding Chris's own unique bank personality code of NKBA. He is very much a Nurturer. Over the years, I made sure to create an environment filled with love, support, and emotional connection through family, friends, and school communities so that Chris always felt valued and cared for.

His Knowledge code (yes, people with disabilities can and do have strong Knowledge codes) led me to foster his curiosity through tailored educational experiences that looked many times like having to find the right teacher, classroom, or school while focusing on interactive and sensory-based learning methods that suited his needs. The blueprint aspect of his personality made it clear that he thrived on structure and routine, so I implemented consistent daily schedules, which provided him with a sense of security and predictability.

Lastly, acknowledging his Action-oriented side, I encouraged hands-on activities and practical learning opportunities, allowing him to engage actively with his environment and develop his skills through direct experiences like summer camps, Scouts, and sports. Reflecting on these newfound BANK insights into my parenting approach, I have been able to support Chris's growth and happiness.

At forty-five, Chris works at a local grocery store. He has worked full- or part-time since he was eighteen. Chris has participated in the Special Olympics at the local, state, and national levels for almost thirty years. His favorite sports for the last ten years have been tennis and golf. In 2017, Chris was chosen for the National Team to represent Ohio at the National Special Olympic Games in Seattle, Washington.

TIPS TO UNLEASHING YOUR OWN SUPERPOWERS

1. Don't jump to conclusions about a child (needs an IEP, needs medication, etc.).
2. Sit down and have a conversation (not a blaming game, not a shouting match).
3. Try interventions. Don't just do it for a day but for a couple of weeks minimum.
4. Document. Document. Document.
5. Monitor schedules, sleep patterns, eating habits, social media, and family dynamics.

SUMMARY

In November of 2023, I had the good fortune of meeting Cheri Tree in Pittsburgh, Pennsylvania, at an event where I went to find tips to enhance and grow my business. When I walked in, folks started asking me about my code. What code? I thought. Human? Teacher? Female? Retired? "No," they said. "Look at these cards and their values. Decide which one describes you in an order from one to four." After processing the value words on each card, I decided on NKBA and figured I had passed the test!

Cheri started talking about BANK and her journey. I was truly mesmerized by the content of her story. After the event, we all got together with Cheri for dinner and spent a good deal of time talking. Everyone shared what BANK meant to them, their families, relationships, and jobs.

My aha moment came the next day when we gathered again. I picked up the red Action card and told Cheri we needed these BANKCARDS in the classroom big time. I continued, "Do you know how many times a teacher would come to me asking me to get a child out of their classroom, and they were talking about this code?"

She smiled her big smile and said, "Yes! We are starting a movement in education. Would you like to be a part of it?" It was right then and there that I decided to become a coach and trainer. I realized that educating educators, administrators, and parents about the BANK framework could profoundly shift how all children are perceived and supported. Rather than trying to fit them into a standardized behavior mold, I saw the potential to create environments that honored and accommodated their individual personalities.

By helping others see all children through their appropriate lenses, we could empower teachers, parents, and administrators to better meet the needs of every child in their care. This movement would foster a more inclusive and supportive educational experience for all children, with or without an IEP.

My challenge to you is to act at your local school level. It doesn't matter if you are a parent, grandparent, aunt, or uncle. Our children need you right now. All students need the BANK program to help them with the process of telling others who they are and how they need to be understood. Help your local administrators get the BANK program for themselves, their teachers, teacher's aides, and all employees. Need help? Reach out to me or anyone at Codebreaker for advice on how to start. We can offer you Masterclasses for Educators, Parents, Relationships, etc. We do in-person classroom and faculty training at schools, districts, and universities.

DEB CASH | NKBA

Deb Cash is a retired elementary, junior high, and high school teacher. She is a regular education and a special education intervention specialist with forty-two years of experience. Deb supervised Special Education teachers for the University of Toledo and has been an adjunct in the English Department at Owens Community College. Deb worked as an intervention specialist for Henry and Lucas County educational service agencies. She also taught for Toledo City Schools, Defiance City Schools, and the Diocese of Toledo. A huge adventure was teaching for the Diocese of Nassau in the Bahamas, where she met and married her late husband.

At present, Deb owns businesses with both Codebreaker Global and Farmasi USA. She is a Certified and Licensed BANK Trainer and Coach for Codebreaker and has used techniques learned from Codebreaker to expand her Farmasi business. Deb is also a certified provider for the State of Ohio and Director of Operations for a non-profit called Connecting People & Places. She launched a pet treat business in the fall of 2024 called CP&P Pups. Deb lives in Maumee, Ohio, with her son Chris and their doodle, Lucy.

Website: linkedin.com/in/Deb-Cash-SuperPowerTrainer

CHAPTER 18
REDEFINING SUCCESS THROUGH CHALLENGE

BY JAIME TAETS

> "Success is to be measured not so much by the position that one has reached in life as by the obstacles which he has overcome."
>
> — Booker T. Washington

How do you define success? What would you do if you weren't afraid? What do you regularly do that helps you shift your perspective? What do you consistently do that helps you challenge your own beliefs and judgments?

INFLUENCE + INCOME = IMPACT

I was thirteen years into my career before I reevaluated my definition of success. For the first ten years, I had a leader I looked up to and admired. She had achieved what I thought was success, and I remember wanting to follow in her footsteps. That all changed one day when I was in a meeting with her where a lot of politics were being played; people were jockeying for position and credibility.

Afterward, I brought it up to her for mentorship, and her response was, "You need to start playing the game." "What game?" I asked. "The politics game—it's the only way to get ahead."

At that moment, my definition of success changed forever. I realized she was not the definition of success and what I wanted to achieve was something very different from what she wanted. Ever since that moment, my life has been a series of challenges that have helped me continue to refine my definition of success and step deeper into my authentic self as a leader, mom, and community member.

Not until I was introduced to Cheri Tree and Esther Wildenberg and the BANK methodology did I realize there was another whole level of success, one where you could create wealth and influence, but with the outcome of creating more impact. The deep values of the entire system and team at Codebreaker Technologies aligned with who I was and who I wanted to be.

Here are the biggest lessons I've learned on this journey with the BANK methodology and its training and masterminds.

1. **Growth comes from reflection.** For years, I thought that going to trainings and reading books was where I would grow. Through the BANK training curriculum, I learned that my greatest learning came in the reflection and application of what I had learned. When I chose to really examine my own responses and feelings, I started to see the power of the BANK system.

2. **Get comfortable being uncomfortable.** Since meeting Cheri and Esther and being introduced to BANK, I have been on a constant search for personal evolution, starting with finding my spiritual practice, which has helped lead me to success in my business endeavors and applying the BANK system to all aspects of my life to improve relationships to taking on the biggest challenge ever in 2023 by climbing Mt. Kilimanjaro, one of the seven summits.

3. **Find your guides.** Throughout your life, people and ideas will come in and out. Each of these people has a season and something they are there to teach you. I learned the people drawn to creating impact are the ones I want to spend more time with. Sometimes, we have to create time for the people who are steps ahead of us on the journey; we have to find the guides who are going to help us on the next leg of the journey. That's what Cheri, Esther, and the BANK community have been for me—a guide to greatness.

4. Life doesn't wait for you. I used to think I could wait for the "right time" to make hard decisions, and throughout my success journey, I've realized that life doesn't wait for my indecision. Opportunities come and go quickly. While I lived in fear, waiting to make the decision, others quickly accelerated their businesses because they were confident and focused. The path to success is paved with tough decisions, and the quicker you make them, the easier the path becomes.

WHAT I LEARNED

The BANK methodology gave me the confidence to bet on myself and lean on my experience to help me find the path forward. It helped me understand that who I am matters, that I am a unique combination of all four codes, and that I now have the power to better understand the people around me. Success comes easier when you are curious about others, and the BANK system helped fuel that curiosity.

Being involved in BANK masterminds also helped me with the tools to stay centered and navigate the hard times. So much of success lies in weathering the storms, not in living in the easy seasons. When you focus on knowing yourself better, it allows you to see the world and others in a different light.

Knowing your strengths and how you are perceived allows you to adjust your approach, to soften the edges of those parts of you that might create angst in others. As a leader, having this BANK methodology information about myself and my team has proved invaluable in helping us leverage each other's strengths and understand how we can impact each other and our business in a positive way.

We have control to influence others more than we realize, and when we seek to understand, it allows us to create the environment also to be understood. I now feel like it's my responsibility to show up authentically as myself and help people understand the BANK methodology to show up authentically. When each of us strives to understand ourselves and how we are perceived, we soften the edges of our judgment of others.

For our world to heal, each of us can do our part to understand ourselves and others at a deeper level. I now see that my BANKCODE plays out in everything I do and how I make decisions, and I can look at the situation from different perspectives. If everyone had this power, we would fundamentally shift the pain and intolerance in our world. If we could see our success as understanding each person's code and serving them according to it, we would heal the communication issues and create another definition of success for society, where we are all focused on Making People Matter.

I use the BANK methodology to Make People Matter by:

- Understanding my team and how to communicate better with each of them individually.
- Deepening relationships with our customers because we are serving them according to their code.

- Increasing our close rate, because we can adjust our proposals and sales conversations to align with the code of the prospect.
- Improving marketing copy, because we now write it to speak to all four codes.
- Improving relationships with my family members, because I can respect their code and adjust my communication approach.

BANK is the secret to true and lasting success across all aspects of your life. It's the way to achieve growth, impact, and joy all in one. But to understand others, you need to spend the time understanding yourself first.

Before you can effectively lead others, you need to know how to lead yourself.

EXERCISE

Write down one fear currently holding you back and what actions you can take to move past it.

Make a list of your guides—who are the top three to five people you need to spend more time with to achieve your next level of success?

Identify one additional area of your life where you can introduce or use the BANK system to create an impact for yourself or someone else.

TIPS ON USING THE BANKCODE

Shift your perspective—put yourself in a different room or do something outside your comfort zone and see how it helps you see the world and yourself differently.

Find and focus on your purpose. When you know why you are doing it, it helps you stay true even during tough times. The journey will be full of obstacles, but when you have a solid foundation, it's easier to weather the tough parts of the journey.

Double down on you. When you feel stuck, instead of looking outside for the answers, go inside, and you will be amazed at what you already have the answers for. You are here for a purpose, and the answers are within if we are willing to be quiet and listen for them.

SUMMARY

There is no singular definition of success. To truly achieve a level of success that fulfills us, it must be based on our definition. We have to stop looking at other people's journeys and the top of their mountains and thinking that is the only definition of success. I challenge you to create your own definition of success, one that inspires you to work harder, go further, and be filled you with energy as you work toward it. The world needs you to live into your strengths, to channel your innate strengths, and to bring your gifts and talents to the world.

I challenge you to identify the greatest sources of your own energy and find a way to spend more time in those areas. When you are energized, you have the power to energize others.

I challenge you to move beyond your biggest fears by finding faith in your own potential. Where can you increase your faith in yourself to make the fear that is holding you back smaller?

I challenge you to examine your life and find the opportunities to inspire others and also be inspired yourself. You cannot inspire others unless you first find those points of inspiration yourself.

I challenge you to find time to go inside—to find the quiet of your mind and listen for the answers to your biggest obstacles.

JAIME TAETS | NABK

Jaime Taets is the dynamic CEO and Founder of Keystone Group International. With a passion for cultivating strong leadership and fostering change-resilient cultures, Jaime leads her team in guiding leaders and organizations toward sustainable growth.

Beyond her role at Keystone, she extends her influence as the host of the *Superpower Success Podcast* and as the author of two bestselling books, *You Are Here* and *The Culture Climb*. As a regular contributor to *Forbes, Authority Magazine*, and the *Minneapolis/St. Paul Business Journal*, Jaime shares her unique perspectives on how leaders can cut through the noise and learn to evolve their leadership approaches to help their teams perform at the highest levels.

Jaime has served on the boards of several for-profit and non-profit organizations. She has been named to Inc Magazine's 200 top Female Founders list, a 100 Women to KNOW in America, and Twin Cities Business Notable Female Entrepreneurs. Her company has been named to the Inc 500 fasting growing companies in the Midwest.

Author's Website: JaimeTaets.com

CHAPTER 19
THE FAMILY BANKING BUSINESS

BY KYLE FULLER

"Everything rises and falls on leadership."

— John C. Maxwell

BANKCODE helped my family communicate better through our Family Banking System. It brought us closer together by understanding each other's BANK-CODES. We now have everyone's BANKCODE attached to our names on our family text message thread. We meet once a quarter for our Family Banking Business to develop as leaders in the Spiritual, Personal, Family, Financial, and Occupation areas of life.

Great minds talk about ideas, and one of the most compelling ideas I have encountered is building the Family Banking Business. This conversation starts with leadership, specifically with Mom and Dad leading the family. My wife and I have three young boys, and at this stage of life, we're in what's called a dependent state, where the children are 100 percent dependent on Mom and Dad for everything in life.

As children mature, get older, and start growing up, they become independent, typically a very proud moment in our society. When our children grow up, move out of the home, get their own mortgages, and buy and drive their own vehicles, we usually celebrate. What's really happening here is we're separating from the first family unit and becoming independent to go build our own family unit. Essentially, what happens here is a wall is created between generation one and generation two.

Then our children go out and purchase things like vehicles. The average American will drive about thirteen vehicles in their lifetime and spend roughly $400,000 on those transactions as something they have to have in life. When this happens, we've become independent as a family unit. This is when the big banks move in to create relationships with our children just like they did for us. You see, these big banks are masters at controlling the flow of money.

With all of their profits, these banks intentionally choose to store their wealth in permanent life insurance. For example, Bank of America has about $24 billion of cash-value life insurance, Wells Fargo has $19.5 billion, and Chase Bank has a little over $12 billion in life insurance contracts they use to protect themselves and put at their foundation.

Banks are more than happy to take our deposits and then lend our money out to other individuals for things like vehicles. All they're doing is positioning themselves to ensure the $400,000 each of our children will spend in their lifetime on vehicles, whether they pay cash or finance, comes directly to them. What's really happening here is we have given up the opportunity to transfer our leadership and our principles to our children and allowed that to go to the banks. They are more than happy to develop a relationship and lead our children through the financing in their lives.

The problem is not just that $400,000 is going to transfer, but that we finance everything in life. What could that $400,000 have done for us if it had flowed through a more efficient environment, where we could have captured and harnessed the earning potential of all those dollars by using a Whole Life Insurance contract?

If that money had flown through whole life insurance for that same time period, it would have yielded about $1.5 million in future value, or what we call interest cost. When we take three kids times $1.5 million, the true lost opportunity cost for a family, by not understanding this, is $4.5 million for just vehicles. So, there's a small fortune sitting right there if we would just change the way we think.

I recommend changing our thinking and creating interdependent relationships within our family instead of moving from a dependent state to an independent state. This change would bring us closer as a family unit and allow us to capitalize or save into our private banking system. The leadership principles, our core values, our vision for what our life looks like when we have abundance in every area of life, and the financial education and awareness we've instilled in our children can now be transferred to Generation Two. When they buy vehicles, our children know we can tie into a Family Banking Business to get our loans. As a result, that $400,000 of cash flow they have to spend on vehicles can flow into the family instead of away from the family.

Now, this $1.5 million interest cost, which is $4.5 million for a family of three children, can be kept directly within the Family Banking Business. All we're really doing here is changing a couple of things: our mindset, how we view this flow of money in our lives, and the environment in which we choose to store wealth. We have to capitalize on our own private Family Banking Business to be able to handle the financing needs of the family in the future.

If we do that, we will be able to control this flow of money for vehicles and anything else that the family might finance in the future with 100 percent certainty because our children have to drive vehicles, and the product we're using is guaranteed. So, it gives us all the certainty in the world to control and harness this cash flow in our lives. Now, one question you might be asking is: Why would my children want to come to me and pay me interest to use Generation One's private Family Banking Business? I'm going to show you exactly why because there's also a multi-generational wealth transfer happening at the exact same time. So, once again, this goes back to a conversation about leadership.

My wife and I were the first leaders in our family. We started saving more money, storing it in several whole life insurance policies, and working on this idea of a Family Banking Business. Now our current death benefit is $12 million. So, as soon as my wife and I had enough cash value and Death Benefit in our Whole Life policies, we felt comfortable and protected. We started buying policies on the next generation, so we started savings accounts for our three boys, Ryker, Ridge, and Remington, and then moved that wealth inside of policies for them.

The earliest you can buy a whole-life policy on a child is about fifteen days old. Currently, our three boys are insured for about $2.6 million total. As soon as we had the immediate Fuller family protected and our savings strategy in place, we shifted and started buying insurance policies and saving money for the previous generation. We own insurance on my mother-in-law, Carol, and my parents, Cindy and Kempton. Their current death benefit is $2.2 million.

So, why would my boys want to come to Diane and me in the future for their financing needs? Could they possibly pay Diane and me a higher interest rate for the use of that money than a commercial bank? I will tell you, my boys would be thrilled to pay me a higher interest rate than to use a lower interest rate at a commercial bank, and here's exactly why. Every single one of us in America has to have access to cash, and every single one of us will die. Those two things are guaranteed, so by creating this Family Banking Business, we're also creating and ensuring a multi-generational wealth transfer.

When Generation One or the previous generation for Diane and I passes away, that death benefit will grow from $2.2

million to about $3.2 million. Now that transfers to Diane or me income tax-free, so $3.2 million dollars is transferred to us. When you have seasoned twenty- or thirty-year-old policies, that is the best place to start putting extra money into those policies because of the compounding effect inside that asset. You're going to need a system that can handle a wealth transfer like that.

Now, assuming Diane and I live to a projected age when we realistically should have passed away, our future death benefit will grow from $12 million to about $34 million. That, coupled with what we get from the previous generation, means $37.5 million, assuming we don't buy any more insurance, and we're not even close to being done buying these policies. We're just getting started. A transfer of $37 million to our three boys is guaranteed at a certain time in their lives, and their future death benefit at that time, assuming they live to an age when they would realistically pass away, would grow from $2.6 million to about $10.6 million.

We've already insured a $47 million wealth transfer minimum to their children. When we take a step back and look at this, the reason my boys will want to tie into this system is because for every dollar they pay and finance with Diane and me, they will get that portion back first when we transfer this wealth.

So, imagine walking into a bank, and the banker says, "We're running a special right now. If you use our bank for your vehicles and your mortgage in thirty years or forty years, we will write you a tax-free check, reimbursing you for 100 percent of the principal interest you gave our bank during that period." If that deal existed, I would exclusively and loyally use that bank for the rest of my life. This type of thinking also helps us build stronger relationships within the family that are centered on education, awareness, and trust.

So, what we're really doing here is buying net worth for pennies on the dollar. Every dollar I save into the policies that we own on my parents, we transfer back to us for forty-seven cents on the dollar. It only costs me forty-seven cents to get that $3.2 million back, so we only put in half of what we'll get back when my parents pass away. We're just ensuring a future windfall for us through a very efficient savings environment.

A lot of people are very focused on building net worth, which is not a bad idea, but I prefer to buy it for pennies on the dollar. When Diane and I pass away, all the premiums we put into our policies and the savings will only cost us twenty-two cents on the dollar to transfer that death benefit to our boys in the future. And my children will transfer their wealth for ten cents on the dollar to their children, which is why it's beneficial to start this process as early as you can in life. We are guaranteeing our future estate will be created by our savings environment.

Think about that for a second. What I just showed you is we are not calculating any of the investments we have or the business we own. This entire wealth transfer and all of this money was created and generated, guaranteed by our savings environment. This is why you really have to start looking at Whole Life Insurance for what it is, which, in my opinion, is the world's greatest place to store wealth. However, none of this means anything without proper stewardship and interdependent relationships.

We can't build this amount of wealth and just transfer it. The education, the relationships, and the leadership have to be there to make sure our children understand these principles so they can perpetuate them. To me, this is what our founding fathers in America did and why we're all so blessed today. Someone back then had an idea big enough to allow us to live as abundantly as we do right now. I feel obligated to perpetuate that forward with my family. We start by teaching our kids the non-negotiables of the wealth-building game: financial education, awareness, a saving strategy, and the protection elements of the money game every single one of us has to have.

We also have to instill that Family Banking education so they understand how to own and control the banking function in their lives. Then they can invest in their unique abilities early in life and become who they need to become to have the greatest impact early in their lives. You see, just because I'm in business or might be a decent investor or a good private banker does not necessarily mean my children will get into the same business I started. They might have a completely different path in life. Their freedom and their abundance will look different than it did for me, but the foundation is the same for every single one of us, which is why we have to focus on education.

The sooner they learn these elements of the money game, the sooner they can invest in their unique abilities and become who they need to be, whether that's a business owner, an investor, a nonprofit runner, or a missionary their whole lives. They will have the resources and education to do that for themselves and perpetuate it for their children's children. So, what can one family accomplish with this idea of a Family Banking Business?

Well, number one is the principle of being stronger together. This will unite and empower your family like it has for mine. Money has actually brought us closer together. It has strengthened the relationships through trust, education, and awareness. We have more self-reliance within our family now through intentional education and awareness of our money. It has allowed us to Beat the Banks.

This has created private banking solutions for our family's financing needs. Therefore, we keep millions of dollars within our family's control for things we have to purchase anyway. This has empowered us with self-reliance. Our family can now opt out of government-sponsored programs in the future. We just will not participate in them because we've built this Family Banking system that allows us to live with a 100 percent self-reliance, and that's why we teach our children to do the same thing.

The second principle, what I call infinite thinking, replaces the idea of retirement with purpose for American families. Our family will not talk about retiring because we are living abundantly in all areas of life, and when you are living the perfect life, that's not something you ever want to retire from. You just keep going to create more impact and more influence for good in our world.

I just want you to imagine for a second what this would look like if a million families had this idea and were implementing the Family Banking Business. It would unite and empower our nation. Through the principle of being stronger together, we would do this through intentional education and awareness of our money, which our country desperately needs right now. It would allow us to Beat the Banks and create private banking solutions for all American households. It would allow us as a nation to be more self-reliant so that everyone has the option and the ability to opt out of government-sponsored programs. And it would allow us to instill the idea of infinite thinking for future generations by replacing the concept of retirement with purpose for American families.

During our quarterly family meetings to review our family banking business—which we emphasize is built on strong relationships—we introduced BANK to the entire family. Everyone took the BANKCODE assessment, and we shared our results and insights together. We knew improving communication would be critical to the success of our family banking business, and this tool gave us a common language to understand one another better.

One moment that really stood out was when my dad had a major light bulb go off. He realized he'd been struggling to connect with one of my younger brothers because their BANKCODES were complete opposites. He had been communicating based on his own code, not my brother's. That simple insight opened up a deeper connection between them, and it was a powerful moment for all of us.

In the end, integrating BANK into our family banking business has had a far greater impact than we ever expected. Strong communication and relationships truly are the foundation of successful family banking.

As a business owner, I use BANK as often as possible when interacting with potential life insurance agents or clients. As part of our system for building lifelong relationships, we send out a link to capture someone's BANKCODE before our first meeting. Knowing their "buyology" upfront has been a tremendous way to strengthen connections from the very beginning. It allows us to communicate more effectively, in a way that actually resonates with them.

We also attach each client's BANKCODE to their profile in our CRM, so anytime we follow up, we tailor our communication to match how they prefer to receive information. One of the best parts about BANK is how quick and simple it is—it takes less than ninety seconds to crack someone's code. Unlike other personality tests that take thirty minutes or more (and let's be honest, nobody has time for that), BANK makes it easy to implement without being a burden on anyone's time.

These concepts and ideas have literally changed my family's financial destiny forever. If you take the time to educate yourself and implement this, you can have the same effect on your family as well. When we have enough individual families who are doing this, we can start putting families together and influencing communities to eventually influence a state, to eventually influence a nation by getting enough families to understand that this education is out there and exactly how they can implement it to impact every future generation that comes after us.

Here we go!

KYLE FULLER | NBAK

Kyle Fuller started in life insurance in 2013 but was overcome by the power of Infinite Banking the following year and has been practicing ever since. He founded Factum Financial in 2016, a life insurance agency that has served more than 2,000 families and created more than $750,000,000 in legacy for future generations.

Today, Factum has a strategic partnership with Keller Williams, giving them the exclusive educational rights to teach whole life insurance and foundational wealth to their Wealth-Building Community.

As an authorized Infinite Banking Practitioner, Kyle specializes in working with big business owners and families who want to create private banking systems. Focusing on education, Kyle and his team are dedicated to guiding clients toward a prosperous future that supports their ambitions in all areas of their lives.

Author's Website: FactumFinancial.com

CHAPTER 20
EMERGING FROM THE SHADOWS

BY MAMIE-JEAN LAMLEY

"You never know how strong you are until being strong is your only choice."

— Bob Marley

THE BEGINNING—STRUGGLING TO BE SEEN

Have you ever felt like a shadow in your own life, moving through a world blind to your potential and indifferent to your self-worth and future self? I have, and that feeling pushed me to a point where I had no choice. Discovering new pathways to make more impactful decisions helped me reshape my life.

How would uncovering the depth of your actual potential change everything for you? Could this awakening turn your struggles into a legacy of hope for those still lost in the shadows, empowering you with newfound confidence and self-assurance?

RECOGNIZING THE MASTERS OF INFLUENCE

> "The number one reason most people don't get what they want is that they don't know what they want."
>
> — T. Harv Eker

Transitioning from the shadows to visibility often requires guidance and inspiration from those who have achieved what you aspire to. Their journeys, marked by resilience and vision, serve as roadmaps. Learning from their experiences is not just beneficial; it's crucial. It provides clarity and a surge of motivation to pursue your dreams with renewed vigor, inspiring you to step into the light and feel the power of transformation.

Like me, you may feel trapped in the shadows despite your efforts. After a decade in event management for a top personal development organization that hosted speakers like Tony Robbins, T. Harv Eker, Gary Vaynerchuk, and Nick Vujicic, I felt stuck as an event supervisor. Then, everything changed at The Masters of Influence event in 2012, where

I experienced a powerful gathering of speakers focused on leadership, communication, and authentic connection. The energy was electric, and each speaker offered insights on creating meaningful influence. This experience reshaped my view of personal development, emphasizing that authentic influence lies in genuine connections with others.

Imagine encountering a proven process by masters who influence. Their stories of overcoming challenges and realizing dreams can inspire you to step into the light. These encounters can shape your direction and clarify your impact on empowering others. True transformation begins with taking responsibility for your change and actively pursuing growth.

REFLECTIONS

Reflecting on these encounters, I feel both inspired and humbled by the power of authentic connection and genuine relationships. Seeing the transformative influence of these figures firsthand has sparked a desire to grow personally and cultivate that exact authenticity in my connections. Imagine being able to shadow such powerhouse speakers; who would you choose to model, and what impact might that have on your journey?

REALIZING THE VISION: A CALL TO LEAD

"It always seems impossible until it's done."

— Nelson Mandela

Reflect on your life's journey. Every experience has shaped your purpose. From uncertainty to empowerment, your story can be a beacon for those seeking to redefine their destinies.

Fueled by the BANK methodology, I've seamlessly integrated it across every aspect of my work—from texts and emails to book and article writing, presentations, signature talks, podcasts, and websites. This powerful tool allows me to connect deeper, tailoring each interaction to resonate with diverse personalities and maximize impact. It has become essential in shaping messages that engage, inspire, and drive results, helping me create content that speaks directly to the values and motivations of my audience.

In leadership roles at Codebreaker Technologies and Empowerment on Fire, I envisioned a future where empowerment is accessible to all. Together, you and I can break chains and ignite inner fires, making every voice heard and every dream validated. Are you ready to Make People Matter?

BREAKING THE CHAIN

Becoming a Certified and Licensed BANK Trainer and Coach in 2014 was a true turning point. It liberated me from the constraints of corporate life and paved the way for a full-time career in public speaking and training, where I could use my corporate skills in more transformative ways. This shift was a moment of "breaking the chain"—a powerful step away from limitations toward fully owning my potential and purpose.

After seventeen years in a corporate software role, I faced a downsizing during an acquisition. Applying BANK insights, I was able to reallocate team members strategically, safeguarding their positions and securing a multimillion-dollar contract. This experience underscored the real-world impact of BANK principles and reinforced the importance of adaptability and strategic thinking in creating meaningful change. Integrating BANK as a tool across texts, emails, book and article writing, presentations, talks, podcasts, and websites has become essential, allowing me to build deeper connections, engage diverse audiences, and empower others with clarity and purpose.

REFLECTIONS

When you integrate the principles of BANK into your conversations, speaking engagements, and leadership training, you will create environments that are pulsing with empathy and mutual understanding. Embracing change while honoring your values is not just a task; it's an invigorating journey that will prepare you to break barriers and reach new heights to fulfill your passion and dreams.

EXPANDING HORIZONS

> "Only those who will risk going too far can find out how far one can go."
>
> — T. S. Eliot

As I embraced my new role and vision, my journey took me to new places and experiences, broadening my horizons and deepening my expertise.

Energized by the courage to redefine my professional identity, January 2015 marked the establishment of year one of Empowerment on Fire, LLC. I engaged in lifelong learning courses like Train the Trainer, Guerilla Business School, Life Directions, and Never Work Again, deepening my knowledge and extending my influence.

INTEGRATING VALUES AND VISION

Insights from these experiences led me to infuse BANK values into my programs, such as Heroic Voice Academy, a platform where individuals can discover and amplify their unique voices, and TEDx Speaker Coaching, a program designed to help aspiring TEDx speakers craft and deliver powerful talks. I created a curriculum that merges these values with innovative methods to enable game-changing engagements, showing how personal values boost professional practices and drive societal change.

A MOMENT OF SYNCHRONICITY

In 2016, at Guerilla Business School, an unexpected opportunity to fill a speaker's slot revealed my capacity to inspire from the spotlight. This pivotal moment marked my journey from anonymity to recognition. As I stepped onto the stage, I felt a profound shift within me. The audience's response was overwhelmingly positive, validating my belief in my message's power and ability to make a difference.

REFLECTIONS

I invite you to take a moment and reflect on your journey. Did you leap into the light or hold back in the shadows? This reflective exercise will help you understand your path and choices, making you more self-aware and prepared for the future.

REVOLUTIONIZING SALES STRATEGIES AS AN EVENT MANAGER

Zig Ziglar, motivational speaker and author of *Secrets of Closing the Sale*, said every sale has five fundamental obstacles: no need, no money, no hurry, no desire, no trust.

While I revolutionized our approach to sales, a personal revelation awaited me. This revelation would challenge me to transform myself significantly by highlighting the interplay between professional practices and personal development.

Recognizing the crucial role of effective communication and connection in driving sales, I introduced the revolutionary BANK Value System to our team of volunteers. Implementing this methodology empowered us to deeply understand our clients' needs and preferences, tailor our communication, and significantly enhance client satisfaction. The impact was immediate, with notable successes ranging from $3,999 to an impressive $25,000 in package sales.

This personalized, values-based approach not only improved sales outcomes but also earned me the privilege of handling sales at all events where Cheri Tree was a featured presenter—a clear testimony to the effectiveness of the BANK methodology.

CHANGING TIMES

"Be the change you wish to see in the world."

— Mahatma Gandhi

As I revolutionized sales strategies, I faced a pivotal personal challenge that spurred further transformation.

A conversation with a dear friend in Atlanta, Georgia, sparked this change. He looked into my eyes and said, "Mamie, you are your biggest obstacle. There's a reservoir of untapped potential within you, waiting to burst forth. It's time to shed the excuses and embrace your purpose."

His words pierced my self-doubt. Despite orchestrating events for thousands, I felt invisible, tethered to the convention hall floor, my voice only heard through the walkie-talkie. The prospect of stepping into my power seemed daunting yet irresistibly tantalizing.

Imagine standing on the sidelines, gazing at the stage, bathed in possibility. You can feel the electric energy coursing through the room as you watch others in the spotlight; a fire stirs within you, urging you to break free from invisibility and claim your rightful place on that stage.

TAKING THE LEAP

Moved by my friend's words, I made a pivotal decision that evening. I committed to overcoming my self-doubt and stepping forward. It was no longer about being behind the scenes but embracing the spotlight and sharing my voice and vision.

A PERSONAL BREAKTHROUGH

The following months went by quickly. I began speaking at smaller events, gradually scaling up as my confidence soared. Standing before a crowd, the weight of my past fears lifted as I spoke with clarity and conviction. I realized my self-doubt no longer confined me; I embraced my purpose with every word.

REFLECTIONS

Now, looking back, that conversation was not just a moment of change; it was the beginning of a new chapter where I could finally lead with conviction and inspire others.

What would it take for you to step out of the shadows, shed your excuses, and confidently embrace your purpose? As you ponder this, consider the journey ahead as you break the chains that bind you and unlock the full extent of your potential.

IGNITING THE FIRE WITHIN

"Our deepest fear is not that we are inadequate. Our deepest fear is that we are powerful beyond measure."

— Marianne Williamson

Your leap from comfort to challenge can be life-changing. Imagine the possibilities if you take bold steps toward your dreams.

My leap from event supervisor to assistant trainer at T. Harv Eker's Warrior Training Camp marked another major shift in my career, opening doors to significant opportunities. Empowering women to claim their space on international stages became my focus.

Over a year, ninety-seven women committed to honing their skills and overcoming challenges; in March 2018, twenty-seven women traveled internationally for the first time to The Women's Economic Forum in New Delhi. Integrating BANK principles into our preparation amplified our impact, resulting in all twenty-seven women receiving an International Award for their contributions.

Consider your path—what's one step you can take today to ignite your fire within and advance your goals while inspiring others?

TRANSITIONING FROM EMPOWERING OURSELVES TO EMPOWERING OUR CHILDREN

The personal transformations and leadership roles I've embraced have led me to a deeper understanding of the importance of nurturing the next generation, beginning with our homes. Transitioning from focusing on my empowerment to the empowerment of our children has been a profoundly moving journey. It's shown me that the true impact of leadership and communication extends beyond personal success; it lies in guiding our children with the same principles—nurturing their individuality and championing their unique paths. This shift has deepened my sense of purpose because I've realized that empowering the next generation is a legacy that begins with us in the daily choices we make at home.

The principles of leadership and communication that have fueled personal and professional growth also hold profound implications for how we nurture and understand the next generation. This journey of empowerment leads us to a fundamental truth: nurturing individuality and respecting each person's unique journey isn't just a professional practice; it's a personal commitment that begins at home.

PARENTING THE CHILD YOU HAVE

> "The biggest job in the world, the most important one, is raising your children. It's who they are. I'm not interested in them being a reflection of me."
>
> — Angelina Jolie

Do you understand and accept what your children genuinely enjoy, or do you impose your expectations upon them? Are you fostering an environment where your children feel empowered to pursue their passions, or are you inadvertently steering them toward your aspirations?

These questions challenge us as caretakers—parents, guardians, aunts, and uncles—to reflect on our approach to guidance.

Consider Kevin, whose interests diverge from his mother's expectations. They attended one of my BANK Personality Workshops.

Kevin's mom, Ava, a social butterfly, learned the difference during an activity that took only fifteen minutes to complete. As the participants selected the personality that best suits them, Ava skipped to the Action section of the room, her daughter Nancy walked over to the Nurturing group, and Kevin headed to the Knowledge section.

When Ava turned around to see that her children were not behind her, she called, "Kevin, son, what are you doing over there? You're not a Knowledge personality; you're Action, like Mom!"

Kevin bowed his head and shuffled his feet, unsure if he should move toward his mom or stay where he was. His sister Nancy stepped behind an adult to hide from the limelight.

At that moment, I moved to block Mom's view and asked, "Ava, would it be okay if I ask Kevin a few questions?"

Ava took a deep breath and nodded.

Turning to Kevin, I asked, "Kevin, what drew you to choose the Knowledge group?"

He peeked around me to look at his mom. I smiled and said, "It's okay. I think Mom would love to know, too."

Kevin stood straight, thoughtfully touching his chin. He said shyly, "I like to read and play games on my computer. And, sometimes, it's nice just to be alone to do my own thing."

"Excellent," I replied. "Mom says you are the captain of your Lacrosse and football teams and get good grades. Would you like to tell us a little more?"

"Yep," Kevin replied. "I play all those sports I'm into, but if I could choose, I'd instead take a break and not have to go from one place to another."

I heard another intake of Ava's breath behind me. I looked directly at Kevin as he sheepishly smiled and asked, "Why do you play all those sports, Kevin?"

Kevin bit his lower lip and began reshuffling his feet. He slowly looked up, and I nodded to encourage him to continue. "Well," he said, "I play sports to keep my mom and dad happy."

The room got quiet as we gave Kevin time to find his words. I smiled, winked at him, and asked Kevin, "If you could share with Mom one or two things that could help her understand you a little better, what would you say?"

He smiled, shrugged, and said, "Mom, you could listen to me better and see that reading is not bad—I like it. And that I don't have to be outside all the time, and being in my room isn't so bad."

Kevin looked up to see his mom wiping away a tear. With a newfound understanding, she opened her arms wide. As Kevin ran into her embrace, she whispered, "I'll listen more, son. We'll figure this out."

As Kevin settled into his mother's embrace, the room filled with a new understanding. Ava's eyes once clouded with expectations, now shone with the bright light of genuine appreciation for her son's honesty and the unique person he was becoming.

A NEW CHAPTER FOR KEVIN

As they left the seminar, Kevin and Ava embarked on a new chapter characterized by mutual understanding and acceptance. Their story serves as a reminder for all caregivers to nurture the individual spirits of the young ones in their care. As Kevin and Ava discovered, listening and understanding can transform relationships and foster a more profound connection that respects each person's individuality.

Kevin and Ava's story is a gentle reminder of our pivotal role in shaping a child's self-esteem and identity. It compels us to ask: How can we better nurture the individual spirits of the young ones in our care, ensuring they feel loved for exactly who they are?

NOT ON MY WATCH - GRANDMA SAGE'S RESOLVE

> "It is easier to build strong children than to repair broken men."
>
> ~ Frederick Douglass

At one of my BANK Seminars, Grandma Sage, motivated by a desire to connect with her introverted grandson Lucas, shared her aspirations to break through his quiet walls.

Lucas was brilliant but introverted, a deep thinker who preferred books and puzzles to playgrounds and parties. He didn't open up easily, and no one in the family knew how to reach him.

Grandma Sage came to the training, took notes feverishly, asked questions, and left inspired and determined, armed with the tools to connect with her grandson.

A CALL THAT CHANGED EVERYTHING

But just weeks later, life delivered a devastating blow. Lucas, her quiet, beautiful grandson, had taken his own life. She called me, her voice shaking. "Mamie, I didn't even get the chance to try. I thought I had time."

The loss was unbearable. But amid her grief, she found her purpose. With a fragile voice, she said: "I have another grandson. He's six. And he's just like Lucas. I won't miss this chance. Not this time. Not on my watch!"

Grandma Sage highlights the critical need for vigilance in supporting the emotional and mental health of those around us. In memory of all the unseen Lucases, let us commit to ensuring no one ever feels invisible or alone.

How can you watch closely, care deeply, and act courageously? Let us create communities where everyone feels valued, heard, and seen. On our watch, let no one slip through the cracks.

FROM SHADOWS TO SHINING LIGHTS

From the depths of invisibility to the heights of empowerment, our journeys define the strength we find within and the connections we make. As we rise from our struggles, we unlock the boundless potential to inspire and elevate those around us. Kevin and Lucas's stories underscore the transformative power of understanding and decisive action. Let us vow to ensure every individual feels valued, heard, and seen. Together, we can forge a world where no one remains in the shadows, and every dream has the opportunity to shine.

MAMIE-JEAN LAMLEY | NABK

Mamie Jean Lamley is an international award-winning author, dynamic speaker, and visionary leader who has empowered global audiences.

As a top sales leader and master trainer for i3 Empowerment Solutions, Codebreaker Technologies, and Heroic Voice Academy, Mamie blends sales mastery, AI-driven business growth, and personality science to elevate leaders, driving unprecedented influence and profit. Globally recognized as an Iconic Woman Making a Difference and a Special Olympics Hall of Fame Inductee, she is building legacies to lead, teach, and inspire 21 million leaders through her signature talks, "Ignite Your Passion" and "Tell Me What You Stand For." Mamie's mission is to disrupt the status quo, guiding leaders from invisible to invincible with powerful conversations and bold, strategic actions.

> "The key to unlocking greatness lies in daring to ignite your passion and stand for what matters."
>
> — Mamie-Jean Lamley

Author's Website: I3EmpowermentSolutions.com

CHAPTER 21
LIGHTEN THE F UP AND LIVE LIFE FULLY

BY NICK RYAN

"If we could read the secret history of our enemies we should find in each man's life sorrow and suffering enough to disarm all hostility."

— Henry Wadsworth Longfellow

In my opinion, we are all born with an innate personality. I have no idea whether that is God-given, through a system like the signs of the Zodiac based on our sun sign, moon sign, and a myriad of other signs, or just is. Our personality can certainly be refined or squashed, fully displayed or hidden, depending on our circumstances.

The fact is we are all some combination of BANK, and over time, it can adjust based on our experiences. That is for sure, but generally, we are who we are. You can't change a zebra's stripes, and that is awesome. I love all types of people. Relationships define me. True…it is easier to hang around with people of similar personalities, mine being a mixture of Nurturing and Action. I was probably more Action when I was younger, but now I am more caring about all beings, whether they be plants, animals, or humans, so I am more Nurturing—yet I do still like some Action.

So, all that said, this brings me to my point. We need to lighten up in order to live life fully. Trying to change people, argue with people about their opinions, and judge people is essentially a waste of time. My first wife and I married very young, and we had many good reasons for choosing each other. We both wanted to have a nice home, kids, and a dog, plus drink a little wine and travel.

We thought we could change each other to mold the other person into whom we wanted them to be. Good luck with that! What we really needed was a better understanding of what the codes in BANK meant and how each of us needed to be communicated with. That lack of awareness and acceptance led to our downfall as a couple, but not as co-parents. Over time, we have learned to admire the good in each other and accept differences with a humorous undertone.

So that brings me to one of my mom's favorite sayings: *If you can laugh and smile away the little trials of today, you will live to laugh and smile away a greater trial another day.*

As we go through life, we will face greater trials, the magnitude of which depends on how much we take on. The more relationships you have, the greater chance some will go through suffering and even death, ultimately including our own. The more challenging situations we try to make a difference in, the more criticism we will face, and sometimes failures will occur. That is again where the concept of lightening the f up comes in. It doesn't mean we don't care; it simply accepts the concept that shit happens, and it is worth going forth anyway.

Picture this situation. I am a real estate investor and developer who has partnered with some other guys and a not-for-profit to develop an amazing community called Highpoint. The idea stemmed from asking, "How do you create a genuine community without a golf course?" I love golf, by the way, but it was just a question. What evolved is a seven-hundred-unit-rental and for-sale community, anchored by a town square with a community center, performing art center, and Montessori school, all run in partnership with a not-for-profit called the Institute for Community.

Four different churches hold services in the community, and there are performing arts centers, providing numerous mentors and volunteers who do amazing things within the community. It is truly outstanding. One church that meets in the community center is a Hispanic church with a connection with an inner-city pastor. His daughter initially worked for the Institute for Community, which is a not-for-profit that runs community programming, and now works for us, the apartment owners. She and her dad drove four inner-city refugee families from downtown Chicago to Highpoint to attend church every Sunday.

Being an urban development company also, our company has seen a significant influx of refugees and migrants in Chicago, and they are being sheltered in empty office buildings, tent cities, shelters, etc. As a Nurturing personality, I saw the opportunity to help change the stars for some of these families, and our company decided to fund four apartments for these displaced families, in conjunction with a partnership with World Relief. The plan is to get the families into a safe home, get their kids into school, and have them become part of a community supporting them until they can get on their feet.

The first two families moved in, which has thus far been a great success. The kids are in school, one of the moms was baptized and is volunteering, and the husbands are learning English and preparing for a job. One resident even donated a car to one of the families. It is going so well that it would be great to offer up two more apartments to two more families fully screened by World Relief to get them on a pathway to success. I reached out to my retired partner of thirty years, whom I dearly love, with the idea, and wow... did I get an earful. He blasted the idea, saying what we are doing is hurting America, entirely against what our country stands for, and passionately stated there was no way he would help; however, he still loved me, and I do him.

When we first joined forces in our late twenties and early thirties, he was a recovering hippie architect with all kinds of ideas for changing the world. His personality type is similar to Elon Musk's; I believe he is a very Knowledge-based person. Over time, apparently, the Knowledge perspective changed, and he has become an ultra-conservative instead of a hippie. Politically, I believe I am a moderate independent. I believe in a hand-up, not a handout. Coming from a family of six kids, one of whom was deaf and one blind, we were expected to contribute fully. I learned early on that people, given a chance and maybe a little boost, want to work, step up, and do what they can. I definitely don't believe in long-term handouts that will weaken a person when they become strong enough to stand on their own.

What I see in these immigrants is that they definitely want to work, contribute, and become self-sufficient. The system needs some revamping for sure, especially in getting work permits quickly. It is crazy that we need workers, especially in the trades, hospitality, transportation, etc., and it takes so long to get them into a position where they can work, pay taxes, etc., when they want to so badly. Instead, we fund their costs while they sit around and twiddle their thumbs. Let's get this fixed now!

Okay, enough ranting…. The point is my partner and I are looking at the same situation through two totally different lenses. That seems to be the case with a lot of things in our current world. The power does not lie in confrontation or the continuous pursuit of persuasion—neither of those works. We are who we are until we choose to see things differently. That is why we all need to lighten the f up. That is the only way we can ultimately solve challenges. We need to come from a place of openness and acceptance.

My wife, Teresa, and I married thirty-three years ago, blending a family of five kids between the ages of ten and fourteen. Teresa is an ANKB personality, which aligns much more closely with my BANKCODE. However, she is higher on the Blueprint numbers than me. My level of detail is very low, and I can definitely whip up more chaos in a hurry.

BANK is a great tool that helps us understand each other and communicate more fully. However, there are other factors, as well. What family background did we each come from? That is a big one. Are you from a patriarchal or matriarchal family system? What is your spiritual background? What is your financial background? Those are all components that will factor in.

I wrote a bestselling book about a lot of those things—*From Jackass to Joy: The Art and Science of Love, and Marriage and Blending Families*—and can honestly say that there are several factors in making marriage and any relationship work for a long time. Two of the most important are your level of commitment and your level of acceptance. For example, when Teresa and I first married, I was a lot like Mrs. Doubtfire in the Robin Williams movie. I loved my wife, and I loved my kids, and I whipped up a whole lot of stuff.

I let a buddy and a nephew move in with us. I took sixteen to thirty family members and friends on vacation with us, often to a big lake or ocean house under one roof. I often invited family and friends over for dinner at the last minute because I knew my lovely wife had prepared a big meal. After a couple of years, she went from this amazingly attractive, fully dressed-to-the-nines lady to Goldie Hawn in

Overboard, an overworked, somewhat haggard version of herself. Fortunately, some good counseling, honest conversations, personal development, and a strong commitment and a level of acceptance got us to a great place: a fully loving family, now with eleven grandkids and a lifelong relationship of passion.

Okay, so you thought that would be how it would end…but not so fast! My sweet Action/Nurturing wife tried to outdo my early marital antics by jumping headfirst into the dog rescue world right when I was about to turn seventy. Again, it is time to lighten the f up and accept it. We have always had dogs, sometimes two and sometimes three. About two years ago, we were down to our last old beagle and thought that maybe that was it for us owning dogs. We could now have grandkids and granddogs. But it didn't quite work out like that. Two years ago, one of our three Nurturing/Action daughters called and said she had the perfect dog playmate for our old beagle, Sylvie, a little rescue hound in the city. I must admit she was cute, so we took her. I didn't know that would open up the floodgates.

About fifteen months ago, Teresa received a call from the foster of the hound we took. The foster said there was an emergency and asked Teresa to fund the transport of eleven dogs to save them from being euthanized. I am also a Nurturer, so what can you do? The person who was supposed to rescue those dogs bailed on Teresa, which was just the start. It turned out she bailed on two other good-hearted ladies, who unfortunately didn't have the financial means to keep them.

Over the past fifteen months, Teresa has directly rescued and placed more than seventy-five dogs and helped fund another 700 nationally, including Darrell, a sixty-five-pound English Staffie that Teresa and I drove to Colorado for one of our other Nurturing/Action daughters to adopt. (By the way, Darrel is a huge hit with her other dog and kids.)

Teresa has formed a not-for-profit called Angel Dog Alliance. It has become her life's mission, with full support from me after I lightened the f up. We now have five dogs of our own, including two young males, who get picked up for doggie daycare to wear themselves out three days a week. Our backyard, which was once a paradise, sometimes looks like a hayfield. There are dog adoption events every weekend at Pet Supplies Plus or other pet stores, and a whole lot of vet and other bills on a weekly basis. It is insane but actually fun. I initially tried to put a cap on it, but how do you slow down an Action? You don't. You help them instead.

Teresa now has a network of doggie-loving friends helping foster, walk, market, and care for the dogs, and we have a whole new group of people to go to dinner with and celebrate life with! My mission statement, developed thirty-five years ago at Landmark Education, is *"All relationships are partnerships for accomplishment, acknowledgment, and fun."*

That statement was supplemented at a Tony Robbins Date with Destiny conference eight years ago: *Live life fully in joyful and generous celebration with others.* I just didn't know so many of the others would have four legs! Have a blessed life, and lighten the f up!

NICK RYAN | NAKB

Nick Ryan serves as Marquette's Executive Chairman. As one of the founding partners, he has been with Marquette since its inception in 1983. With more than forty years of experience in real estate development and investment, Nick has been involved in more than $3 billion in transactions, primarily in the multifamily sector, but also including office, industrial, hotel, retail, student, and senior housing.

Nick is a civil engineer by profession, bringing engineering and analytical skills to new acquisitions and developments. Still, his biggest asset is his commitment to forming win-win relationships with major companies, institutional partners, and clients. He is a member of the Pension Real Estate Association and the National Multi-Family Housing Corporation and serves as the Board President of the Institute for Community. Nick is a licensed Real Estate Broker and holds a civil engineering degree from the Rose-Hulman Institute of Technology.

Author's Website: MarquetteCompanies.com

CHAPTER 22
SERVING THE BEST

BY PAM KRANHOLD

"Make each day your masterpiece."

— John Wooden

Have you ever touched someone so deeply that it surprised you how powerful you actually are? When you made that impact, what part of your best did you tap?

My role models for making people matter and serving the best of myself and the best in others came along early. Both my parents grew up in humble, hard-working families. The mottos "No time for nonsense" or "There's never a second chance to make a first impression" seemed to be passed along in their DNA. Three older sisters also showed me how to do things right and how to avoid doing things wrong.

In adolescence, I learned to listen. Sometimes, it was for all the warning signs in a stress-filled household. Learning when to give another person space or to fly under the radar would bring a feeling of safety. I learned how conflict got resolved with grace and forgiveness or stayed a raw and open wound.

By the time I was born, my mother's father had suffered several strokes. He was unable to form words and was bedridden in the community hospital or care center for sixteen years. Just imagine—his most precious ability was to listen, as his children, grandchildren, and great-grandchildren visited him routinely with dedication. My grandmother walked four miles and back to and from the senior care center daily to feed my grandfather his lunch. Children across generations would take him out on drives.

Even though our family lived 1,000 miles away, my parents, who didn't spend extra money on much, made sure we made the drive a few times a year. We would read the guestbook signed by visitors to that one-room life. Their notes of appreciation and sweet regard for my grandfather showed that he mattered. I read the words—both what they said and didn't say. As a young girl, looking up to previous generations, I learned bits and pieces of each person's style and story.

On those road trips, we listened to iconic (and not-so-iconic) songs on eight-track tapes, over and over. I learned each song's emotion, the perspective of the lyrics, the mood of it all, or what sparked a memory. I read books by Toni Morrison, Maya Angelou, and John Irving, all with their unique and vivid characters woven together. They shared the greatness and sometimes weakness of each soul. Those songs and stories showed that people remember how you make them feel. Did the words share misunderstanding, heartache, or crushing disappointment? Was there endless love, forbidden love, or passionate longing? Those words whispered and sometimes shouted, "Give from your heart. Do your best. Be kind. It matters!"

On each road trip, we would visit people my parents had met when they were transferred to different towns for work. They may have met as neighbors, church members, or community members in a philanthropic organization, but they became life-long friends. Those visits were the networking of the time. It was keeping in touch. We would pull into town almost unannounced! If the people weren't home or away from their office, we would leave a note—a sign that we cared. My parents passed down simple pleasures and the joy of enjoying people. I didn't know that someday there would be a code for connecting with each soul we touch.

SERVING THE BEST (AND WORST) IN OTHERS

My family's business served the people and businesses throughout our region. But this wasn't just any business; it was a credit bureau—credit scores and bill collecting. We knew the financial character of most people in town. Before computers, a manila envelope held the personal history that would define their fiscal futures! Each spoke volumes about what they valued. Even newspaper articles were cut out and saved to build a picture of the person's integrity.

As a kid, my favorite news article was about a vengeful woman who, Carrie-Underwood-style, poured sugar into her husband's gas tank while he was at a local bar. I wasn't rooting for her apparent revenge; I was just amazed she had that much passion, frustration, and anger, combined with the gumption to do it!

Each person's report and story differed, yet many themes were repeated. Both good and bad snippets of data created a picture like a puzzle half-solved. It was up to the reader to decide how the bigger picture would likely shape up and how the person would show up from there.

Each holiday season became a humbling experience as parents out shopping for brand-new bikes or a car for their kid would have their credit requests declined. They had planned to pay over time and had faith they were good for it. They would come to our office very frustrated. They felt desperate to have that moment of joy and pride from being able to give such an important gift. But they were stalled by a bank of data they felt didn't represent them or misrepresented their credit history. Many people didn't know a credit report existed. Many were stressed out. How could they salvage their plan?

You can probably imagine there were topics people protected when under stress. It's good to know what not to talk about—the tripwires that grate across the nerves of different personalities. I didn't have the easy tool of BANK back then.

By fourteen, I was at the front counter, handling walk-ins and phone calls. Often, I would be the face of the bad guy, denying credit and putting them on the naughty list. So many people were apprehensive about sharing personal financial business with a "kid." When you're perceived as less than or don't meet expectations, you learn to connect and empower others with patience and grace.

Characters ranged wide! There were single parents with a brood of kids, a high-roller real estate developer in a rush for the opportunity to make the deal as soon as possible, and so many marriages playing out their best and worst interactions before my eyes. Serving the best and worst in times of stress was a great foundation for seeing the humanity in us all.

Learning BANK back then would have been a game-changer! When people were unable to be kind under stress, I would have had a better tool to help put a stop-gap on disrespectful behavior. Even at that young age, I understood the best someone can do is limited by their perspective and their natural reaction. But the concept of Emotional Intelligence (EQ) was just being brought into classrooms and boardrooms. BANK would have provided me with the language to listen just a little bit closer and respond to the spoken and unspoken signs of people being their best in the moment or sometimes their worst.

BEING BETTER

Over the past ten years, my sisters and I, now with no parents to blame, have clearly heard the language each of us was raised with. We depend on it when we want or expect a given outcome. Nuances of different parenting and personalities show up over and over. And we can empower, break down, or even deny relationships through our connections.

With BANK, you've already learned that it's not personal; it's personality science. Once you hear it, feel it, and see it, you can't unlearn it. You'll have the language, tools, and ability to create better outcomes in business and relationships.

Each connection is an opportunity for engagement and impact. Connect with the mission of making people matter. Use the BANK system and know the steps to get to yes. Raise self-awareness. Understand motivations. Tap empathy. Build self-regulation. Get skilled at connecting.

Start with Make People Matter. The value is timeless!

- You'll be ready to be your best.
- Your relationships will be stronger and healthier.
- You'll find what is working and not working for you or your business.
- You'll make the kinds of changes you've valued since you were a kid.

SERVING FOR A HIGHER PURPOSE

Serving a power higher than yourself or a mission bigger than yourself can bring out your best. Think of a leader, mentor, or historical figure who rose to great heights by serving a higher purpose than themselves. For example, Robin Sharma's leadership messages are aligned with serving the best, too! Concepts like ethical ambition, work you can be proud of, and wealth money can't buy—guide you toward a quality approach and clear goals. Think about how you can incorporate these into each day in tangible and intangible ways.

Serving the best requires awareness of the opportunity to innovate and grow. Seek people who inspire you to share your best with the world, too!

BANK technology and tools tap your limitless potential, show you the strengths and opportunities for improvement, and give you actionable steps to serve your best and the best in others.

FINDING THE BEST IN OTHERS

By midlife, even though I had gone through many iterations of leadership and communications training in corporate life, the tools I used were classics. When I discovered BANK, I realized they were also outdated.

Have you had an experience that opened your awareness to a new way?

Sometimes, old ways just won't get you where you want to go. When you're a life-long learner, you can use examples all around you to level up. In the business world, competitive benchmarking crosses industries. For example, a car dealership may look at the best call center response times or satisfaction ratings and approaches of an upscale hotel chain to improve its own customer experience.

I worked for a major insurance company in leadership roles in quality management and performance excellence. While there, we created our own quality mission statement. My statement tied my love for people and cooking together, a metaphor for Serving The Best.

I volunteered as a senior examiner for California's Malcolm Baldrige Award program. The National Institute of Standards and Technology program was developed in response to other countries beating the United States at developing and sustaining greatness, such as Japan and Germany. They had cultures that stood out for their focus on quality. The award criteria framework has evolved over time to focus on best practices and proven systems to continually innovate. Stakeholder engagement is key, and meeting them where they are or where they want to go is essential.

Each evaluation team would get a comprehensive report from the organization outlining strategy, leadership, customers, workforce, operations, results, measurement, analysis, and knowledge management. Sometimes, we would go on-site to mine additional information about the organization's best outcomes or the opportunities for improvement.

With every evaluation report, we shared what we found great or found as a gap, we included the "So what?" It kept things simple to understand and relevant for a leadership team to consider the next steps. We were trained to see their limiting and limitless potential. Innovation was at the heart of so many great companies. Don't you think that kind of flexibility and adaptation is required to connect one-on-one, too? Innovation helps give a standing ovation to another person's uniqueness.

That spirit of innovation championed by Cheri Tree captured me from day one! There was a better way to find the best for the company through customer-, staff-, team-, partner- supplier-relationships. A company's culture speaks volumes about what it values through who it values, how they do it, the results it gets, and how it celebrates its wins or approaches failure.

My passion is sparked! The path is clear when BANK helps create a better story. Serving my best is sure to include integrating BANK into best-in-class, world-class companies and people who want to show up as world-class.

In one of my consulting roles, I had the occasion to attend a school staff meeting. The nation's education system marketed a "No Child Left Behind" motto, which the school readily adopted. Yet I found the teacher molding the discussion for students with disabilities with incredibly defeating doubt about expectations and outcomes. The qualification was a sobering reminder that it only takes one person to not believe in another and not see their best. It made me wonder if their approach and measures for making these kids matter were the best they could be.

Has there been a time when you knew a culture or system around you was giving up? How did it affect the people around you?

Being a school board chair, especially during incredibly disruptive times for the learning community, made me wish everyone had knowledge about BANK. We all needed to level up our skill sets to start with What Matters Most. Speaking one language would have helped so much. We were keeping up with a very dynamic time.

We all know how important self-esteem, family dynamics, peer relationships, and conflict resolution are, and it all starts at a young age. Then, there are the adult kids we all are, bringing our unique values to each matter at hand.

Codebreaker Technologies has captured the best practices for using patented tools for empowerment and connection to the education arena. Codebreaker's leadership, planning, commitment, and bold passion to create a profound and enduring impact on humanity is going to bring innovation to education systems. It will touch the lives of countless kids, teachers, and parents with the transformative power of BANK.

Sharing BANK at Back-To-School nights or through one-on-one coaching to administrators will inspire school leadership, teachers and staff, parents, and students. This toolkit can shift the depth of education, build emotional intelligence, and make a difference in the classroom, on campus, and for many kids and families.

What makes me happiest is this isn't just a movement; it's a legacy in the making! With the most basic understanding of BANK, my goal of someday bringing BANK to performance excellence organizations, like those who level up using the Baldrige criteria, was just taking shape. I, along with Codebreaker and teams of educators from pre-school to PhD-school, are going to Make Kids Matter!

How will you make the next generation matter?

EXERCISE

The commitment to making people matter is unique for each of us. What motivates us to truly serve our best is unique. What's needed in a given situation or for a given project varies, as well. Stephen R. Covey, the author of *The 7 Habits of Highly Effective People*, encouraged readers to look at all the roles in life and plan tasks and time with consideration for how to best serve in each role. Start with what matters—the big rocks. For example, if you are a student, could you do your best by turning in your part of a group science project early? If you are an executive, is getting the right buy-in to support a critical, impactful change the priority?

As I use the BANK methodology, I realize it isn't just the values I love most that can help me serve my best. I can be the best-of-me all day; but am I serving others with my best? Sometimes, I need to tap values that I use more often when I'm in a pinch, when the going gets tough or when it's forced. I need to keep myself flexible and be willing to stretch to serve in each role. So, I encourage you to take on the habit of not just listing the roles and ways to connect and be your best, but also, to apply the BANK values that will matter most. Using the BANK methodology to consider which values you can bring forward to be better and connect with others is a true gift. Get started!

Step 1: Make a list of the important roles in your life (e.g., self, child, parent, caretaker, leader, team member, friend).

Step 2: Next to each role or relationship, note one or more ways you can do your best (e.g., be dependable help for homework, give garden produce to neighbors).

Step 3: Note the BANK values of the people you connect with in each role (either a BANKCODE or the specific values you see them needing more of from you, like fun and spontaneity).

Step 4: Make a plan for delivering what matters most for each role and the people you'll connect with.

Step 5: Serve Your Best!

Making people matter will bring an undeniable light to their world and yours!

SUMMARY

In conclusion, you can and absolutely will make people matter when you serve your best. We can make a profound impact by dedicating ourselves to the values of service and connection. Success is more than personal achievement; it is about embodying a mission that prioritizes others and building a legacy that resonates with compassion, grace, and excellence. Through the heartfelt stories and lessons shared, we recognize that serving our best is a journey shaped by empathy and stewardship. By embracing both our strengths and vulnerabilities and leveraging methodologies like BANK, we unlock a deeper understanding of how to serve more authentically and effectively.

The roots of these values, much like those of a mighty tree, provide strength and guidance. They nurture the relationships that define us, and when we commit to serving selflessly, they leave an indelible mark on the world. Remember, our roles are intertwined with opportunities for engagement, empowerment, and growth—from personal connections to professional collaborations. We must continuously ask ourselves the questions that guide our path: What core virtues are we embodying? How are we building bridges in our communities and organizations?

With intentional practice and thoughtful reflection, we make people matter and enrich our lives. Doing so fosters a culture of mutual respect and inspiration, a testament to our role models' influence and the enduring power of service. Serve with devotion, commit to excellence, and lead with empathy. As you proceed to the next chapter in your story, remember the great potential within. Make the choice to serve your best—for yourself, others, and future generations that will look to you for guidance and grace.

PAM KRANHOLD | NKAB

Pam Kranhold is a seasoned business consultant with more than thirty years of expertise in government healthcare administration, business development, performance excellence, and quality management. She specializes in helping teams innovate, grow collaboration, and integrate best practices into business strategies to drive positive and sustainable results. She is also a Certified and Licensed BANK Trainer and Coach.

Pam has held key leadership roles at Delta Dental, contributing to major state and community healthcare programs, including California Medicaid Fiscal Intermediary, Texas Medicaid/CHIP, and Utah Medicaid. A recognized leader in performance excellence, she was the first Delta Dental's Quality Award recipient and is an Alumni Baldrige Examiner.

Beyond her professional achievements, Pam is dedicated to grassroots community efforts and education. Her contributions have been recognized by the City of Sacramento, notably for her role in funding and developing a twenty-one-acre community park and initiating the city's annual Park Day.

Author's Website: PamKranhold.com

CHAPTER 23

MAKE PEOPLE MATTER BECAUSE THEY MATTER TO GOD

BY PATTY SHIH-MEI LEE CAMPBELL

"Treat others as they want to be treated."

— The Platinum Rule

Have you ever wondered how people become the way they are? What was their childhood like? What experiences and environments shaped them into who they are today? Why were some people so strong and able to overcome tough obstacles while others crumbled at the weight of their circumstances?

Ever since I was little, I wondered about these questions. I always wondered why my mom was different from my friends' moms. Why did my mom fight with me over who got the larger piece of cake when other moms gave selflessly to their children and nurtured them? They seemed to care for, cook, clean, and listen to their children's needs, while my mom couldn't look beyond herself or understand other people's points of view. I was "made in Taiwan," raised by nannies and housekeepers, and grew up in Taiwan and Singapore with my sister, parents, aunts, and uncle.

CHILDHOOD

For the most part, I had a great childhood. I remembered playing outdoors all the time with my sister, uncle (who was only two years older than me), and friends. Back then, we were considered raised well if we had full bellies, a roof over our heads, and a safe environment with a great education. I remembered my dad telling me once that he was raised very poor on a farm, and food was scarce. His parents were very tough on him and used to burn him with a hot iron if he misbehaved. My grandfather was a tailor, so the hot iron was always hot and available. There were eight brothers altogether, which explained how Grandpa and Grandma managed to keep all of them in line in the poor countryside of Tainan, Taiwan. My dad told me years later that he never even thought of raising us with emotional support and self-esteem. There was no fostering and nurturing confidence in your children. They were to be seen and not heard, especially if they were girls. Children's sole responsibility was to listen and obey their parents and elders. They did not have a voice, and it was discouraged. In the Chinese culture, there was only us and our community. The concept of I, me, and mine was a Western concept, not an Eastern concept.

SINGAPORE

I didn't remember growing up in Taiwan very much. I mostly remembered how we lived in Singapore, where I went through kindergarten to fourth grade in an all-girls school. We had to wear ugly, green coverall dresses as uniforms, and most of us had short black hair. We lined up every morning in the school field, sang the national anthem, and exercised. Then, we would go to our classes and brush our teeth with no toothpaste after lunch every day.

Girls could be so cruel and such bullies that they tore up my school papers in class. I cried to the teacher, but I don't remember if the girls got disciplined or not for what they did to me. I also remembered when I talked out of turn in class with several classmates, my teacher lined us up and slapped our hands with a ruler. You can bet we never talked out of turn again.

We played outside and swam at the pool most days while growing up. We climbed trees, plucked and ate rambutan fruits, and played with ants, wild cats, and dogs. We even raised baby chicks while living in a nine-story high-rise with balconies. We were pretty free to play as long as our homework was finished. My dad was busy working as a real estate developer and business owner in Singapore, while my mom studied at a beautician school. She entered competitions and won Best Make-up Artist back in her glory days. She was also a famous ballerina since childhood in Taiwan and taught ballet to some of my classes in Singapore.

NEW YORK, USA

When we migrated to New York, USA, in 1978, life changed a lot for us. All of a sudden, my sister and I were given new American names. Overnight, my name changed from Shih-Mei Lee to Patty Lee. My sister changed from Shih-Chen Lee to Kathy Lee. My mom said she saw a black-and-white American TV show with twin sisters, so we were named after them. We found out on March 17, 1979, that I was born on St. Patrick's Day, which befits my American name perfectly! It wasn't until years later that I realized I was named after the Patty Duke show called *Identical Cousins*. The cousins in the black-and-white TV show were named Patty and Kathy. My mom thought they were identical sisters because she didn't understand English and named us that before we arrived in New York. Because Singapore was at one point a British colony, we all had to learn Mandarin and English in school. By the time I started sixth grade in Queens, New York, I already knew English and even skipped fifth grade.

In Taiwan and Singapore, it was very inexpensive to have nannies and housekeepers. When we moved to New York, it was too expensive to have outside help, so my sister and

I had chores right away, like doing the dishes, cleaning our own rooms, and helping to vacuum and dust the house. We walked to school and took public transit to and from school. I remembered being shocked to be in the same class as boys, and I couldn't talk to boys (and later men) for years.

MENTAL ILLNESS MAGNIFIED

My mom continued to have bipolar episodes where she would release all her pent-up emotions, talk incessantly, and complain non-stop for days. She would try and run away with us girls and lock herself in the bathroom for hours, etc. She would frustrate my dad so much that they would fight and yell in front of my sister and me as we cried in fear and helplessness. My dad didn't know how to handle my mom's mental illness, and back in the day, in the Asian countries of Taiwan and Singapore, they didn't know how to deal with my mom's periodic outbursts either. They hospitalized her and treated her with electric shock therapy, which traumatized her and worsened her condition. She developed physical scars of tic behavior and other neuropathy issues. She also never sought counseling and therapy with a psychiatrist because of the stigma of being "crazy." When we came to America, my dad's solution was to take my mom traveling on vacation for weeks at a time to calm her down from her manic episodes. They pretty much traveled the world and even took a whirlwind trip around the world on the Concord supersonic airplane back in the 1980s.

GREW UP TOO SOON

While my parents traveled, my sister and I were left to fend for ourselves. Our parents stocked the fridge with TV dinners, and we grew up fast, having to take care of ourselves at an early age. During our teenage years, my sister went to the High School of Art and Design, and I auditioned and attended the High School of Music and Art, later renamed LaGuardia High School of Music and the Arts—the *Fame* movie school in Manhattan. We lived near Long Island in Queens and took the Long Island railroad into the subway systems of Manhattan to get to both our schools. Many things could have endangered us, but God protected us for the most part. I had men flash at me, was almost robbed once, and almost got scammed once.

GOD, CHURCH, AND ME

One of the best things my parents did right was take us to church since we were babies. They were both born-again Christians and had introduced my sister and me to Jesus, God the Father, and the Holy Spirit since birth. We were baptized as babies and grew up in the Chinese churches of Taiwan and Singapore. When we moved to Queens, New York, we continued to go to a Chinese Church where my sister and I continued to speak our native tongue of Taiwanese and some Mandarin.

In our Chinese church in Queens, I found Jesus as my Savior, and I began my lifelong journey and relationship with the living God. My youth group leader, Emily Hsieh, was such an encourager, and she led by great example. I learned so much about myself and my purpose, calling, destiny, and place in this world. I asked God all those questions I mentioned at the beginning of this chapter, and He always answered my questions and downloaded insights to me as I read the Bible and worked through my struggles in life. He explained to me that my mom had a traumatic life growing up and was stuck in her childhood wounds. She never grew up and matured normally, like most people did. He wanted me to see my mom as a wounded person, trying her best to be my mother in the capacity she had. I was able to have compassion for her and forgive her for all the years she couldn't love me and my sister the way she should have.

My journey with God gave me my Father's eyes. I was able to see people the way God sees people. I was able to love people the way God loves people. This became my superpower. I had an uncanny ability to intuitively connect with people of all ages—from babies to teenagers to adults to the elderly.

My quest for understanding people led me to study Human Development and Family Studies at Cornell University. I then pursued my Master's teaching degree at Bank Street College of Education in Manhattan. I believed prevention was better than rehabilitation. It would be better to reach children while they were young before they were damaged by the harshness of life and needed therapy.

OVERCOMING OBSTACLES

Because I didn't grow up with a voice or self-esteem, I let many people silence me and put me down for years. I allowed people to take advantage of me because I didn't know how to set boundaries and defend myself. I allowed my ex-husband of eleven years to abandon me and my son. I took on teaching jobs that only paid $16,000/year, $23,000/year, and office administration jobs that only paid $33,000/year. Friends, coworkers, and people of authority took advantage of my gifts and talents. Growing up, I had so many fears because I had to learn everything myself without parental guidance. I was afraid of men and authority figures.

Because I inherited my love of real estate from my parents, I became a successful investor in 1998, which sustained and supplemented my meager income. In 2009, I decided to leave my job working for a boss to embark on my entrepreneurial journey. I took real estate investment courses in Arizona, where I "met" and saw Cheri Tree standing on stage as a successful entrepreneur. I thought I was on my way to building my real estate empire when the market crashed in 2009 and 2010. I lost all of my properties and had to fight the bank when they tried to foreclose on my house.

All of us in real estate crashed hard as we scrambled to make money, but we couldn't because all our houses had half the equity they had when we bought them before the crash. The big banks not only didn't help people; they also got bailed out by the government, but they still turned around and foreclosed on families and millions of Americans. They took people's basic need for shelter and turned it around for profit on the backs of hard-working Americans.

I also trusted all the wrong people with my investments. All these so-called "Christians" came out of the woodwork, promised me a return on investment, and basically took my money and ran. I basically went through hell and back for fourteen years, from 2010 to 2024. Again, I continued letting people take advantage of me, and I was unhappy. The Bible says, "Hope deferred makes the heart sick, but a longing fulfilled is a tree of life" (Psalm 13:12 NIV). My hope was so deferred that my heart was very sick.

I also struggled with depression for fourteen years. I have been through several months of depression every year since 2010 when I lost my baby girl Chloe Joy Campbell (due Sept 28, 2010) at six months pregnancy. As the years went by, the depression months grew longer and longer. In 2023, my depression lasted eight months! I didn't recognize myself anymore; I had changed so much over the years. I isolated more and more and had fewer parties or friends at our house. I ate and snacked a lot at night and gained more than thirty pounds, and I didn't like who I was becoming.

I now have a newfound appreciation for those who struggle with this epidemic we call depression, anxiety, bipolar, and mental illness. Before 2010, I never understood why people got depressed because I was always so peaceful and joyful growing up. When someone is depressed, the chemical in their brain changes, and it feels like molasses. The things I used to know how to do left my brain as if I didn't remember how to do anything anymore. I would wander in the grocery store for half an hour and come out empty-handed because I was too overwhelmed by everything on the shelves. I could barely cook, drive, or do laundry, and my anxiety level overtook me and rendered me helpless.

Sometimes, we must hit rock bottom before our epiphany moment happens—2023 was my rock-bottom year.

On January 5, 2024, God woke me up at 1:30 a.m. I couldn't go back to sleep, so I started talking to God like I always did. God told me the fourteen years of losses and famine were a thing of the past. He told me he would replenish tenfold all the years the locusts have stolen! No more losing babies. No more losing houses. No more depression. No more being gullible and naive. No more losing hundreds of thousands of dollars. No more being like Hello Kitty without a mouth and a voice.

I'm now a warrior and a lioness roaring with pride, confidence, and strength. The year 2024 was the year I transformed. I have taken full responsibility for my life, and I recognize full well that I can either give up my power to others or stand fully in my own power in the LORD. I can walk out my calling in life and the purpose for which I am created—to help coach people into their full potential and passion in their life, relationships, spiritual journey, inner healing, financial healing, business, and work life.

BANK SUCCESS JOURNEY/MINDSET

Thank God that in this journey, I found Hermie Bacus, my mentor and coach in both real estate and financial businesses. Through his training, patience, guidance, and many motivational books by John Maxwell, Darren Hardy, Jim Rohn, Robin Sharma, and Robert Kiyosaki, I started developing the positive mindset and confidence I needed. It took fourteen years of moving forward one step and falling backward two steps, climbing the steep learning curve of transformation from a mother and teacher to an entrepreneur, a businesswoman, and a financial and life coach.

I also found BANK with Cheri Tree and Esther Wildenberg. Before BANK I didn't know I was an NBAK—a Nurturing, Blueprint, Action, and Knowledge person. I didn't know I could tailor my marketing and presentation skills to speak more effectively to people using their dominant language and personality.

I didn't know I could use artificial intelligence (AI) to interpret clients' personality types and cater my approach to them accordingly. Years of experience have also helped me become a better public speaker and well-rounded writer. I am so thankful I can integrate every tool available through BANK. I am so grateful I have built the network I now have through BANK and other business networking groups like Novato Chambers, Rotary Club of Novato Evening, FinFitLife, LinkedIn, Facebook, Instagram, YouTube, Alignable, and other social media platforms.

My loving husband, Billy Campbell, has stood by me through thick and thin for eighteen years now, and we have just renewed our vows from 07-07-07. Because I went through a painful divorce before, I was so afraid and hesitant to give my heart away again. His patience and persistence in pursuing me sealed his love, which became the constant and solid rock that held our marriage together. I am forever grateful for the life we built together with our children, family, and friends. I know we have made people matter in our lives by being there for them whenever they need us. We have always served our family, friends, and community. We have hosted annual Chinese New Year potsticker parties for years to unite people of multiple cultures. I love people, and I intend to make people matter every day because people matter to God.

EXERCISE

Thank you for letting me share my journey with you. Here's an exercise for you:

- Describe how you felt when you read this chapter.
- What were your aha moments?
- What did you learn that was new or different?
- What is your story? Your journey?
- What will you do to make people matter to you?

TIPS

- Meditate and pray/talk to God every day.
- Everything else will fall into place.
- Be mindful and self-aware of what you say, do, and how you treat people.

- Take five minutes every day to breathe deeply and relax so you can clear your mind and focus on the tasks at hand more efficiently.
- Write down your thoughts and journal every day for five to ten minutes. You will be more in touch with yourself and God.

SUMMARY

I encourage you to make people matter every day in your life. Things come and go. Money comes and goes, and your business and work come and go. You can't take your things with you past this life. You can't take your money with you past this life. Your work and your boss will not likely be there on your deathbed. Who will be there for you in the lowest times of your life and on your deathbed? Hopefully, the people who matter most to you and the people you made matter in this life.

PATTY SHIH-MEI LEE CAMPBELL | NBAK

Patty Shih-Mei Lee Campbell is, first and foremost, a child of God. She has overcome a lifetime of obstacles to make people matter every day, including herself. She has had a lifetime of teaching and coaching experience as her family and friends come to her for advice over the last thirty years. She has been through the "school of hard knocks" for fourteen years, emerging as an expert in her field of real estate, financial services, life insurance, emotional healing coach, life and joy coach, and business coach.

Patty Shih-Mei lives in the San Francisco Bay Area with the love of her life, Billy (William Nathan Campbell Sr.), and their smart, handsome, and fun-loving son, Liam (William Nathan Campbell Jr). She also has an amazing thirty-year-old adult son, Jeremy Liu, who is thriving in every way and with whom she is so proud. Her mother "Queen Mary" also lives with her now and has just turned eighty years old.

Author's Website: www.AbundanceGroup.us

CHAPTER 24

CUSTOMER APPRECIATION: EVERYTHING YOU NEED TO KNOW TO SUCCEED

BY SUSAN GONZALEZ-MILLIRON

"Every company's greatest assets are its customers because, without customers, there is no company."

— Michael Lebequf

Do you remember the best customer appreciation you have experienced? What made it special? How did you feel?

Do you remember the worst customer appreciation experience you had? What happened to make the experience terrible? How did you feel?

While reflecting on the answers to the questions above, think about what you expect from the person helping you make a purchase that would bring you back as a repeat customer and a referral partner.

I began my sales career at the tender age of sixteen, selling film and cameras in a store at an amusement park. I loved interacting with the park's visitors. I transferred that love of sales into the retail arena in high school through college and my first few years of teaching. My biggest reward for helping people with purchases came from the last twenty-nine years in direct sales, where I created loyal customers and a referral program to receive new customers through word of mouth.

A year ago, I was introduced to Codebreaker and the BANK methodology. The phrase, "It's not personal, it's personality," resonated strongly with me, as did "Make People Matter." Knowing what I now know, using this methodology has increased my level of customer appreciation to being the best it can be. Knowing the personality code of the person you are interacting with takes the guesswork out of their values and how they approach buying.

Here, I will explore the Who, What, Where, When, How, and Why of customer appreciation.

WHO IS YOUR PERFECT CUSTOMER?

People have the freedom and choice to purchase from anyone. How do you stand out as the person of choice? By knowing the personality code of your customer, you can capitalize on your approach. Every customer can now be your "Perfect customer." The person who has Blueprint as their first code wants to know the value they are receiving and if there is a money-back guarantee. They want to know the facts about what they are purchasing and the contingencies for what might happen.

The person with Action as their first code wants to know the bottom line. Don't waste their time with everything a Blueprint wants to know. Does this purchase align with their core values of flexibility, fun, image, and excitement?

The person with Nurturing as their first code is interested in how this purchase supports both you and them. The person with Knowledge as their first code wants to know everything about the purchase. They will only make a commitment after thoroughly researching their choice.

The bottom line is that once you know your customers' personality codes and how they purchase, you can tailor your customer service to their needs.

WHAT CAN YOU DO TO CREATE THE BEST CUSTOMER APPRECIATION EXPERIENCE?

Now that you know your customers' personality codes, you can prepare for your interactions with them. The Blueprint thinks inside the box: You must be on time for your meeting—fifteen minutes early is even better. You must have all the facts about your product, including guarantees and how to contact you to answer questions that might come up. They must see the value (a discount or sale price is excellent), and your product needs a money-back guarantee.

The Action personality wants to know how this benefits them and their lifestyle. Don't get bogged down with all the particulars. Highlight the benefits and close quickly. Action personalities do not believe in the box metaphor. They ask, "What box?"

The Nurturing personality cares about you. How can they help you with the sale? Nurturers recycle the box.

The Knowledge personality wants all the facts, links to product reviews, and links to product benefits because they must do their own research. Do not expect a quick sale, and be prepared for a lot of questions. Knowledge personalities create the box. Once you understand your customers' core values, you can create the best experience for them based on their needs.

WHERE DO YOU FIND YOUR PERFECT CUSTOMER?

Does everywhere sound way too broad? Does having a target market help you create the perfect customer experience? If you sell high-end intimate clothing, your target market is most likely women. You can break that down even more into age groups and go deeper into the type of intimates, such as activewear, professional wear, or everyday around-the-house wear. It is good to know who will benefit from your product. Pick a group to focus on to understand and give the best buying experience.

Networking groups, chambers, and professional organizations can all be good places to find new customers. Have your thirty-second commercial run through KAI (Codebreaker AI) to hit all four personality codes.

WHEN DO YOU START THE CUSTOMER APPRECIATION PROCESS?

It's said you make a first impression within the first thirty seconds of meeting someone. Before doing business with someone I do not know, I ask them to help me help them by sorting the BANK values cards in order of which values mean the most to them and which mean the least. This allows me to serve them better and saves us both some time. I take note of the order of the values cards, and I ask them if I can take a picture of them holding the BANKCARDS in their order for my contact information. Right from the start of our interaction, I know their code, understand how and why they buy, and can tailor our interaction to meet their needs.

HOW DO YOU CREATE THE BEST EXPERIENCE FOR YOUR CUSTOMER?

Now, the fun really begins. You know your customer's personality code and you have prepared for your meeting. You are dressed according to each code's expectations, know which handshake is the most appropriate, and understand how and why they buy.

Follow-up after the sale is extremely important. Calendar your time for follow-ups. A phone call, text, or email within twenty-four hours of the purchase is crucial. You are checking in to verify they are happy with their purchase. Sending a handwritten note is also a game-changer. I was at a networking meeting, and after my one-minute commercial, a customer stood up and announced to the group that they would receive a nice handwritten note in the mail. Another customer stood up and mentioned that I would call to ensure they had received their purchase and had tried it on and was happy. Another customer stood up and said I had a great referral program. It was very heartwarming and exciting to have several people comment on how I appreciate their business.

Some follow-up tips:

1. Calendar the time for phone calls, handwritten notes, texts, and emails.
2. Handwritten notes are always a plus.
3. Have a referral program that rewards your customers for referring new people to you.
4. Create a birthday club where they receive a postcard with a gift to redeem or a discount for a future purchase (good for thirty days or in their birthday month).
5. Create a BONUS card where they receive a free item or a huge discount after so many purchases.

6. Have a system set up where you check on your customers quarterly to see how they are doing, whether they need anything, or whether they have a referral.
7. Do random notes and giveaways. If your company has samples, send them a sample of a product they haven't tried. Buy book markers or affirmation cards to slip in a random note.
8. If you have a VIP page on Facebook or any social media, highlight a customer of the week or the month.
9. Have a quarterly, twice-yearly, or yearly customer appreciation get-together with fun games, prizes, and food.
10. Send out a quick survey asking for input on how to offer better service or for fun giveaways.

The bottom line is that keeping in touch with your customers makes them feel special and appreciated. It creates loyalty to you and your brand. Sharing new product lines, sales, fun events, and discontinued items (in case they want to stock up if it is a favorite) keeps them in the loop and interacting with you.

WHY CUSTOMER APPRECIATION IS A MUST

People have choices. There are many companies out there selling what you sell or offering the same service you offer. By Making People Matter, you are creating a loyal customer. A loyal customer who will refer you based on their exceptional experience. Knowing their personality code and buying habits helps make your job easier. You cannot build a successful business without the help of your customers. Without customers, you have no business.

Having Codebreaker and knowing how to use the BANK methodology to understand how and why customers buy has improved my customer service. I have always prided myself on my customer service, but BANK has allowed me to take it to the next level by understanding my customers' personality codes and what they value. Thus, I can customize my level of service to their individual needs.

SUSAN GONZALEZ-MILLIRON | NABK

Susan Gonzalez-Milliron has dedicated more than fifty years to empowering others. With forty-four years as a special educator and six years as a high school administrator, Susan has taught every grade level, supporting students with diverse needs. Her work spans mentoring new teachers, developing programs for at-risk students, and advocating for special needs families. Susan's unwavering passion is rooted in helping others thrive. In addition to education, Susan has more than five decades of sales experience, excelling in both retail and direct sales. She has won numerous awards for sales, sponsorship, and team building and has been a featured speaker and panelist at conferences.

Susan's achievements include receiving the "Student Teacher of the Year" award and serving on committees for curriculum development, teacher hiring, and leadership initiatives. She is now focused on building a coaching business centered on social-emotional learning. Susan lives in Sylvania, Ohio, and remains dedicated to helping others reach their fullest potential.

Author's Website: CrackMyCode.com/Susan.Milliron

CHAPTER 25
LIVING YOUR BEST LIFE NOW

BY TARA RYAN

"To live is the rarest thing in the world. Most people just exist."

— Oscar Wilde

When you were young, did you have dreams of changing the world? Did you believe you would do something big, something crazy, something amazing? Were you living your best life each and every day? How old were you when you stopped? Do you console yourself by thinking you'll do it *someday*? Perhaps when the kids are all grown up, or after you finish paying for their college, or you meet the dynamic person who will complete you? Or maybe when you retire and have all the time in the world? Then you'll live your best life. Then you'll have the resources. Then.

When I was eighteen, I moved from my Pleasantville upbringing in the Chicago suburbs to attend an extension school of Moody Bible Institute in Spokane, Washington. I didn't have a clear path or vision, but I knew one thing for sure: I would make my life meaningful. I was going to do something big! I was going to make my mark on the world! I was studying and preparing myself to be a missionary and was beautifully naive. After classes, I would ride my bike to work at an after-school program for elementary-aged students whose families were what most would consider living in poverty. It was eye-opening. My heart was all in for these kids. We would spend the afternoon making progress on schoolwork, creating silly crafts, and having full-on bean bag tag battles in the classroom when the boss wasn't around. They were not growing up with the privilege and opportunity I had, yet their hearts were as full as their ear-to-ear smiles.

At the time, I was sharing a small one-bedroom duplex with my friend and classmate, Dorcas. We lived minimally and dreamed big. She was a hot mess of a roommate. I couldn't live with her clutter, so I painted the concrete floor in the small basement, bought a cozy rug, and moved my little twin bed down to the cellar. My dad thought I was nuts, but I slept better in the cold air anyway. I remember vividly waking up at an ungodly hour, by any college student's standards, to the robotic jingle of my new and first-ever cell phone. It could only be one person calling at that time: my dad. He was a morning person through and through.

When I was a kid, he would bust through my door on the weekends at sunrise, chipper and anxious for someone to rise and shine and join whatever ambitious project he had for the day. He has always been a beacon of love and inspiration for me. Those who know him would be familiar with his common exclamation, "Go for it, baby!"

My father's chipper voice drew me out of this vivid dream. The dream had felt so real I needed to tell him about it immediately before the details faded. In my dream, I enjoyed the pristine view of Lake Rosseau at the sports camp I had attended several summers in a row as a high school student. My kids from the after-school program were with me. This was no ordinary camp! Muskoka Woods Sports Resort was truly a resort and expensive to boot. Yes, we slept in bunk beds in cabins in the woods and had bonfires, but that's about all that would align with your typical summer camp. Goldie Hawn and Kurt Russel had a vacation home just down the shore. I heard that their son attended hockey camp the same year I was there. I never confirmed this, but that didn't stop me from claiming it as truth and name-dropping to my friends back home. My students would have no business attending a camp such as this. They would stick out like a sore thumb. I described the details of this dream to my dad, and I felt inspired. He could feel the emotion in my whole being as I unfolded the details as best as you can describe a dream.

The kids were having the time of their lives and experiencing the elaborate gymnastics program with a full spring tumbling floor, bars, and rings, trampolines with training harnesses, balance beams, and horses enclosed in a temperature-controlled all-seasoned dome. Waterskiing behind brand new Master-Craft boats with top-of-the-line skies and wakeboards, pristine beaches with sailboats and kayaks, idyllic nooks, and paths leading to firepits and performance stages beneath manicured forest canopies.

They had it all! In my dream, these kids built friendships and memories and joyfully inspired everyone around them. I said something to my dad, "Wouldn't that be incredible if they had that opportunity? If they could really go?" I shouldn't have been surprised by his reply, "Go for it, Baby!" *What?*, I thought. I didn't know what he meant. I was still in la-la land. He went on, "Make it happen. I'll donate the first one thousand dollars if you can raise the money to take those kids to camp."

The seed was planted. I mulled on it, chewed on it, not really believing at the time that I would pursue such an ambitious task. But I couldn't let it go. It was like a nagging fly on my face. It made my heart beat out of my chest every time I considered it, but I kept swatting it away, shoving it down. I was losing sleep over it. Could I really pull something like that off? I finally folded; I had to try.

I presented the idea to Judy, the director of the after-school program. I believe she had the impression I was just a big goofball, always being silly and pushing the line by provoking the kids to plastic sword battles and snowball fights. It would be an understatement to describe her round face as contorted. She was confused. She could not wrap her head around the vision. I imagine my insecurity and lack of developed communication skills didn't help! "Why would you possibly want to raise money to take these kids from Spokane to a camp in Ontario, Canada, when there are plenty of more affordable and local options?" she asked.

"If I had the ability to raise that kind of money, wouldn't there be better stewardship for the funds?" All good questions! She flat-out said no. I persisted. She rejected. I can be quite pesky when I want something! I didn't let it go and eventually redirected, requesting her permission to approach the families outside of the program, releasing her of any responsibility or liability. She granted me that, at least.

I wanted to gauge the interest levels. Would any families even be interested? I was scared to death. I had zero experience in fundraising or planning group trips. Not to mention, I was just out of high school, and my parents intimidated me a lot. What possible rapport did I have? The meeting was held the following week, and to my surprise, the room was full of curious parents. I stumbled through my first presentation on what it might look like to make this dream actually happen. It was embarrassing. I had done minimal research on real costs or logistics or details. Questions came at me that I didn't have the answers to. Despite my inadequacies, the interest and support were overflowingly positive. So, it began.

I thought it was essential for everyone involved to have a stake in the planning, so I suggested that parents contribute $200 per camper. We would raise the rest of the funds. My dad connected me to a non-profit that aligned with our vision; they would be willing to take donations on our behalf, ensuring they were tax-deductible. I had been a World Vision sponsor for a young boy in Africa for several years and was familiar with their model of sponsorships. I replicated it. I interviewed each student to learn about their dreams, favorite activities, heroes and role models, and their favorite colors. They helped me create sponsorship profiles with their picture, and I headed to Kinkos to make copies. (Remember Kinkos?)

I presented them everywhere I went. I asked my professors, aunts and uncles, fellow students, coworkers, strangers on the street, and family friends. I had them with me wherever I went and just kept asking. As the months went on, money was flowing in! I contacted the camp to see if they would consider just donating the camp fees or providing scholarships. They hadn't considered that at the time, but let's just say they were getting to know my name. Remember, I was pesky! I was registering nine campers, after all. We bought airfare and finalized our travel logistics. We made matching bright yellow T-shirts to travel in so I wouldn't lose anybody! The students affectionately dubbed me "Top-Dog," a title proudly displayed on the back of my shirt.

In the summer of 2001, it all came to fruition. This was happening! At the ripe age of nineteen, I boarded the plane as the only adult chaperone for nine excited campers ranging from eight to twelve years old. For many of them, this journey marked numerous firsts—their first time flying, their first time away from home, and their first goodbye to their parents. It was a milestone moment.

During the flight, I was in the middle seat between two girls, one of whom, Tory, was experiencing her first-ever flight. It was a rainy day, and she squeezed my hand hard enough to cut off the blood flow. She was such a chatterbox, but I don't recall her ever saying a word in the thirty minutes between boarding and taking off. The plane began its shaky ascent, the force pushing us into the backs of our seats, and before long, we were above a white blanket of clouds, the sun shining bright in the blue sky. She released her iron grip on my hand, opened her clenched eyelids, and glanced out the window. She whispered, "It looks like heaven." Witnessing her wonder brought tears to my eyes, reminding me to take time to experience this beauty as if it were my first time.

After successfully navigating through our layover in Denver, we finally arrived in Toronto. The customs process was a bit overwhelming and something I hadn't prepared for, but we made it through. The camp staff were waiting on the other side with a van to take us on our final destination, a two-hour journey to the campgrounds. As we pulled onto the familiar grounds, memories flooded back—from deep fireside chats with counselors to the majestic mornings on the still water learning how to waterski barefoot. I was full of anticipation for these kids to experience the magic of this place.

Some anxiety arose as they received their cabin assignments and realized they would not be together. They were separated by grade and gender. As soon as they caught sight of the lavish food court, the swimming beach with sailboats and kayaks, the infamous water BLOB inflatable launching pad, MasterCraft speed boats and ski program, brand new basketball courts, and the pristine grounds, their nervousness turned to excitement.

Amid this excitement, a realization struck me: I hadn't made any plans for my own accommodation. The camp director noticed my confusion and worry and offered me a bunk in the staff housing for the week. The camp founder happened to be there that week and heard wind of this unlikely crew of kids who were attending camp. He asked for a private meeting with me. He had a very philanthropic heart and was intrigued with the story. He confessed he had contemplated bringing in underprivileged campers, but he had never followed through because he didn't think they would feel comfortable. He was inspired. He stayed for the week and watched firsthand how my students and his campers built genuine and strong friendships. My students were beyond grateful to be there. It showed, and it was contagious. Their attitudes were of joy, gratitude, excitement, and wonder. They brought that sense of wonder to every camper they came in contact with. It was beautiful!

The week came to an end. We made the journey home, and life returned to normal. They continued to live in difficult circumstances. I moved the following year to Denver and lost touch with the whole crew. Life kept moving onward, and the adventure of taking these kids to Muskoka Woods Sports Resort became a distant memory—just something I did once.

I graduated college, got married, worked for a grassroots non-profit, and had three amazing kids of my own. My husband and I struggled financially and relationally. I was living life in the trenches, just trying to make it to the end of the day without having lost my temper on someone. Dreaming of how to change the world became a sweet thought but no longer seemed possible. I'd get excited here and there about something big, but I'd quickly lose heart as my emotional and physical resources were tapped. It became obvious that my marriage was over, and I got divorced.

I was now a single mom, running my own business and doing a deep dive into the meaning of life. This new identity threw me head-first into self-discovery and becoming intentional about how I wanted this next phase of my life to look. I had a choice to make. I could continue settling for daily existence or take control of my life and start dreaming again. But where do you start?

I began by committing to growing my library, a challenge from the iconic 1980s leadership guru, Jim Rohn. What was something small I could commit to daily that would be investing in my self-growth? I purchased two classy bookshelves and committed to filling them with old classics like *How a Man Thinketh*, *Think and Grow Rich*, and *How to Win Friends and Influence People*. I picked up reads from spiritual leaders across religions, like Richard Rohr's *Universal Christ* and Paramahansa Yogananda's *Autobiography of a Yogi*. I woke up and read. I read on my lunch break. I listened to audiobooks in the car. The more I read, the hungrier I was. My deep desire to experience the fullness of life through contribution and big dreams was rekindled.

My kids were becoming more independent, and my business was growing. As I became financially stable, my dreams grew, but I felt alone in my passion. I wanted to surround myself with like-minded people. People who were excited about life, dreamers, visionaries, who not only thrive but also want to help others thrive. People who were living their best lives now and inspiring others to do the same. I intentionally looked for this community for over a year.

Then bonus mom, Teresa, invited me to attend a Codebreaker conference she was hosting. There, I witnessed passion, connection, vision, and leadership. I was hooked.

Growing up in a family that values connection, relationship and accomplishment, I had been exposed to many forms of personal growth materials and philosophies. I must have been just ten years old the first time I took a Myers-Briggs assessment. Since then, I've been introduced to many more, including StrengthsFinders, Enneagram, and DISC.

When I first heard of BANK, I was naturally interested. What I love most about BANK is the simplicity. It's easily digestible even to folks who have never done a personal assessment and to children! I can break down the four personality profiles in less than a minute in a way that nearly all people can relate to. I now carry the four values cards around with me that define each personality: Blueprint, Action, Nurturing, Knowledge.

Often, when I meet someone new or work with a team, I'll pull out the BANKCARDS and let everyone take a few minutes to discover what type they resonate with. It's a beautiful thing to witness someone have an aha moment about a coworker, family member, or friend whom they may have misunderstood this whole time. I've done this exercise with my team of therapists, and to this day, they feel it was one of the most impactful meetings we've ever had. Learning how to appreciate each other's differences and communicating with intention in a language that resonates makes relationships more enjoyable and creates exponentially more value! It reduces conflict, increases connection, and creates trust. Imagine how much more efficient your time and energy could be when you have exceptional relationships!

BANK has brought in a new presence and awareness of how I communicate with others and receive communication. I find I'm curious to understand others. I'm less inclined to take offense or be defensive. My relationships have experienced what I can best describe as a blossoming. What is the result of great relationships? Joy, intimacy, thriving and confident children, an incredible business team, influence in my community, and doors opening for all of the dreams I can dream!

EXERCISE

What is one dream you had in your youth? Did you follow your dream? If not, do you remember when you let it go?

What happens when you feel most inspired?

Do you experience deep connections in relationships? Is it natural or difficult to find a connection?

TIPS

When you feel inspired, take action. Overthinking takes you in the opposite direction of inspiration.

- Invest in your self-growth.
- Be Courageous.
- Go for it, Baby!

SUMMARY

I have spent the last year identifying my values and crafting my personal mission statement to live a life of adventure and shared abundance in line with my core values of charity, courage, freedom, and authenticity. The BANK philosophy is now part of my team, and we dream of bringing inspiration, well-being, and even transcendence to our community. We are in the midst of creating a rejuvenation center founded on creating beautiful spaces and experiences that will inspire. It will be a place where people can transcend life's immediate realities, roles, and responsibilities to experience being. Our authentic selves live in the space where wonder and magic happen. Then, what is possible for us, our community, our world? What would it be like if we each brought our best selves to our family, coworkers, and community? What would it be like if we could leave our stress behind? We could take time to dream, touch the mysteries of the universe, and find true inspiration.

I'd like to find out. I am choosing to live my best life now! How about you?

TARA RYAN | NABK

As a seasoned businesswoman with a visionary approach, Tara boasts a proven track record of leading teams to success. Before becoming a massage therapist and acquiring Evergreen Massage, Tara led a non-profit development department, orchestrating large fundraising events and major donor campaigns. She was honored with the eWomen's Network Femtor Award for young professionals in 2005.

Deeply passionate about her community, Tara has served on the Evergreen Chamber Board of Directors, participated in Leadership Evergreen, and is an active member of the Downtown Business Association. She is dedicated to creating a haven of respite and inspiration, encouraging people to live their best lives!

Author's Website: EverGreenCoMassage.com

CHAPTER 26

UNCOVERING YOUR PATH TO FINDING YOUR PURPOSE

BY TIFFANY ANDERSON

> "The only way to do great work is to love what you do. If you haven't found it yet, keep looking. Don't settle. As with all matters of the heart, you'll know when you find it."
>
> — Steve Jobs

Are you feeling stuck in a rut, like you're just going through the motions of life without a clear sense of direction or purpose? Do you long to make a meaningful impact in the world and leave a lasting legacy? If so, you're not alone. Discovering your path to a bigger purpose is a journey that requires self-awareness, patience, and courage.

I am here to take you through an exercise that will help you start to discover who you are and what your purpose is, leaving you feeling ready to make a bigger impact.

DISCOVERING WHO I AM

My name is Tiffany Anderson, and I've traveled this path of identifying my bigger purpose in life. I can't wait to take you on this journey as well. It took me more than ten years of self-discovery and asking, "Who do I want to be when I grow up?" Despite having a master's degree and a successful career, I felt unfulfilled and knew something was missing.

Let me take you back to one of the worst days of my life—the day I got a call from my parents that my mom had lung cancer. From that moment on, everything changed. At the age of fifty-two, the doctors gave my mom only two more years to live. Unfortunately, we only got another four short months with her.

If you've gone through losing a parent, especially at such a young age, you know the pain, heartache, and struggle even to be present in life. My mom was a Nurturing; she cared for everyone and always put herself last. Looking back over the last ten years, I can now see that losing her is what developed me into who I am today. Sometimes, it takes losing someone before you see the bigger impact they had on your life. From this experience, going forward, I vowed to be the best version of myself, to show up for others, and to live my life as completely as I could. My mom was now my guardian angel, and she would guide my journey. I'm grateful she gave me this gift and was there for me through the spirit to help me find my passion and transform my life.

My mission started two months after she passed away. I feel it was not by chance but by her guiding spirit. When a friend introduced me to a health and wellness product and community of support, I began my journey, which I had no idea would lead to finding my purpose.

At that time, my days consisted of work and being with my family. I didn't have any real big dreams or aspirations beyond being a speech therapist and a mom. When I started my health and wellness journey, I didn't realize I was stepping into a business opportunity that would sculpt my future into what it is today, where I have been able to build a multiple-figure income, retire from my career, be home with my kids, and create my own coaching program where I can help others achieve their goals.

As I embarked on this new path I'm still on today, I kept coming back to one thing: my desire to help and support others. I loved making others feel good, and I felt empowered being on their journey with them, helping them overcome their struggles. I realized I was just like my mom because I cared so deeply for others. Soon, I created a health coaching business called "Fun and Fit with Tiff," where I shared my struggles with having an eating disorder and how I overcame it to inspire and support others with theirs.

What I didn't know was what was about to come next.

Something even bigger was in store for me. As I continued to serve and support others, my areas of expertise expanded as I developed new skill sets to learn how to connect and scale my business. An exciting shift was happening, and I started to become more focused on coaching other women in their businesses due to the success I was having in mine.

It was energizing to know I could help other moms have more time and more money so they could do more with their kids and be more present in life. I knew I had found my zone of genius and that I had a gift to make an even bigger impact in this world.

That was when Create Success Coaching was born. Soon, I was asked to be a keynote speaker and trainer, and I even became a bestselling author. This next-level version of me was fun, and I had no idea I had this strong desire to make this big of an impact. Finding my purpose and my joy has been a road of self-discovery, and truthfully, I can say it's just beginning.

WHAT I LEARNED

Through my journey of self-discovery, I learned that it's a journey, not a destination. Uncovering what brings you joy takes time, experimentation, and personal growth. It wasn't until I dove deeper into my values, what mattered to me, and who I was that I could truly embrace my potential. I challenge you to have an open mind, keep opportunities open, and be ready to explore personal growth because you never know what lies ahead.

However, I first had to confront my own doubts and fears. I questioned whether my motivations for helping others were genuine or driven by financial gain. This idea of being driven by money felt uncomfortable, so I questioned my motives.

Through some self-discovery of the BANK methodology, I transformed my understanding of myself and my purpose to make it even clearer than what I thought it already was.

BANK focuses on personality science to identify the values of each person. The company's mission to #MakePeopleMatter echoed my own vision. Through a simple ninety-second assessment and learning more about myself, I could truly see my values centered around supporting, helping, and inspiring others. This awareness allowed me to lean into what brings me joy. Making money was a by-product and a great incentive, but it was not my driving force. I learned that money is not a bad thing. Money allows good people to do even better things.

This transformation empowered me to embrace my role as a catalyst for others' growth and success. I now dedicate myself to helping others achieve their goals while navigating their own personal development journeys. Understanding myself through personality science freed me from the mindset that held me back. I can now focus on what matters to me and understand what matters to others at a deeper level.

I often wonder if my mom's journey would have been different if she had focused on herself sooner. As Nurturers, we frequently neglect our needs, resulting in our inability to live at our highest potential. I have learned that self-care should always be a central to our continued growth to live at our highest potential. What BANK helped me do was reclaim my true self, focus on who I was, and understand what was important to me. When you can do this, you will start to see the value of the unique gifts you have to offer the world. With my new self-discovery, I was ready to walk alongside others and support them on their journey, empowering them to find their passion and make a difference for others.

EXERCISE: DISCOVERING YOURSELF

Let's do an exercise together to help you discover your purpose and make the impact you want to make on the world.

FIRST, IDENTIFY YOUR VALUES

Your values are the foundation of your purpose. They are the beliefs and principles that guide your decisions and actions. To identify your values, ask yourself:

- What matters most to me in life?
- What do I stand for?
- What do I want to achieve in my life?

It wasn't until I took the BANK personality assessment and started to focus on myself and who I truly was that I began to understand my motivations. I had been struggling with the feeling of inauthenticity, wondering if I was only doing what I was doing for the money or if I was genuinely driven by a desire to help others.

When I gained insight into my values and realized they were centered around being a Nurturer and bringing people together to support one another, everything clicked into place. I saw that my actions were aligned with my true values and not driven by external factors. It's crucial to take the time to discover your own values and understand what is most important to you. When you do, you'll find a sense of purpose and fulfillment that can't be shaken.

SECOND, START EXPLORING YOUR PASSIONS

Your passions are the things that bring you joy and fulfillment. They are the activities that make you feel alive and engaged. To explore your passions, ask yourself:

- What do I love doing?
- What activities make me feel the most engaged and fulfilled?
- What topics do I enjoy learning about?

Only after I achieved success in my personal business did I find my true passion. My passion was expanding my knowledge and skill sets to guide others in growing their businesses and achieving success. Sharing my product was just a part of my journey that led me to find greater satisfaction in helping others learn how to grow their businesses by authentically showing up and connecting with others.

I am passionate about training and helping others create tools and systems that save them time, money, and energy in their businesses. Seeing others succeed after receiving my support brings me tremendous joy and fulfillment. It's incredibly rewarding to know I've contributed to helping someone else achieve their goals and build a successful business.

NEXT, DISCOVER YOUR STRENGTHS

Your strengths are the skills and abilities that come naturally to you. They are the things you're good at that you can use to make a meaningful impact in the world. To discover your strengths, ask yourself:

- What am I naturally good at?
- What skills have I developed over time?
- What do others appreciate about me?

Your strengths have a lot to do with your personality. I'm good at creating connections and supporting others through the knowledge I have learned. I have the superpower of uncovering what's holding someone back from living their full potential. What is your superpower? Maybe you haven't discovered it yet, but I know you will as long as you continue to have an open mind and heart and surround yourself with like-minded people who will lift you up and inspire you.

Make a list of what you feel you are really good at, or ask others to tell you what they think you do well and how you've helped them. Sometimes, it's hard to see our own strengths.

LAST, DEFINE YOUR PURPOSE

Now that you've identified your values, passions, and strengths, it's time to define your purpose. Your purpose is the intersection of these three areas. It's the thing that you're passionate about, good at, and aligns with your values. To define your purpose, ask yourself:

- What problem do I want to solve in the world?
- What impact do I want to make?
- What legacy do I want to leave behind?

You are almost there. This is where the fun begins. This is where you really start to see and feel the impact you can make. I want to solve the problem of helping women see their own greatness, step into what brings them joy, and become unstoppable. When I am able to do this, it will have a huge ripple effect worldwide.

SUMMARY

Take as much time as you need to discover who you are; it took me more than ten years, and I am still on the path to building my purpose to make a bigger impact in the world. It is not an overnight discovery, and I encourage you to start the journey today.

If you are feeling stuck, continue your path; I know you are meant for something greater, and you are going to impact so many people. Sit with the questions above and take some time to discover what's possible for you. You have amazing gifts and talents inside of you that bring you great joy, and you will soon uncover how you can use those gifts to make a bigger impact on others.

Discovering your path to a bigger purpose is a journey that requires patience, self-awareness, and courage. By identifying your values, exploring your passions, discovering your strengths, and defining your purpose, you'll be well on your way to making a meaningful impact in the world and living a life that truly matters. Remember, your purpose is not a destination. As my mom would always say, "Life is a journey and only you hold the key." I give you permission to embrace the process. Trust the journey. I know you will uncover your path to find your purpose.

TIFFANY ANDERSON | NKBA

With more than a decade of direct sales experience, Tiffany has established herself as a trailblazer, consistently ranking Top Ten in sales and holding the coveted number-one sponsor spot for an impressive four years. Building on her remarkable success, Tiffany launched her coaching business in 2020, dedicated to mentoring women and direct sellers in achieving their goals.

Tiffany shares invaluable expertise as a bestselling author, keynote speaker, coach, and trainer, empowering women to soar to new heights in their businesses.

Partner with Tiffany to tap into her proven strategies and unlock your full potential.

Author's Website: TiffanyAnderson.org

CHAPTER 27

CONNECTING FOR NEXT LEVEL SUCCESS

BY TRACIE HASSE

"The best and most beautiful things in this world cannot be seen or even heard, but must be felt with the heart!"

— Helen Keller

Do you remember your first day of school? Were you nervous and afraid of the unknown? Were you concerned about whether other kids would accept or reject you?

I still remember my first day of school. I had moved away from all my friends in Cody, Wyoming, to Las Vegas, Nevada. On the first day of school, I was terrified. I felt scared at the thought of being away from my family all day. When it was time to go, my parents found me hiding under the bed and carried me across the street to the kindergarten, kicking and screaming. I was in a full-blown meltdown. This behavior carried on for about a week. Years later, my mother reminded me that my breakthrough happened when I finally made my first friend. After that, I was excited to go to school and meet my friends. What a way to kick off my life as a networking super-connector.

I was stuck at the same level of success for years and wanted to break through to the other side, but I couldn't figure out how. My work ethic has always been beyond amazing. I have a reputation for giving it all I've got in life. I didn't know what I didn't know.

To the outside world looking in, I was successful! I was awarded Affiliate of the Year three years in a row and awarded the top sales awards. I was well-known in my industry. How could I not be happy with that?

With a champion's mindset driving me to reach my best, I knew deep down I hadn't yet reached my full potential. I didn't know what was missing or how to get there. I had the desire for more understanding; however, it seemed to evade me. It was elusive to me. I felt like a dog chasing my tail, a hamster on a wheel.

Have you ever felt that way about your life, relationships, finances, or weight? Do you ever feel like you're stuck at a plateau that's never going to change, no matter what you do? How did you overcome those situations?

Well, I sure was stuck and thought, that's life. As my life coach, Bob, always says, "Acceptance is the Key." Acknowledging and accepting I was stuck at these plateaus was the first step. Next came being open to possibilities to move beyond this new acceptance and understanding.

Being open to new ways of thinking and being is an inside job. With this concept in mind, my philosophy is to remain open to receiving and experiencing miracles. From this mindset, I have more to give and share with others to *make people matter*.

When I reflect on my life, I think of the people who made me matter along the way by helping me move through difficult situations. By doing so, I learned how to assist and be there for people going through difficult situations that we all encounter. It's the nature of being human.

Having said all that, I'm here to share my story from the day I met Cheri Tree and Esther Wildenberg, Co-Founders of Codebreaker Technologies. What I've learned and continue learning from them has been a miracle for me. It's given me the knowledge to take my life to that next level of fulfillment and success, both personally and professionally!

As I look back on that moment, what has transpired since then has been miraculous for me. I have truly taken my life personally and professionally to that next level, which I didn't even know was possible!

It hasn't always been easy for me, and I still have my challenges. I've had my fair share of self-doubt along the way, too. For me, it was the big decisions and big investments I've made in myself that made the difference and allowed me to gain the knowledge for the growth and success I've achieved. And for that and so much more, I am grateful every day!

In the summer of 2017, I had the good fortune to attend a Debbie Allen event in San Diego. I first connected with Debbie when writing my first book, *Go Big and Stay Home: Connect, Refer, Create Your Road to Riches*.

That day, my good friend Valerie and I were about to witness a very special, yet unexpected masterwork-level presentation.

Cheri Tree stepped onto the stage. She spoke with a true and open heart, delivering an inspiring, activating message with words of inspiration to be my best and live my boldest, brilliant dreams. Cheri said, "I'm going to teach you how to increase your sales up to 300 percent by using personality science and emotional intelligence." I was on the edge of my seat, soaring with the angels. It was music to my soul.

And when this whirlwind, force for good, finally put down the microphone, Valerie and I both knew we had just seen creative magnificence. Cheri left us with a vision for a new level of excellence. Enlivening my champion heart to achieve the greatness I knew I had. We felt the entire room light up with passion and inspiration. We were inspired and on fire, lit up by the expanded possibilities of becoming legendary. From that moment, I knew I had to learn everything Cheri was teaching! Something amazing had just taken place. It was a brush encounter with greatness.

It is hard to put words to what I was experiencing. My mind was racing as thoughts and realizations came one after the other, flooding into my mind. It was an after-effect of encountering true genius.

Now I realized why I was stuck at a ceiling with my income. I had been living my primary code, Nurturing-Action, to its fullest without regard for the other two non-primary codes. When I encountered these personality types, I was unable to connect, and it made me feel like a failure. I didn't have the language or system to express that then. Now, with the understanding of four personality types, the possibilities are unlimited. I knew this was different; it felt so right, and I could tell it was going to be big.

That evening, when I returned home, I was still on fire, smoldering with exuberance over the possibilities and grandness of it all. How was I going to convey something so big, so brilliant? It all seemed beyond words. I burst open the front door and proudly announced to Reed, the love of my life, "You won't believe who I met today. I saw the most amazing speaker and learned about a spectacular system, so get ready to *Crack Your Personality Code and Take It to the BANK!*"

I didn't know it then, but my life would never be the same. The simple act of attending Cheri's talk set off an amazing chain of events that set me on a journey of discovery, leading me to where I am today.

Getting my first set of BANKCARDS, purchasing a training, and attending the next live event was one of the best decisions I have ever made. I can now look back and credit much of my success to deciding to invest my money, attention, focus, and determination into learning, applying, and mastering this new skill set.

The following weekend, Reed and I attended our first Codebreaker Summit, where Cheri Tree and Esther Wildenberg led the training. The event was spectacular, and we were offered the opportunity to invest in a Codebreaker Trainer Certification Program. It was easily the biggest personal investment I've ever made, and it challenged my commitment to becoming my best. I had become the Nevada State Champion Gymnast at twelve years old, and I continue to this day to fulfill my champion heart with all I do. The promise of a potential increase in my income of up to 300 percent and the challenge of becoming my best self was calling out to my champion heart. I had to *GO BIG*. I was in!

JOURNEY INTO NEXT LEVEL PERSONAL DEVELOPMENT

In 2012, I was at the top of my professional career as a sales executive. I had just won my third consecutive North San Diego County Association of Realtors Affiliate of the Year award. I was well respected in my industry. My stellar reputation as the in-the-know resource for realtors and the hostess of the best must-attend events.

Life was leading me to a decision point. I needed to make a change if I were to grow and take my life to the next level.

As a seasoned sales executive, after ten years with the top escrow company, I made the decision to leave. I realized if I stayed, I'd just be doing the same thing for the next ten years. So, I took a leap of faith and resigned. I have a true Action personality style, not exactly knowing what the future holds without a job lined up. My family thought I was crazy. But in the end, it turned out to be one of the best career decisions I've ever made.

It allowed me to take a breather and pay more attention to living a life well lived. These are the heartfelt highlights of the many miracles and accomplishments that took place when I took time for myself. I was able to spend quality time with my parents and be with them up to their last breath of life. Reed and I took an epic eight-month road trip adventure from San Diego to Vancouver, Canada, spent several months in Las Vegas with my parents, and then back to our heaven on earth, San Diego, California.

The opportunity came knocking when the founder of the leading escrow company in Southern California found out I was available. The founder had been a mentor to me in the past when he hired me in 2003 to work for the previous escrow company. Now he was the top decision-maker for his own company. He wanted to recruit me as the sales executive to build the San Diego office.

My decision was easy. The founder was a trusted mentor who had proven himself a successful leader. His company was the best in the industry. And I would be working with a brilliant and dedicated world-class team. Only this time, I had a new wealth of knowledge and life experiences. My passion was renewed. I would have a chance to apply my new skills to this exciting opportunity to do what I love: connect, empower, and build a business with a proven team of the best of the best.

I was empowered with the ability to connect with individuals more authentically for greater, more prosperous relationships. As a result, I had an increased level of emotional intelligence and increased empathy and understanding of everyone around me. Now, I have new eyes to see the world through BANK-colored lenses and genuinely connect with all four of the personality codes.

WHAT I LEARNED

I was unaware I had a next level. I had been lulled to sleep by my success. And I had drifted into autopilot at work, even if it was at a very high level of performance. There is always a next level. Authoring my first book and committing to certification training with Codebreaker was just what I needed.

The strength of a Nurturing personality is in their Network.

Who are the Influencers in your network? What's their BANKCODE?

When you are connecting with someone new, it is incredibly fulfilling to secure new business by closing the sale. When people feel seen and heard, they open up in ways that deepen the relationship and allow you to make a difference in their lives. That's the true benefit of a deeper connection for me as a Nurturing personality type. It's the strength of that connection that builds your confidence and makes you the best at what you do.

Networking events and hosting epic events fuel my fire. When it comes to networking, I rock! Meeting new people, seeing friends and clients, and connecting people to prosper for more success makes me happy.

The mentors and coaches in my life each helped me take my expertise to the next level, starting with my parents, gymnastics coach, third-grade teacher, business mentors throughout my career, and life coaches.

> "If you want to double your income, triple your investment in personal development."
>
> — Robin Sharma

Investing in myself meant taking my super-connector skills to the next level with the Codebreaker Signature Series Training.

Along the way, I have shared BANK with well over a thousand people. One of my greatest aha moments came from the feedback I have received from many of those people. I asked a few dear friends to share the impact BANK has had on their lives, which I will share now.

I love the success story Jonna shared with me and the results she achieved: "In 2019, I was introduced to using the BANK methodology just before the pandemic forced my business to shut down. I had to transition to a new job in a different field. During my interview, I was asked about how I build rapport with clients. So, I brought out my BANKCARDS right then and there and was able to use them to demonstrate my expertise in understanding people, which impressed the interviewers. They hired me as a national sales representative! In less than three months, I set new sales records. The BANK training has greatly enhanced my skills in working with diverse personalities for business success!"

John shared: "The concept of *making people matter* is the cornerstone of my success both in my career and my interactions with friends. I believe people are always, consciously or subconsciously, looking for others to verify their thoughts and opinions or to validate them. The greatest gift you can give someone is to listen very carefully, reflect on what is said, and comment on something meaningful that will clarify their thoughts or opinions, whether you agree with them or not. It tends to be a form of praise or reverence in their minds, which always makes a good foundation for good friends and clients."

My friend Christina said BANK impacted her life in the following way: "In my professional life, BANK has enabled me to achieve success faster. As a NABK, when I meet other NABKs, we simply just connect right away. I am blown away by my ability to describe so many personality traits in a comprehensive and compassionate way. I now have a tool to bring understanding among us all and create stronger relationships. It has helped me learn about others and appreciate our differences.

FIVE TIPS AND EXERCISES TO CONNECT FOR NEXT LEVEL SUCCESS

Practicing the habit of implementing BANK daily increases your emotional intelligence and confidence. You become masterful at *making people matter*.

Success is an inside job. Take note of your thoughts about yourself. What are you thinking? Do you have limiting beliefs? Are your thoughts and beliefs in sync with the success you're looking to achieve? If not, change them.

Are you investing your time and money in coaches and personal development programs to maximize your potential and achieve your next level of success?

What kind of legacy would you like to leave? Write it down.

Be the leader and create your own leading events. What events will you host to grow your business and increase your client base and sphere of influence?

CHALLENGE

Crack the personality code of a family member, work colleague, friend, hot date, new acquaintance, client, or prospect who you are meeting for the first time. Remember to always ask that person, "Why did you select that order?" because that is where the gold is!

Take time today to dream big about your heart's desires. Write down your dreams and career lifestyle and visualize it happening.

THINGS TO REMEMBER

Cracking the personality code in person is one of the best ways to demonstrate to others your elevated level of emotional intelligence and command of personality science. It helps to break the ice and creates a memorable connection with the people you meet.

BANK is an amazing tool to strengthen your network and achieve your next level of business and relationship success.

SUMMARY

I learned that when I summon the courage of my convictions, stand firm in my true passion for networking, host epic events, and commit to serving others with an open heart, I can impact people's lives. That's what it's like to *Make People Matter* every day! Because ideas without action are worthless.

The reality is we all have a next level no matter where we are in life!

So, GO BIG! Connect, refer, and create your road to riches!

I challenge you to invest in yourself, meet new people, make an impact, and make more money, changing people's lives while having a blast doing it!

Cheers to Your Success! With Love!

TRACIE HASSE | NAKB

Tracie Hasse is an award-winning escrow sales executive with more than twenty-five years of experience in the real estate industry. She is celebrated for her exceptional ability to connect people and inspire growth. A Certified and Licensed BANK Trainer and Coach, Tracie has a deep understanding of personality-based sales and communication techniques, helping clients build stronger, more authentic relationships.

Known as a "Super-Connector," she has an innate talent for networking and empowering others to create lasting connections. Her first book, *Go Big and Stay Home*, guides readers on how to connect and build a thriving network, cultivate referrals, and create their unique path to success. Tracie's passion for sales excellence and strategic growth has made her a trusted mentor and leader in the business world.

Author's Website: linkedin.com/in/TracieHasse

CHAPTER 28
THE ART OF INTENTIONAL CONNECTION

BY VICKI PARKER

"I've learned that people will forget what you said, people will forget what you did, but people will never forget how you made them feel."

— Maya Angelou

Have you ever had the experience that you were invisible? Going through life without anyone in particular taking notice? Maybe you were at a shopping mall, walking down a city street, or making your way through an airport. Have you ever felt like, even though you were in a room with people you have known for years, they really did not know you or how to communicate with you? I sure have!

THE UNKNOWN

In college, I studied dance. I attended a small Catholic college on Detroit's north side, and we had only a handful of dance majors. I was standing in the dressing room after ballet class, and a few of the older girls were talking about senior projects and their auditions. They were all strong dancers in jazz, ballet, and tap. And they had strong personalities to match. I remember contributing to the conversation from across the room, and one of the leaders of that group just looked at me, turned her head away, and didn't acknowledge me or my comment. At that moment, I felt left out, unwanted, and alone.

Several years ago, after a devastating breakup with a man I thought would one day be my husband, one of my best friends and I were shopping for clothing in a department store. As we were perusing the racks, I was rehashing the breakup story. She turned on a dime, standing toe-to-toe with me, her face about eight inches from mine, and yelled very loudly, "Get over it!" I'd never felt more invisible in my life. This was one of my dearest and closest friends, and she did not understand me, nor did she know how to speak with me or support me. That was a heart-wrenching moment.

The feeling of not being known by those you encounter on a daily basis, the closest of friends and family, can leave you bitter, uncaring, and unloving. On the other hand, when someone really meets you where you are and leaves you feeling like you mean something, it can give you a perk in your step, a feeling of confidence and confirmation that who you are is important.

BEING SEEN

A few years ago, I was sitting in the Delta Sky Club Lounge at LaGuardia Airport in NYC. Being a seasoned traveler with more than a Million Miles on Delta alone, I've been exposed to some lovely experiences in this lifetime and have witnessed varied levels of service and customer service, in particular. At one point in my travel career, I did not have home internet services, so I would often remain in the Delta lounge until closing. As you can imagine, being on the road 250-plus days a year, I've spent quite a few hours in those clubs and am pretty much at home when I'm there. On this particular afternoon, I was sitting at a counter overlooking the tarmac with an empty glass beside me because I had finished my sparkling water. I was totally focused on completing my weekly invoices, gathering the receipts, and wrapping up my week before flying back to Chicago. "Excuse me. Would you like an hors d'oeuvre?" I was startled by this interruption to my thoughts. "Pardon me?" I asked. "Would you like a stuffed mushroom with white sauce?" asked the club attendant.

In my thirty years of travel on Delta and twenty years or so as a Sky Club member, I do not ever recall being served in the lounge. Typically, everything is set out in a buffet fashion. I was literally, and pleasantly, taken aback! I'd been a

Customer Experience (CX) Trainer for eleven years at this time and was very impressed with Delta's newest delight! I arrived in Chicago with a great story to tell and the feeling of being valued and appreciated for my loyalty. I was surprised and delighted and felt like Delta knew exactly what I needed after a long week of travel. Simply to be seen, served, and appreciated.

Surprising and delighting customers is an area of emphasis for the top-tier automotive brand dealership personnel I coach. When I found myself delighted, it was really rewarding. I felt like I mattered, and Delta, knowing exactly what I needed at that moment, came through with flying colors!

Years before, during the middle of rehearsals for a musical I was choreographing, I tore my ACL (anterior cruciate ligament) on a ski trip. I drove a manual shift Volkswagen Beetle then, and with my knee in a full leg brace, there was no way I'd be able to drive my car. My best friend, Julie, who had dealt with sports injuries of her own and knew the impact of an injury on your daily life, immediately offered to swap cars until I could use my left leg again. Wow! I hadn't experienced that level of generosity from anyone before this. I was moved by her thoughtfulness and willingness to learn to drive a manual tranny. At that moment, I realized I mattered to my friend, and she was willing to make sacrifices for me.

During the pandemic, my in-person training was sparse, and my twenty-year-old car was showing signs of wear on the engine and other mechanical parts. I began to pour money into this solid and very loved vehicle. My brakes went out at one point, and then somehow, my rear windscreen shattered, seemingly from the inside to the outside, and my radiator needed replacing.

A year into COVID, my mom was involved in a serious car accident, leaving her with broken C1 and C2 vertebrae. Fortunately, I was in Detroit at her home at the time. Because of my freelance lifestyle, I was able to stay with her for about eight months while she was recovering.

During that time, my car wound up needing new tires, glow plugs, and several other powertrain attributes. My mother and four brothers paid for the repairs because they knew I hadn't been on the road working for about eighteen months at that point.

I was embarrassed to be in such a financial state that I couldn't comfortably pay for my own vehicle maintenance, but I was keenly aware that *I mattered!* I mattered to my mom, well, because I'm her daughter. In this case, however, she wanted me to understand I mattered to her and that she valued this time we were spending together, that she knew all that I had given up to be there with her for so long. I had that same experience with my brothers. I am still incredibly moved by my family's love for me and for one another. I am truly present to the blessing of being a part of the Parker family.

IN THE BACKGROUND

After completing my education in dance and psychology and during my twelve-year tenure with Hyatt Hotels and

Resorts, I spent a year as an ambassador at the Century Hyatt-Tokyo, working with all non-Japanese guests. During this time, my verbal skills became clearer. I had to really think about how my words would land for those for whom English was not their native language.

When asked by a female colleague how she might be able to participate in an exchange program to the States as I had in Japan, I told her she should speak with the human resources director. She could *put a bug in his ear* and let him know of her interest in an exchange. She looked perplexed and told me she didn't understand why she would put a bug inside of his ear. We had quite a laugh. That was when I began teaching American slang in exchange for polite Japanese.

My non-verbal observation and listening competencies were also greatly enhanced while living and working in Japan. I was responsible for *all non-Japanese guests*. I got to support and communicate with guests from around the world who did not speak Japanese or English. This was in 1989, pre-Google Translate. Fortunately, my charade skills paid off, and I somehow muddled through some pretty interesting situations.

Upon my return to the Hyatt Regency—Dearborn, in Michigan, I was part of a team of trainers for Business as Unusual. We trained staff on internal communications within and between departments. This was totally up my alley since I strive for clear, effective communication. It also expanded my capacity to work with adults and have seemingly difficult conversations.

After moving to Chicago to pursue an acting career in 1994, I landed an automotive gig, which led me, once again, to training. Since then, I have been training and facilitating in the automotive realm for new vehicle launches, sales processes, service processes, and the elevation of customer experience.

> "Think as little as possible about yourself. Think as much as possible about other people."
>
> — Eleanor Roosevelt

BEFORE BANK

Before discovering BANK, I participated extensively in transformational work with Landmark Worldwide, where I had the opportunity to coach participants in many of their courses. And, most recently, through all of their Communication Courses and the Team, Management, and Leadership Program.

Through the years, I have learned how to be *with* people how they are and how they aren't, to be with *any* communication, not to make everything about me, and to see where and how I *embrace or resist* communication. I have also learned how to release or *give up* certain things, for example, that I don't have to be right.

I believed I had a pretty good understanding of people. And I put to use several tools to purposefully leave people with the experience that who they *are* matters. These include careful use of words, intonation, inflection, body language, and timing.

CREATING THE EXPERIENCE THAT OTHERS MATTER: TEN PRACTICES FOR MEANINGFUL CONNECTION

At the heart of every authentic relationship is the desire to be profoundly seen and valued. Whether in our personal lives or professional settings, people crave the feeling that they matter. When we show up with the intention of making others feel heard, appreciated, and respected, we lay the foundation for deep, meaningful connections. In my journey as a Women's Empowerment Coach, I've come to understand that relationships are built on the simple act of making people feel significant.

Here is a summary of ten practices I've embraced to create an experience where others feel they genuinely matter. These principles can transform your interactions and help you forge stronger, more authentic bonds with the people in your life—whether family, friends, colleagues, or clients. (For a fuller description, visit the author's website).

1. Active Listening

Listen deeply to understand; then paraphrase to show you're fully present. This creates a space for others to feel heard and valued.

2. Express Appreciation

Regularly acknowledge others' efforts with simple gratitude. A genuine "thank you" reinforces their sense of worth.

3. Personalized Attention

Treat each person uniquely by remembering details or celebrating their milestones, which shows they're valued as individuals.

4. Empathy and Understanding

Recognize others' emotions without judgment. Empathy fosters a safe environment for them to feel valued and supported.

5. Create an Inclusive Environment

Embrace diverse perspectives, creating a space where everyone feels welcomed and valued for who they are.

6. Provide Constructive Feedback

Give growth-focused, respectful feedback that shows belief in their potential, reinforcing their value to you.

7. Empowerment and Trust

Trust others to make decisions and act confidently, showing that you believe in their abilities and worth.

8. Foster Meaningful Connections

Engage in deeper conversations by asking about passions and struggles, which lets them feel valued for who they are.

9. Recognition and Visibility

Acknowledge others' contributions—whether big or small—so they feel seen and celebrated.

10. Consistent Support

Be a reliable source of support, reinforcing that their presence matters to you over the long term.

These practices build the foundation for relationships where people feel profoundly seen, valued, and understood.

CREATING THE EXPERIENCE OF BEING VALUED: TEN PRACTICES TO REINFORCE THE EXPERIENCE USING BODY LANGUAGE

Non-verbal communication is just as important as verbal communication when it comes to making others feel like they matter. Here are ten body language practices to ensure your physical presence reflects your intention to make others feel valued:

1. Maintain Eye Contact

Looking someone in the eye shows them you are present and engaged. It conveys that they have your full attention and their words and feelings matter to you.

2. Open Posture

Keep your posture open and relaxed. Avoid crossing your arms or legs because it can appear defensive. Facing the person fully and keeping your body open shows you are welcoming and interested.

3. Nod and Smile

A nod of acknowledgment and a smile communicates warmth and empathy. These gestures show you are engaged and understanding, making others feel heard and appreciated.

4. Lean In

Leaning slightly forward while someone speaks shows you are actively listening and engaged in what they're sharing. It signals you value their perspective.

5. Appropriate Touch

In certain contexts, a gentle touch or handshake can convey warmth and trust. Always be mindful of personal boundaries and cultural differences when offering touch.

6. Mirroring

Mirroring someone's body language subtly can create a sense of rapport. This non-verbal cue can help people feel understood and connected to you.

7. Use of Space

Respect personal space while remaining close enough to show you are engaged. Being too distant can create a sense of disconnect while being too close can make people uncomfortable.

8. Active Gestures

Using gestures while speaking helps to reinforce your enthusiasm and engagement. It's important to avoid overly dramatic gestures that may seem distracting, but expressing yourself with your hands can make the conversation feel more alive.

9. Facial Expressions

Your facial expressions should align with the tone of the conversation. A sincere smile or a thoughtful expression can convey empathy, interest, and understanding.

10. Consistent Attention

Putting away distractions, such as your phone, and giving your full attention shows the other person *they* matter. *By staying present, you convey they are the most important focus in that moment.*

By integrating both verbal and non-verbal communication practices into your daily interactions, you can create an environment where people truly feel they matter. This intentionality will deepen your relationships and foster a sense of connection that supports empowerment, trust, and mutual respect.

My intention is for all people to have the experience of being seen, heard, known, and respected for who they are and what they've accomplished. That *they matter!*

EXERCISE: SELF-REFLECTION

What are some of the *actions* you take that have your acquaintances, friends, and family experience that *they matter*? (Write their names next to the actions.)

What are some of the *actions* you take that might give them the impression that *they do not matter?* (Write their names next to the actions.)

What are some of the *words* you have used that leave your acquaintances, friends, and family with the experience that *they matter?* (Write their names next to the words.)

What are some of the *words* you have used that leave them with the experience that *they do not matter?* (Write their names next to the words.)

WHERE WE FALL SHORT

When we leave others with the experience that they *do not* matter, how do we shift *this* narrative? How can we have others *have* the experience that *they matter* in the world?

We can get to know what is *most important* to them, how they want life situations to occur, and how they like to be presented with communication.

WHEN WE TAKE IT TO THE BANK, WE CAN TAKE IT TO THE BANK

What BANK has brought to the table for me is a deeper understanding of the *values* of people. This has made a tremendous difference in how I assess situations, determine my communication style before communicating, and choose my words.

I've often stated that *words matter*. When using BANK, you learn which words will have an immediate impression given each personality type, have the greatest influence, and leave a lasting impact on people based on their values.

Here is a brief summary of the four personality types of BANK and their unique preferences in communication and decision-making:

Blueprint: Values structure, stability, and details. They appreciate thorough planning and reliability.

Action: Energized by opportunities, excitement, and competition. They respond well to dynamic and enthusiastic pitches.

Nurturing: Motivated by relationships, empathy, and shared values. They seek genuine connection and mutual benefit.

Knowledge: Driven by data, expertise, and autonomy. They appreciate logical, well-researched insights.

You learn which personality type needs more information, less information, or a different type of information. For example, for someone who holds dear the Blueprint values over values within the other personality types, you'll know they're not likely to be risk takers. Knowing this will serve you when you let them in on your process and share warranties or guarantees. Be sure to allow them to know upfront any procedures or protocols. In more personal situations, allowing your Blueprint-focused friend to be in on your itinerary, timing, and know what to expect will put them at ease and excited to join you. They are likely going to be upset or triggered by spur-of-the-moment changes in schedule.

For me, BANK has provided a new dimension in understanding people and a quick, easy way not only to communicate with my family and friends but to have a lasting impact on my customers' experiences as well. When understood and engaged in the right way, using BANK can lead to deeper trust and rapport in both personal and professional contexts. And, by speaking to a person's true preferences, you foster a meaningful, authentic connection that naturally enhances sales outcomes.

Since using and coaching others in the BANK methodology, I have been able to impact the lives of many leaders, clients, and teams. I've increased my scope and reach while increasing my income exponentially. And I've expanded my capacity as an entrepreneur, now leading multiple teams and streams of income with ease and financial freedom.

My mission is to empower successful businesswomen who have lost confidence in themselves, and my varied business ventures allow me to do so on multiple levels.

SUMMARY

One of the most powerful lessons I've learned through the BANK methodology is the importance of genuinely understanding the values that drive the people around us. The key to connecting with others in a deep, meaningful way lies in making them feel and experience being seen, heard, appreciated and known. Whether you're communicating with a Blueprint personality who values structure or an Action personality who thrives on excitement, the more attuned you are to their preferences, the more you can create authentic connections. BANK has taught me that by speaking to someone's values and communicating with intention, you not only enhance relationships but foster trust, respect, and lasting impact. And your influence and income are quickly elevated.

I challenge you to take the time to understand the people around you—whether family, friends, or colleagues—and learn what truly matters to them. Review the basic BANK personality descriptions. Identify what values you think are highest for each person on your lists. Or, make your way to the author's page and crack the code of each person.

I challenge you to review the Ten Practices for Creating the Experience That Others Matter. Incorporate the practices of active listening, empathy, and personalized attention into your daily interactions. Be sure to cross-reference their BANKCODE and take actions that complement their code or use words that support their values.

I challenge you to review the Ten Practices for Creating the Experience of Being Valued. Add in non-verbal communication, maintaining eye contact, leaning in, and mirroring. The way you make people feel will shape your relationships and influence the world around you.

I challenge you to measure your success in deepening your relatedness with each person. Identify if you incorporated new actions and words, how comfortable you were with this new process, and did it make a difference for the other person? What was the impact on your relationship with each person?

Finally, I challenge you to go to the author's page and crack your code and the code of your ten closest family members, friends, or colleagues within the next forty-eight hours.

Print out and share your Free Personality Reports with one another. This step alone will increase relatedness, deepen your relationships, and have your loved ones get it that *they matter!*

VICKI PARKER | NAKB

Vicki Parker, author, speaker, and coach, is a known relationship and confidence builder with a broad background spanning leadership, coaching, and hospitality. She specializes in growing confidence in successful female leaders, leadership development, management, performance, customer experience, and teamwork. Vicki is a Certified and Licensed BANK Trainer and Coach, and neurolinguistics programming (NLP), blending these techniques with her experience as a trainer, coach, and hotelier. She focuses on holistic wellness, addressing both personal and corporate dynamics.

Vicki has co-authored three books, Amazon Bestsellers *Overcoming Mediocrity*, *Unstoppable Women*, and *Building Bridges of Hope, Overcoming Trauma in Family Law Cases*, and her most recent release, *Bringing New Words to Your Body Conversation*. Additionally, she is the inn-keeper at the Inn at Brandywine Falls in the Cuyahoga Valley National Park, where she provides a sanctuary for relaxation, fitness, and personal renewal.

Author's Website: VickiParkerUnlimited.com

CHAPTER 29

MAKING PEOPLE MATTER IN THE WORLD OF BUSINESS AND MAKING MONEY

BY WINN CLAYBAUGH

> "Imagine that every person is wearing an invisible badge screaming, 'Make me feel important.'"
>
> — Author Unknown

How attractive is your workplace culture? Do people support and contribute to your company values, or are they only there for the paycheck? Does your work environment address the three basic human needs? How do you define leadership in your company? Are you sometimes perceived as a jerk at work? Do you sometimes show up as a resistor at work, someone who brightens up a room by leaving?

A RIPPLE TURNED INTO A MOVEMENT

Far too many people hate their lives Monday through Friday because they're treated poorly at work, forced to operate in a toxic environment, left feeling unappreciated by the boss, or even worse. I can only imagine those individuals leave work and take that energy home to their family members, where they amplify and spread the heartbreaking message that people do not matter.

Fortunately, the opposite of that toxic culture and its impact can also exist. In a company that makes people matter, the positive energy spreads way beyond a virtual work environment or a brick-and-mortar building. If you're part of a company with ten employees who go home to four family members, the impact of a positive culture can spread to forty people. If your company touches one hundred people every day, how many will they impact? In my organization, where 13,000 people spend time in our Paul Mitchell Schools across the country, making people matter is not just a platitude or mission statement: it's a movement that started as a ripple, influenced in part by an incredible mentor of mine.

Many years ago, I had the chance to interview a Catholic nun named Sister Bonnie for my MASTERS podcast. Sister Bonnie decided to become a hairdresser and do hair for the homeless. She graduated from beauty school and set up a shop, which she named The Pearly Gates Salon, located in the tiny bathroom of a shower facility in downtown Cincinnati. Over the next seven years, she cut hair for 10,000 homeless people in that tiny bathroom until a group of amazing individuals built a wonderful salon for her and her guests.

Before meeting Sister Bonnie, I had a difficult time seeing beyond the dirty exterior of the homeless, and I could easily jump into judgment about how those people ended up in the position they were in. That wasn't the person I wanted to be, and I realized Sister Bonnie was a great example and a mentor for me and my company. After I spent time with her, talked about her in my seminars, and helped raise money for her organization, her lovely mentoring finally started to seep in.

One day, I arrived at one of my schools and found a homeless man in front of the building. Normally, because of my own fears and prejudices, I would have ignored him. Or worse, I would have called the police to have him removed. Because of Sister Bonnie's influence, I began talking to him and invited him into the school for a hair service. I had him take a seat in the reception area, then walked to the back of the school and asked a group of students, "Who wants to be a day maker?" Ten students immediately raised their hands. I chose one, brought him to the reception area, introduced him to the homeless man, and asked him to take good care of his "client." Two hours later, after being shampooed, conditioned, groomed, and cared for, the homeless man left the school.

I honestly don't know how this affected the homeless man, but his experience is not the point. The point is this: Because of Sister Bonnie's mentoring, I made a little, tiny shift in my thinking. I let go of a fear and a belief system that didn't serve me or anyone else. The person who changed was me, and ultimately, the culture of my company—by activating and shifting into the Nurturing part of my code.

IF YOU WANT THE SPOTLIGHT, YOU MUST DO THE WORK!

If making people matter is important to you and your business, it must be part of your belief system, your mantra, your mission statement, and your daily conversations, whether one-on-one at the water cooler or in a team huddle.

You need more than lip service or words on a poster hanging on the wall. You need systems for every interaction, from the moment they walk in the door, all throughout their workday or customer experience, and even your process for showing gratitude and appreciation for their service or their business. And, if there's no system in place for handling an unhappy customer or employee, then your behavior does not align with your values.

By the way, every business has unhappy customers and employees now and then. How you treat that person throughout the encounter demonstrates whether your company truly focuses on making people matter. With people-focused systems and training, an unhappy customer or employee can become your most loyal and vocal fan—even more than the person who never experiences a challenge or complaint. "Fixing" a bad experience can turn into the best word-of-mouth promotion.

BUILD IT AND THEY WILL COME!

One of my favorite movies is *Field of Dreams*, with its message "If you build it, they will come." To fill your company with hardworking, loyal, creative, and passionate team members, you must build a culture that attracts people like that.

The word "attractive" simply means that things will come to you. Customers and new team members won't choose your business, product, or services because of your impeccable accounting system. You have to work on being attractive. When you and your culture are attractive, passionate team members and loyal customers will find you.

Is your culture attractive? Are you attractive as a team member, even if you've only worked there for a month? Are you attractive as a leader?

Whenever two people come together, they create a culture. In your business, you must decide how that culture looks and feels, or it will be decided for you—and often, a culture created by default is a culture that feels toxic.

Have you ever "felt" a toxic culture when walking into a store, restaurant, or office building? Without knowing the behind-the-scenes drama of the fear-based boss who thinks their only role is to dictate, police, and catch people doing things wrong, or the drama between the team members who work there, you can automatically feel it. That restaurant could have elegant marble floors and a top-rated chef, but you're immediately turned off and running for the door! You likely just experienced the dark side of the code, absence of emotional intelligence.

Most people would probably agree that Disney has a culture, identified by adjectives like magical, happy, clean, and fun. More than 225,000 employees—they call them cast members—work for the Walt Disney Company worldwide. Do you think Disney just stumbled across 225,000 people who naturally had the skills to create a magical, fun, happy, and clean experience for their guests? Disney created a culture, and then they trained people within their culture to provide the experience that Disney guests have come to expect and want to enjoy. Please note that Disney did not solidify their culture with just one training, nor will it be just one training in your organization. Creating a positive culture requires you to TRAIN, TRAIN, TRAIN!

DEFINITION OF LEADERSHIP

Leadership is not a position; it's a mindset and an attitude. A leader is someone who has influence over another human being—which basically means everyone can be a leader. You can have power and influence standing in line at the grocery store with a bunch of strangers. How? With a few words or actions, you could make that stranger's day or ruin that stranger's day. Can you imagine the power and influence you have with the people you work with every day?

There is an old belief system that if you want something done right, you must do it yourself. In my opinion, that's the worst advice ever.

If you are the smartest, most talented, and most skilled person working in your company, business, or store, I feel sorry for you because that means that you are now forced to work twelve-hour days, six days a week. A smart person knows how to collaborate. A smart person knows how to bring out the best in others.

I believe collaboration is a skill set we all need to learn. Collaboration is all about bringing out the best in others. It's not about how many points you can score: it's about how many points you can help the entire team score. How do you learn the skill set of collaboration and bringing out the best in others? Practice—practice to build connections, rapport, and trust. It takes repetition.

Without this skill, you could be an expert or master at your craft but end up getting fired. You go to the boss, asking, "Why are you firing me? I'm the most talented person here?" And the response will be, "Yeah, but no one likes working with you."

Here's the deal: some people can be such jerks at work that no one wants to help them, so they're right—they do have to do everything themselves. Or, they may not really be jerks, but if people think they are, they need to own and correct that perception.

HOW NOT TO BE A JERK

I've heard that roughly 50 percent of employees who quit their jobs do so to get away from their boss or from toxic team members. And by the way, the worst employees don't quit; the best employees do because they know they deserve better. The worst employees know they're lucky to have a job. They stay and become part of the problem. In my organization, we call them resisters—they brighten a room by leaving.

People think their boss or a coworker is a jerk when...

- They never have fun at work.
- They're always tired or serious.
- They're always on their cell phone.
- They don't show gratitude—big mistake! Gratitude is another basic human need, right up there with oxygen.

Now, some of you might have the belief system that says: "I don't care what people think about me," but that's no way to make people matter.

A business owner or manager is giving a tour of their store, their office building, or their warehouse, and someone on the tour asks, "How many people work here?" The business owner replies, "Oh, about half. About half work here."

That may sound like a joke, but it happens in businesses when team members are not engaged. Maybe they're engaged with their time, meaning they show up for one thing and one thing only—to receive a paycheck so they can pay their bills. But they are not engaged in sharing their creativity, their passion, or the best versions of themselves. And when people are not engaged, we want to fire them, but you cannot fire your way into building a better team.

SYSTEMS AND TRAININGS

If you say people matter to you, but you have no systems or trainings for employees on how to properly treat each other or your customers, then your mission statement of "making people matter" means nothing. This is where you need to activate the Blueprint and Knowledge parts of your code.

In its simplest form, a system can be defined as, "This is how we do things around here." Personal interpretation cannot enter a system. If you were hired to be in the Disneyland parade, you couldn't show up as your own version of Mickey Mouse. If you're a cook at McDonald's, you can't show up with your own recipe for hamburgers. If you work for companies like these, you join their culture, and you follow their systems.

A system has two qualities: It's written down, and it's repeated continually.

In my company, some of our key written systems include our Golden Rules, Guiding Principles, and Gathering Guidelines. I'm a big fan of lists, so I pulled from those three systems to share some of the ways we make people matter in my organization. We have these on our posters so people can see them every day, and we back them up with frequent repetition in our team huddles and trainings.

Golden Rules:

- Always be in a great mood. (Fake it when necessary.)
- Gossip is not allowed.
- Resolve all personal challenges with love.
- Go to the decision maker with any apparent unsolvable challenges.

Guiding Principles:

- People learn best when they are having fun.
- Making a mistake is not fatal. We make "discoveries," not "mistakes."
- Learning is blocked when fear is present.
- Praise is the best motivator.
- The learning process is not good or bad; it simply is working or not working. If it is working, we improve it. If it is not working, we change it.
- The word "education" means to "draw out," not to "put in."
- A staff that trains together stays together.

Gathering Guidelines:

- Sit in a circle. (This removes hierarchy and the feeling that "I matter more than you do.")
- There are no "problems," only "challenges" and "opportunities."
- There's no such thing as a "complaint"—only "suggestions" with at least two solutions. (People matter more than words. We avoid words that make people feel like they are a problem or a mistake.)
- There are no dumb questions, dumb answers, or dumb ideas. (We're all in the process of learning and growing, and the work environment is a safe place to facilitate that growth.)
- Criticizing, teasing, put-downs, and sarcasm are the only taboos.
- Failure is not fatal!

WHAT IS MY ROLE?

Early in my career, after being in the salon business for a few years, I was approached by an employee who pulled me aside. "Winn," she said, "I want you to know that for the last twenty years, I've been in a very abusive marriage. Because of working here, I now have the courage to divorce this man. For the last two years when I come to work each day, I feel loved, I feel safe, I feel like I matter, and I feel like I'm making a difference. Because of all of that, I now have the courage to divorce this horrible man."

That unexpected revelation was a huge wake-up call for me. Until that moment, I thought my only role was to create a place where people earn a paycheck. That day, I realized every business and every team member working in that business has the opportunity and the responsibility to create a culture that addresses three basic human needs:

1. People need to feel safe.
2. People need to feel they belong.
3. People need to have a purpose.

PEOPLE NEED TO FEEL SAFE

Let me give you a scenario for this. Let's say I'm the boss at your work. One day, I wake up in a great mood, but I have a lot of phone calls and emails to handle. I drive to work, dash through the front door, and rush past the receptionist, team members, and customers. I go straight to my office and shut the door. What's the buzz in that building in about two minutes? "Winn is in a very bad mood. Everybody lay low today. Don't go near the boss."

With that type of energy in the building that day, what happens to creativity, teamwork, sales, and profitability? It diminishes and is compromised. Even if I snuck in the backdoor or built a tunnel from the parking lot, would people know I was in the building? Would they feel the toxic culture I created?

As a member of my team at work, I not only need to be in a good mood every day—and if I'm not in a good mood, I need to own that and take responsibility for it—but if people don't know I'm in a good mood, I still have some work to do.

When I arrive at one of my Paul Mitchell Schools, it can take me thirty to forty-five minutes before I land at a desk and get down to work. What am I doing during that time? I'm visiting every inch of the building and talking to as many people as I can. I'm asking how they're doing and how their family vacation was. I'm giving hugs and expressing my gratitude for their commitment and the work they do. I'm emphasizing and sharing the three basic human needs so they feel safe, they feel they belong, and they feel they have a purpose.

PEOPLE NEED TO FEEL THEY BELONG

I read somewhere that 60 percent of people say, "No one has my back." And by the way, half of them are married.

I don't believe people just come to work for your company or business; they *join* you. I don't believe customers just spend money with your company; they join you. People want something to belong to—something that's bigger than themselves. You undoubtedly have people working with you who have never felt like they belonged anywhere. They did not fit into traditional educational environments such as high school or college. Sadly, some people do not feel they belong in their own homes. Can you imagine the loyalty you can create if coming to work every day is the first time these individuals truly feel like they belong?

In the same way a company needs to establish systems and trainings for manufacturing, accounting, and other important functions, they also need a path for creating a company culture where people feel like they belong. It's just as important as the innate need to feel we belong to family, community, or group of friends. "Can I be myself? Can I express my thoughts, ideas, and opinions? Do I have a voice?"

Each year, the Paul Mitchell School network holds a three-month FUNraising campaign. In the last twenty-one years, this campaign has raised awareness and more than $26 million for a variety of selected charities. Why are we so dedicated to our annual campaign? Because it's the right thing to do and we are here to make a difference.

Our students and team members overwhelmingly tell us they love being part of a company that cares. They want to give back and help others, and they love being able to do that as part of their job or their educational experience.

According to studies by the IBM Institute for Business Value, the Cone Corporate Citizenship Study, and the Points of Light Foundation:

- Three out of four people say it's very important to work for a company that "does good."
- Nearly half are willing to work for less pay for a community-engaged company.
- Forty percent say they would work longer hours for a "socially responsible" company.

- Eight-six percent of Americans say they're likely to switch from one brand to another that is associated with a charitable cause.
- Seventy-nine percent said they are more likely to buy a product that supports a nonprofit.
- Eighty-one percent of companies today view employee volunteerism as directly affecting the bottom line.

With the arrival of Generation G—the G stands for Giving—giving back is no longer a "nice to do" idea—it's a "must do" for businesses. Remember, 86 percent of your customers are looking at you and asking themselves, "Is this company just out to make money and fill their pockets, or are they also taking care of their community, locally and globally?" This has also been validated in the research done on BANK, revealing that the number-one buying (or buy-in) decision for the Nurturing code was whether or not the company was involved in charitable causes that make an impact for others.

PEOPLE NEED A PURPOSE

Imagine that two janitors work for the same elementary school. They have the same boss, responsibilities, hours, and pay. One janitor has the attitude that "These little brats make a mess around here, and it's my job to clean it up. That's what they pay me to do." The other janitor has the attitude of, "It's my privilege and my sacred responsibility to create a clean learning environment for the next generation that will save this planet." They both have the same job description, but one thinks he has a job with a paycheck, and the other has a purpose and a mission.

When it comes to making people matter, any type of business can incorporate all three human needs, whether it's a dental office, a barbershop, a distribution warehouse, and even your company. Take, for example, the pizza parlor employees who come to work with this attitude:

"Yeah, we make pizzas. We also create a safe environment for each other here at work, free of gossip and judgment. Even though our lifestyles, ages, and colors are very different from each other, we truly look forward to connecting with each other and making everyone feel like they belong. As a team, we all signed up to participate in a cancer walkathon. We aren't just selling pizza. We help families come together at the end of a busy work and school day to connect and laugh with each other in a clean, fun environment."

YOUR CHALLENGE: GET CONNECTED

Making people matter requires connecting with people and creating trust to bring out the best in each other. Is there someone at your work, store, or office you have not yet connected with? You've seen them every day for weeks, months, or even years, but there's still no connection. Maybe they look different from you or have a different lifestyle, political, or religious affiliation, so you assume there is no common ground.

Let's consider your lack of connection is just a bad habit, and bad habits are meant to be broken. Bad habits, bad luck. Good habits, good luck!

It's time to make the connection. The first time you try may feel awkward and uncomfortable, but practice, practice!

Here's a sample script to help you get started: "I know I've seen you here every day for months, and we've never connected, and I apologize for that. I'm just curious to know why you chose this career. Where are you from? Congratulations on that huge sale, that beautiful hair color on that client, and the amazing sales strategy you came up with. Good stuff! Tell me more about you. What's your code?"

THINGS TO REMEMBER: DO THE MATH!

Making people matter is not just about not being a jerk at work. It's about using your power and influence to create a culture where people actually feel better about themselves after spending eight hours a day in your building. Do you know each of their BANKCODES, and do you intentionally connect with them based on their codes? How many people could ultimately be impacted if you were to make this philosophy come alive in your work environment?

Do the math:

- Name every employee you work with on a daily basis.
- Multiply that by the number of family members they then influence.

- If you work with ten people, and each one has four family members, your energy, actions, and mood can influence more than forty people. That's the power and influence you can have in your work environment.

Remember, this does not apply exclusively to the boss. Every person has influence, no matter their title, pay scale, or time in the company. How are you using your power?

SUMMARY

Making people matter in business is not about hanging one poster, scheduling one training, or holding one team meeting. It's systems, training, and repetition over and over again. In my company, we're still discussing the same things in team trainings and meetings we discussed forty years ago. You never graduate from this stuff.

WINN CLAYBAUGH | NABK

Winn Claybaugh is the author of *Be Nice (Or Else!)* and host of the *MASTERS by Winn Claybaugh* podcast. CNN's Larry King, who wrote the foreword for Winn's book, called him "one of the best motivational speakers in the country."

A business owner for more than forty years, Winn is the Founder, Co-Owner, and Dean of Paul Mitchell Schools with more than one hundred cosmetology and/or barbering schools throughout the United States. He is also a national speaker for major corporations and a popular radio and podcast guest. Under Winn's leadership and in keeping with their unique culture of giving back and building self-esteem, Paul Mitchell Schools has donated countless volunteer hours and more than $26 million to charity.

Recognizing his contributions to the professional beauty industry, American Salon named Winn one of the five "Industry Leaders Who Helped Revolutionize Education." The North American Hairstyling Awards (NAHA) made him the youngest person ever named to their Hall of Leaders. Winn also received the prestigious Ellis Island Medal of Honor.

Author's Website: WinnClaybaugh.com

KNOWLEDGE

CHAPTER 30
THE AI-ENABLED LEADER: BUILDING QUALITY AND TRUST WITH BANK

BY ANNA PARKER

> "The first rule of any technology used in a business is that automation applied to an efficient operation will magnify the efficiency. The second is that automation applied to an inefficient operation will magnify the inefficiency."
>
> — Bill Gates

Do you have FOMO when it comes to bringing AI performance improvement solutions into your business? Do you have the right mindset to join the AI revolution and become an AI-enabled company? Do you know how to use BANK for amazing AI solutions? Do you even know your business' BANKCODE?

MY STORY

Before I dive into how to integrate the BANK methodology into your business for AI-driven performance improvement, let me share how BANK has been an integral part of my life for the past ten years. In 2014, I attended my first BANK event, and it was life-changing. My ex-husband introduced me to BANK because he knew it would help us respect each other's differences and co-parent our kids.

Now, a decade later, we have new BANK-savvy significant others, and our kids have grown up with BANK and internalized it. Now, we all have high emotional intelligence and an inherent understanding of how the four personality types appear in human behavior. I'm very proud of my harmonious modern family, and I think we're the least judgmental family you will ever meet. We use BANK all the time because it drives effective communication in everything we do, personally and professionally.

I have a unique understanding of the BANK methodology because I have been the lead designer and developer of all the curriculum and reports since 2015. It's been an honor helping Cheri grow her vision over the years as I continued my own personal and professional development journey. With my background in product management, technical writing, leadership, and now AI business solutions, I have insights I want to share with you.

For this chapter, I'm focusing on how to use BANK to prepare for the AI revolution.

ALL PROBLEMS ARE COMMUNICATION PROBLEMS

If you think about it, all problems are communication problems. Think about family arguments; they often start when someone assumes their loved ones understand their feelings without actually expressing them. Without open dialogue, misunderstandings can quickly build up. In the business world, missed deadlines usually aren't about anyone slacking off. More often, it happens because the instructions aren't clear, leaving team members in the dark about what exactly needs to be done and by when. And then there are the workplace processes—if a manager doesn't explain a new procedure clearly, employees might stick to the old ways, inadvertently causing confusion and hiccups.

Clear communication, where everyone understands their roles and tasks, can solve many of these problems, making everything run more smoothly and keeping relationships harmonious. That's why knowing a person's BANKCODE is so valuable in everything you do.

WHAT'S YOUR COMPANY'S BANKCODE?

Thinking about how we communicate can really make a difference, whether with people or within a company. Just like people do better when we talk to them in a way that suits them, companies work best when their style matches a specific BANK persona. This helps ensure the company's vision and values come through clearly, both inside and out, shaping how they connect and make decisions.

Every company operates with a unique persona, intricately woven from its mission, vision, and values. This persona not only characterizes its organizational culture but also guides decision-making, shapes customer relationships, and determines market positioning. Understanding and defining this persona through BANK can illuminate the path to achieving organizational objectives and fostering sustainable growth.

Before you can consider implementing AI solutions in your business, you must consider how those solutions are perceived and what your processes are. This is why, before every consulting engagement, I crack people's codes and then have the team crack the company's BANKCODE.

Which of these following personas define your company?

The Blueprint Company Persona: These companies thrive on predictability, ensuring systems and processes are standardized for maximum efficiency. They prioritize compliance and quality assurance, focusing on creating a stable and reliable framework where every cog in the machine functions with clockwork precision. When a company aligns its mission and vision with these values, it establishes itself as a leader in trust and dependability. Blueprint personas assure customers they're committed to delivering consistent experiences and high-quality outcomes.

The Action Company Persona: Driven by a relentless pursuit of success, Action companies focus on sales numbers, outperforming competitors, and providing the best services available. They are dynamic, energetic, and motivated by challenges—a vision rooted in ambition. These companies embrace a mission that encourages taking bold steps, pushing boundaries, and achieving unparalleled benchmarks. With an Action persona, a company is seen as a frontline leader, ever ready to seize opportunities and elevate industry standards.

The Nurturing Company Persona: Nurturing enterprises build their identities around community and empowerment. Their missions center on setting both employees and customers up for success, supporting them to craft their own paths to personal and professional growth. Values like empathy, collaboration, and mutual support are at the core of their operations. A Nurturing persona ensures the company is perceived as a caregiver within the industry, deeply invested in building supportive communities and shared success.

The Knowledge Company Persona: Anchored in research and innovation, Knowledge companies champion analytics-driven decisions and green technology development. They focus on the big picture, striving to improve and innovate continuously. Their vision revolves around thought leadership—becoming the torchbearers of progress and sustainable solutions. A Knowledge persona positions a company as a visionary, capable of transforming challenges into pathways for a brighter future.

DETERMINING YOUR COMPANY'S BANKCODE PERSONA

To identify your company's persona, start by examining its mission, vision, and core values. Reflect on questions such as:

- What are the fundamental principles guiding your decisions and goals?
- How do you measure success, and what drives your company's achievements?
- What kind of culture do you aim to foster—one based on structure, ambition, community, or innovation?

Aligning these elements with BANK helps crystallize your company's persona. Identifying whether you lead with Blueprint, Action, Nurturing, or Knowledge can clarify where your strengths lie and how you can engage more effectively with your partners, clients, and workforce. It guides strategic planning and communications, ensuring every aspect of your business resonates with its authentic identity.

Understanding your company's BANKCODE is a strategic asset. It enables you to highlight core competencies, align market presence, and cultivate meaningful relationships. Acknowledging this identity fosters authenticity, empowering the company to innovate and deeply and positively impact its industry.

By exploring these aspects, companies can realize their innate strengths and navigate AI integration and other advancements in harmony with their foundational identity.

HOW DOES A CORPORATE BANK PERSONA CONTRIBUTE TO ADOPTING AI SOLUTIONS?

With AI solutions popping up everywhere, it seems like there's a new company ready to help improve your processes based on your current operations. Want a virtual AI receptionist to take calls and book appointments? Sure, it's an option, but what if you're missing an even better fit? If your company thrives on being nurturing and personal, you might want to keep that real person on the phone and just empower them with AI tools to make their job smoother. That's why knowing your corporate BANK persona really matters.

Stepping into the AI world as a small company brings many exciting possibilities. It changes how you connect with customers, handle daily operations, and turn the workplace into a more fulfilling environment for everyone. Imagine being able to offer tailor-made experiences for your customers. AI can look at data, predict preferences, and make recommendations that make them feel genuinely valued and understood. This kind of customization boosts their satisfaction and builds strong loyalty.

For you and your team, AI's more than just a tool—it's like a supportive partner. It can handle repetitive tasks, freeing up your time and energy to be more creative and strategic. Think of AI as your digital assistant, managing tasks like scheduling and inventory so stress goes down across the board. This streamlines everything, boosting productivity and job satisfaction, so employees can focus on what really matters. While some folks worry AI might replace jobs, the truth is it enriches roles by taking care of the mundane, leaving room for human creativity and problem-solving. Your team can concentrate on what they do best—building relationships and driving the business forward.

To truly become an AI-enabled company, getting a handle on your business model and internal processes is key. It means thinking about what makes your business stand out and determining where AI can make a difference. Start by looking at your workflows, how you interact with customers, and any challenges you face. Understanding these things helps spot where AI can boost efficiency, spark innovation, and increase customer satisfaction. By tidying up and documenting your processes, AI can slot right in, aligning smoothly with your business goals. This is where knowing your corporate persona becomes a strategic asset.

By refining how you operate based on your corporate BANKCODE, you lay down a strong foundation for AI, paving the way for sustainable growth and innovation. With new AI business solutions and tools emerging every week, there's always a better fit for your company popping up on the horizon. The best solution might be one you haven't discovered yet. Take this chance to boost your company's potential, ensuring AI truly enhances your business in the best possible way.

Embracing AI is all about reimagining your company's potential and really playing to its strengths. Whether you're taking your first steps into AI or ready for the next leap, there are exciting changes that can flip doubts into excitement. But before diving into AI-driven performance improvements, it's important to have a solid grasp of your corporate BANKCODE, internal processes, strengths, and weaknesses. This sets you up for success and helps you make the most of what AI has to offer.

RUN YOUR COMPANY OPERATIONS AS B-A-N-K

Think of your company's persona as the heartbeat of your organization, shaping every decision and interaction that occurs. But when it comes to the *how* of running your business—your operations—I can confidently say from my experience that the order in which you approach things really matters. That's why I highly recommend running your operations in the B-A-N-K order, always starting with Blueprint.

Beginning with Blueprint lays a strong foundation, providing the structure and clarity that ensures everyone knows what to expect. It's like setting the stage with a detailed plan before launching into action; this helps prevent missteps and keeps everyone aligned with your core goals.

Once the Blueprint is in place, Action naturally follows, sparking momentum and driving initiatives forward. This phase is all about executing strategies with energy and purpose, capitalizing on the secure groundwork established by the Blueprint.

Next, we embrace Nurturing, focusing on the people aspect. Nurturing is about fostering meaningful connections, supporting employees and customers, and creating an environment where everyone feels valued and motivated. It ensures the human element enriches your operations, turning plans and actions into shared successes.

Finally, Knowledge offers depth and insight, using data and analytics to refine processes and inform decision-making. This stage brings a forward-thinking dimension, allowing you to anticipate challenges, seize opportunities, and continuously improve.

By following this B-A-N-K order for operations, you integrate structure, dynamism, empathy, and intelligence, crafting a holistic approach that enhances your business's efficiency and resilience, while staying true to its heart.

Here's a story I have used over and over as an analogy in my consulting as an argument to always lead with Blueprint when it comes to operations.

One incredible trip to New York City taught me a key lesson about business. It was a long-awaited vacation at the beginning of December, and my heart raced with excitement as I finally set off to explore the city's famous holiday season window displays. For years, I had heard about the magical scenes at places like Bergdorf Goodman, Macy's Herald Square, and Saks Fifth Avenue, and now I was there to experience them firsthand.

As I walked down the bustling streets, I could hardly contain my anticipation. As I approached Bergdorf Goodman, famed for its breathtaking displays, I was ready to be dazzled. But as I neared, my excitement quickly turned to disappointment. The glass was covered in dirt, completely hiding the intricate artistry and imaginative storytelling that should have been a feast for the eyes.

This visual makes an excellent business analogy. I believe it is essential to have standards and a system to follow, whether for your business or for keeping famous windows sparkling clean for the holiday season.

No matter how much effort is put into your products and services, without a solid foundation, it's all too easy for the opportunities, creativity, and innovation to get lost and obscured, just like those windows. It is a vivid reminder that driving your operations with Blueprint values ensures all your hard work shines through, capturing attention and delivering joy, just like those sparkling displays I had hoped to see in my story. If you lead with Blueprint, predictable obstructions—just like the dirt on the window—will disappear to showcase your offerings' full spirit and benefits.

LAYING A STRATEGIC FOUNDATION WITH BANK

The journey to becoming AI-enabled is not solely about technology; it's about laying a strategic foundation. This is where the BANK methodology excels, particularly with the Blueprint personality leading the way. Starting with Blueprint ensures clarity in offerings, structure, and predictable systems. This approach stabilizes your enterprise, offering a solid groundwork for AI integration.

Each personality type in the BANK system—Blueprint, Action, Nurturing, and Knowledge—brings significant value.

Blueprint structures the company's vision and aligns everyone around clear, strategic objectives. This clarity is essential when embarking on AI journeys because it ensures everyone understands the path and expected outcomes.

With Blueprint leading, Action personalities thrive in an environment poised for dynamic progress. They are pivotal during the implementation phases, driving innovation and ensuring that AI projects gain momentum. Nurturing personalities keep a close eye on maintaining customer-centric operations, while Knowledge offers deep insights through data analytics, ensuring decisions are backed by evidence.

TIPS FOR EMBRACING AI AND THE BANK METHODOLOGY IN YOUR BUSINESS

1. **Understand Your Corporate BANKCODE:** Evaluate your company's mission, vision, and values to determine its unique BANKCODE. This understanding will guide your strategic planning and communication, ensuring alignment and authenticity in every interaction.

2. **Tailor AI Solutions to Fit Your Persona:** Before rushing into AI tools, ensure they complement your company's unique culture and values. If your organization thrives on personal connections, consider integrating AI in ways that augment rather than replace human interaction.

3. **Adopt AI as a Supportive Partner:** Use AI to handle repetitive tasks and free up time for strategic and creative pursuits. Think of AI as your digital assistant, im-

proving efficiency and leaving room for human ingenuity. Remember, AI doesn't replace jobs—it enriches them.

4. **Follow the B-A-N-K Approach for Strong Operations:** Start with a Blueprint to lay a solid foundation, ensuring clarity and alignment. Build momentum with Action by driving initiatives with purpose. Then focus on Nurturing to foster strong relationships within your team and with your customers. Finally, use Knowledge to continuously refine processes and seize new opportunities, encouraging growth and improvement.

5. **Regularly Revisit and Refine Processes:** As new AI solutions emerge, continuously assess whether updates can enhance your operations. Stay flexible and open to innovations that can optimize your business performance, always keeping your foundational principles in mind.

By following these steps and aligning your operations with the BANK methodology, you'll navigate the AI landscape efficiently and deepen the unique strengths of your company's persona, ensuring growth, innovation, and a lasting impact in your industry.

EXERCISE

1. Based on your company's vision, mission, and values, what is its BANKCODE? Also, write down the company's top four core values.

2. What are your favorite parts of running the company vs. which parts do you want to automate with AI solutions?

3. Which processes need organizing the most, in order of priority, with the most urgent at the top, and why?

4. What's blocking you from adopting AI solutions to improve your all-around performance with automation?

SUMMARY

Embrace the future of business by aligning AI initiatives with the BANK methodology to build trust and enhance performance. Understanding your Corporate BANKCODE positions your business for success in the AI era. By integrating AI as a partner, these strategies ensure tasks are streamlined, creativity flourishes, and human connections are preserved. The journey begins with Blueprint as your foundation, establishing clarity and structure in operations. With solid groundwork, Action propels you forward, motivating strategic executions with energy. Nurturing follows, emphasizing empathy and support, which transform plans into meaningful relationships. Finally, Knowledge leverages data to refine your processes and anticipate future challenges.

ANNA PARKER | KANB

Anna Parker, Chief Learning Officer at Lucid AI Solutions, shapes innovative AI programs with her expertise in product management, technical writing, and instructional design. Collaborating with AI Change Management specialists, Anna ensures smooth AI adoption through strategic communication and training materials. Formerly, as Director of Product Development at Codebreaker Technologies, LLC, she led the product development lifecycle, focusing on sustaining best-in-class curriculum and BANK reports.

Anna's journey with BANK has been transformative, shaping her dedication to the Make People Matter movement, which she integrates into all areas of her life. Introduced by her ex-husband, BANK's principles helped her find harmony in her modern family, including meeting her second husband through the community. This philosophy is evident in both her professional and personal life as she fosters relationships and ensures everyone feels valued.

Author's Website: Comm4Results.com

CHAPTER 31
MAXIMIZE RELATIONSHIPS, BUILD TEAMS, SKYROCKET RESULTS

BY DALIA HARAMI

> "The single biggest problem in communication is the illusion that it has taken place."
>
> — George Bernard Shaw

We all intuitively know that understanding each other's personalities helps everyone to feel seen, valued, and heard, which in turn strengthens personal relationships, improves teamwork in business, and drives better financial results. When we recognize individual strengths and communication styles, we can connect more quickly and effectively, reduce misunderstandings, and work together in ways that maximize performance. We are able to create deeper trust and increase productivity because when we make people matter, relationships thrive, teams collaborate, and businesses grow.

Allow me to share some stories:

REAL ESTATE AND MLS LISTINGS

As a realtor, one of my pet peeves when browsing real estate listings on the MLS is the lack of thoughtful home descriptions. Many listings fail to fully describe the property, leaving out key details that could make a buyer excited. They often list just the basics without highlighting the benefits of the features or the advantages of the location. Without enticing language that appeals to what each type of buyer values most, these listings don't do much to capture a buyer's attention or spark interest, which means some realtors are not maximizing their service to their seller clients.

I worked hard with my business partner, Peter, to complete our first real estate flip. We overcame several challenges, including contractors who quit, contractors we had to fire, and village permits, to name a few. While we bought the house at the right price and executed a fantastic remodel, I believe it was the extra *power-scripted* detail in our MLS listing description that helped set our property apart to sell it fast.

In Chicago, selling a home after Labor Day often means missing the prime listing season, but that didn't hold us back. The detailed, compelling remarks in the listing attracted a surge of interest—tons of views, multiple showings over seven straight days, and two solid offers. We even turned away a third pending offer because we had sold the home *within a week* for $15,000 more than the highest comparable price we set as our goal. Our success was the perfect combination of preparation, execution, and leveraging the power of persuasive, attention-grabbing language to communicate to buyers why they have to make our house their new home.

NETWORK MARKETING

Top leaders in network marketing are often asked, "How did you know what to say to that prospect?" Their success comes from years of experience, so it isn't always replicable for everyone. Most new network marketers don't have any sales experience and often don't know what to say. One of the biggest challenges in the industry is the fear of rejection; it is a large contributing factor to the high attrition rate. The industry promotes getting more nos to eventually earn a yes, but that has never made sense. It's the same faulty reasoning as thinking that if you flip a coin three times and it lands on tails each time, the likelihood of getting heads on the next flip goes up. Why shouldn't we aim for a yes each time by saying the right thing that resonates with each person? When we do this, the process becomes easier to teach, easier to learn, and more duplicatable, the key to long-term success in direct sales.

I remember once when a very successful top leader did a three-way call with a prospect for me. I didn't understand why at the time, but something inside me told me the approach wasn't going to be right. The leader was a strong Action, while the prospect was more of a Knowledge personality. Later, when I learned about BANK, I realized why I had that gut feeling—it was all about aligning the right approach with the right personality. If you truly believe your product or service is the best, sharing it in a way that turns off a prospect does a disservice to both you and them.

LAURA'S ENTREPRENEURSHIP STORY

As a lifelong serial entrepreneur, my friend Laura has always focused on innovation and improvement, particularly in the areas of sales and marketing, the lifeblood of any successful business.

One major realization she had was recognizing her natural tendency to be late. Once she understood how that could offend 25 percent of the population, she was able to avoid losing deals and improved her professional relationships. Applying BANK has also transformed how she builds and manages teams. By identifying personality types, she asks the right questions, hires well-rounded individuals, and creates teams that complement each other's strengths. This approach has ensured she isn't leaving opportunities on the table or alienating potential clients because of communication gaps.

Laura also realized that individuals she might have overlooked or even dismissed in the past have become some of the most valuable members of her team. Embracing the power of respect, inclusion, and adaptability led to greater success. She passionately believes that if everyone recognized the value of each personality and focused on collaborating, learning from, and supporting one another, businesses and schools alike would operate far more effectively.

LAURA AND JEFF'S RELATIONSHIP STORY

Laura (NABK) and her husband Jeff (KBAN) have distinctly opposite personalities. She is highly nurturing, while Jeff has a very low natural nurturing instinct. When she's upset and just needs a hug, it doesn't naturally occur to him to do that. When one of their kids falls, she has to remind him, "Hey, your son is crying—go give him a hug." It's not intentional; he simply doesn't recognize it because he can get overwhelmed by emotions and stress.

Laura used to take offense to his behavior, but now she understands it's just part of his personality. With this awareness, they actively work on their relationship. Laura learned to be more patient, to ask questions instead of jumping to conclusions, and to plan ahead instead of waiting until she's under stress, where she naturally excels. Jeff, on the other hand, has realized his instinct to withdraw during stressful moments doesn't serve their relationship. Now, instead of disappearing, he'll say, "I need ten minutes, but I'll be back."

While opposites do attract, those differences can often lead to significant struggles and even divorce. BANK has helped them identify and navigate these challenges—not just for their own growth, but for each other. By working through their differences, they've been able to grow closer and build a stronger bond.

LAURA'S PARENTING STORY

Parents often see their children through their own perspective, but BANK helped Laura recognize and break that habit and improve how she communicates with her kids. It's also helped them better relate to each other.

Her older son is a very sensitive Blueprint personality; he doesn't like surprises and prefers structure. When they get ready to leave the house, she now gives him a countdown—ten minutes, five minutes, two minutes, then one minute—so he feels prepared and not rushed. This simple approach has completely changed their mornings. He starts his day calmer and more in control, which makes everything smoother for the whole family.

Her younger son is a high Action personality—full of energy and always wanting to play. He didn't understand why his older brother would sometimes need space. BANK helped her to explain their differences in a way they could both understand. Now, Laura is able to balance their needs.

They play games in short spurts with the younger son, or he jumps on a mini-trampoline to burn energy without overwhelming his brother.

This practice has made Laura more patient and intentional as a parent. It's improved how she disciplines, interacts, and communicates with her kids, and she's grateful for the difference these tools made in their family dynamic.

JAGGER'S STORY

When my nephew Jagger was eight I asked him to crack his code using the BANK values cards. To my surprise, he identified himself as Action first. I wasn't convinced. After losing his mom to cancer at the age of five, Jagger became very attached to his dad, seldom letting him go anywhere without wanting to join him. He was also sensitive and caring. I specifically remember a time when his older sister, Alyssa, was teasing him at the mall. On our way out, I joked, "Let's leave her behind!" His immediate response was, "Noooo, we can't leave her!"

I decided to test him again. The next day, I gave him a set of kid-friendly ICON cards and asked him to sort them just like the day before. I thought, "Maybe he didn't fully understand the words or concepts the first time." But, no—he sorted them in *exactly* the same order, with Action first. At that moment, I realized the problem wasn't his understanding, it was my assumption.

Fast forward several years, and Jagger had *absolutely* grown into his *Action* identity. He was constantly active—creating YouTube videos, seeking likes and subscribers, and even taking on hot sauce challenges with his dad, fully embracing his true self. This taught me that although we often believe we understand the people in our lives, truly knowing who they are comes from listening to them and observing how they behave, both when they're in their element and when they're under stress.

MARIA'S DIY PIZZA STORY

My friend Maria (Action) was invited to her son and daughter-in-law's house for dinner. She had a brilliant idea of bringing DIY pizzas, complete with all the toppings, so the kids could have fun creating their own individual pizzas, envisioning an evening of joyful chaos.

The kids were over the moon, ready to dive in. She said, "Grab that cheese and throw it all over the pizza." But before the cheese could fly, her daughter-in-law (Blueprint) swooped in and declared, "No! Use a spoon."

The kids' pizzas went into the oven, and now it was the adults' turn. When the adults' pizzas were ready to bake, Maria said, "Let's pop them in now. The kids' pizzas only have a few minutes left, and then ours will need just a bit longer. Perfect timing!" Her daughter-in-law responded with a hard "no." Maria let it go and left the kitchen, figuring things would work themselves out.

When the oven timer dinged, Maria returned to claim their creations...but wait—where were the kids' pizzas? Gone. Vanished. Like a cheesy, saucy crime scene wiped clean. Her daughter-in-law confessed that she'd tossed them out because they were "too messy" and had remade them into perfect works of art. Picture every pepperoni placed with GPS precision and evenly spaced.

Thankfully, the kids didn't realize their Picasso-style pizzas had been replaced by architectural models.

Maria realized that for her daughter-in-law, control and order brought comfort, while for Maria, messy creativity meant joy and connection. It's a great reminder that we all see the world—and even a pizza—through the lenses of our own unique personality and values.

MARIA'S DISNEYLAND STORY

My friend Maria (Action) wanted to make sure her kids had fun, so she was always coming up with spontaneous surprises. She was the type of mom who lived for the moment.

One day, she said to her kids, "Get in the car—we're leaving in five minutes!" Thirty minutes later, they pulled into Disneyland. "Surprise!" she said, expecting joy and excitement. But instead of smiles, her kids were upset. They didn't enjoy the day, and she couldn't understand why. She thought she was giving them a magical moment, but instead, they seemed upset and frustrated.

What Maria didn't realize at the time was that her Blueprint daughter needed structure and planning ahead. Her Knowledge son needed predictability, but his sense of order was disrupted.

Decades later, Maria asked her daughter, "Why were you so unhappy that day?" Her answer resonated as if the moment just took place yesterday: "Because it wasn't on my calendar. I wasn't dressed right, and I didn't have time to do my hair!"

At just ten years old, Maria's daughter already valued structure and preparation more than spontaneity. Growing up, her kids were often upset that their mom was running late or planning things at the last minute. She carried the guilt of thinking she was a "bad mom" for a long time until she realized they were seeing things from different lenses. While Maria expressed her love through spontaneity and adventure, her kids needed structure and predictability. She was an Action mom raising Blueprint and Knowledge kids, and love often looks different to those who give it and those who receive it. Understanding each other's values can help us better connect and appreciate the ways we care for one another.

JOE'S STORY—TURNING A $600 APPRAISAL INTO AN $11,000 COMMISSION

My realtor friend Joe received a call about appraising a home left in a parent's estate, even though they were almost ready to sign with another agent. He asked if they would allow him the opportunity to discuss his marketing options with them before they signed with that agent, and they agreed.

There were two couples at the meeting. Joe started off as he did on every appointment by introducing the BANKCARDS and saying, "I like to do things a little differently and have some fun at the same time. Is that okay with you?" This statement always piques curiosity! Of course they said, "Yes!" Joe made sure to give each person a set of BANKCARDS simultaneously, and they cracked their codes.

Amber (NBKA) is married to Steve (ANKB), and Kristen (KBAN) is married to Tim (NKBA).

Joe thanked them for doing the short exercise and quickly shared the insights he gained about them.

He told Amber she seems to like to help people and is very structured in her profession. It turned out she was a counselor.

He suggested Steve may be a salesman. Turned out he leads and trains sales teams.

He told Tim he likes being around people and absorbing information. It turned out he was a teacher.

He told Kristen she may be more of an analytical or scientific type. It turned out she was a research scientist.

Joe continued communicating with them in their codes. Not only did he win the listing, but he sold it in forty-two days when the average sale time in the area was four to six months, and he earned an $11,000 commission plus future referrals.

JOE'S REAL ESTATE STORY

My friend Joe's story is a powerful testament to how implementing the BANK methodology can transform success, even for high performers in competitive industries like real estate. Joe had already reached impressive heights in his career as a top-producing realtor. Earning the Realtor of Distinction award multiple times proved that Joe was operating at a level that many agents aspire to. With a 37 percent closing ratio on listing appointments, he was already well ahead of the industry average of 20-22 percent. By all standards, Joe was excelling.

However, even for someone achieving great results, there's always room to improve. When Joe discovered and implemented BANK, his performance surged to a level he hadn't thought possible. Within less than a year, his closing ratio skyrocketed to 86 percent—a remarkable jump that solidified his position as a top-tier professional.

Joe was able to better understand his clients' values and decision-making processes, which allowed him to connect with them on a deeper level. Instead of approaching appointments with a "one-size-fits-all" sales strategy, he tailored his communication to align with each prospect's unique buying preferences since spouses or partners have different needs to feel at ease during the process.

This shift improved his success rate and helped him streamline the sales process. Joe wasn't just working smarter—he was working more efficiently. He was able to close more sales in less time, boosting his productivity and enabling him to better serve his clients, all while reducing the time spent on each deal. At the same time, he reclaimed valuable hours to spend with his wife and family and pursue the activities he enjoys.

ACTIVITY: "CRACKING THE CODE" GAME

I often recommend the Cracking the Code game as an engaging group activity. It's perfect for family gatherings like game nights or business team-building sessions. It helps participants learn more about each other in a fun and interactive way while fostering deeper understanding and connection.

Instructions:

1. Set Up:
- Have everyone privately determine their own BANKCODE (using physical BANKCARDS or visuals, depending on the group size).

2. Spotlight Turns:
- Choose one person to be the "spotlight" for the round.
- Everyone else takes turns guessing that person's full BANKCODE and explaining their reasoning (e.g., observations about behaviors, preferences, or communication styles).

3. The Reveal:

- After all guesses are shared, the spotlight person reveals their actual BANKCODE.

4. Discussion and Insights:

- Discuss any surprising insights or Aha! moments. Participants often realize nuances about the spotlight person they hadn't noticed before, leading to a greater understanding of why people behave or communicate the way they do.

OUTCOME

This activity is a fun way to build stronger relationships, uncover hidden dynamics, and gain new perspectives on others. It's been fascinating to hear stories of people who were sure they knew someone well, only to discover something new they were able to apply to their relationship moving forward.

Are you ready to unlock the full potential of your relationships, strengthen your teams, and accelerate your business results? Let's connect and make people matter to achieve even greater success.

DALIA HARAMI | KNAB

Dalia Harami is a Certified and Licensed BANK Trainer and Coach, Business Success Strategist, Real Estate Managing Broker, seasoned real estate investor, and veteran network marketing professional with a diverse background spanning multiple industries. With more than thirty years of expertise in financial management, collections, e-commerce and commercial treasury analytics, customer service management, and leading a manufacturing organization, Dalia offers clients strategic guidance for achieving growth and financial stability. Her broad experience equips her to drive operational efficiency, enhance team collaboration, and optimize client communication. Dalia's proficiency in persuasive communication ensures the right message is delivered effectively to each audience, fueling client acquisition, satisfaction, retention, and referrals. Notably, she applied strategic messaging to successfully flip a property, selling it in just seven days at $15,000 above the highest comparable price. Known for her results-oriented approach and strategic insight, Dalia is dedicated to helping clients and business partners build sustainable, thriving businesses while fostering meaningful connections.

Author's Website: ItsPersonality.com

CHAPTER 32
DESERVING SECOND CHANCES
BY SUE MANDEL

"Don't think there are no second chances. Life always offers you a SECOND CHANCE... It's called TOMORROW."

— Nicholas Sparks

I am one who has lived the lowest of the lows, and by God's grace, I climbed out of the gutter to become a contributing member of society. The question becomes: Do *people like me* deserve a second chance? Why would someone, anyone, bother to give *me* a second chance? Why would I even want to go through that process? My life had no structure to it. Becoming responsible, starting all over again, why?

Second chances are reserved for people who've never known the struggle, the uphill battle of every step. So said my keen intellect.

A new chapter in the story of life was unfolding. New chances offer redemption, growth, and renewal. They are a turning point where mistakes and setbacks are not the end of the road. They're only what you can see until you turn the next corner. As I turned that corner, I had to make a choice. Will the rest of my life be more of the same?—More incomprehensible demoralization? Or was I finally desperate enough to look for my second chance?

THE TURMOIL OF YOUTH

At twenty-nine, life was a non-stop party. As a bartender in a bustling Navy town, I thrived on the nightly excitement and the constant attention from sailors. I was having the time of my life—until I wasn't.

Like every other morning, he came walking downstairs. However, unlike any other morning, he was looking at us, his wife and I, sitting at the kitchen table. I could see his eyes as he looked down at his watch; then he looked back at us. Shaking his head with such a glare of disgust and contempt, he turned and began slowly walking back upstairs. We'd been up all night, and for me, I was up all night *again*.

For the first time, I felt a crushing wave of shame and remorse. As I saw my friend's husband's disgusted look, it hit me like never before. His normal life contrasted starkly with my chaotic existence, marked by a haze of drugs and alcohol. In that moment, I saw myself through his eyes—a realization that devastated and awakened me. That look of contempt on his face was palpable and devastating. My best friend's husband saw me for exactly what I was—a drug-addicted alcoholic.

I don't know where the words came from since my brain had never even formed the thought, but the words came tumbling out of my mouth as if a dam had burst. "I have a problem, and I don't know what to do about it." I was horrified.

Looking back over my decades of sobriety, I could easily say those years were effortless, but that would be far from the truth. If I said anything even close to that, it would be one of the biggest whoppers I've ever told, and I've told some doozies.

According to *Forbes*, "the biggest whopper ever told is an idea that people will accept a lie as a fact if it's told long enough and loud enough." Remember when the world was flat? Universal truths, like the world being flat, would be considered a whopper today if told as factual, which science has obviously proven false.

It was the perfect storm, and I was desperate enough, thankfully. Today, I get to do my best to live life one day at a time. At times, it's one hour, or one minute, or one second at a time. Every now and then, it's even one breath at a time. My big audacious goal in life is striving for progress, not perfection.

PEOPLE LIKE ME

Living in Seattle, Washington, I had to learn to walk around the alcoholics in Pioneer Square. They were either passed out or drinking *something* from a brown paper bag. They. Were. Disgusting. They were dirty and smelly, and their clothes looked like rags from my cleaning supplies box. I don't think they had too many teeth left in their mouths. Now, that's what an alcoholic looks like, not me. Little did I know.

Somewhere along the line, as I was growing up, I learned people like me—people struggling with alcoholism and addiction and falling so far down the ladder of respectability—weren't destined for success. The societal expectation was that I would end up nowhere; however, I dared to challenge that limiting belief. *People like me* aren't supposed to live happy, productive, and fulfilling lives. People like me are supposed to die in the streets, and if they are alone when it happens, they aren't found for days. I was terrified. I was terrified that if I went back to drinking, I wouldn't be able to stop again. I wouldn't be able to stop again, and I wouldn't be lucky enough to die next time. I had no doubts I would end up like the alcoholics who didn't die from their disease. I knew I would end up in jails or institutions.

But not me! That's not my story. Mine is one of second chances. By God's grace, I've been able to show up for my loved ones. I've stayed sober through the most difficult times and been there when they needed me most.

For as long as I can remember, my mom was my best friend, and I was her little Susie. I didn't know how rare that was to be an alcoholic woman and have a close relationship with my mom. I was only two years sober when she got *the diagnosis*. People like me don't know how to show up when it's especially tough. And then *people like me* miss saying goodbye to loved ones. It's just too hard to be a responsible grownup.

Mom was so afraid. She was afraid of dying, afraid of leaving us, and afraid of what would happen to my dad. Dad was paralyzed on his entire right side from a stroke fifteen years prior. She was terrified that without her there to help, Dad wouldn't be able to get to his doctor's appointments or do his laundry. How was he going to get groceries or cook meals? Was he going to be okay? What if he got sick? Would he survive and be able to get around without her help?

My mother's greatest gift to me was allowing me to be her trusted confidant. Mom could confide those fears in me, being honest about what she was going through. She couldn't talk like that with Dad; he was already devastated knowing that he was going to lose his life partner after so many decades. A few months after that first confidential conversation with my mom, my best friend passed away.

Eight years later, my dad had been so independent that he bought and wore out *three* electric scooters. He volunteered at the local high school and rode his scooter five miles roundtrip to tutor students in English as a second language, even when it was raining. That round trip took him at least an hour. And I never knew about his volunteering; I learned about this from a newspaper article at the bottom of his nightstand.

I eventually became my father's caregiver. Dad and I would sit together for hours, listening to books on tape. He loved playing blackjack and taught us to count cards when I was very young. During this season of our life together, I would load him up in the car with a packed suitcase hidden in the trunk. Although I'd tell him we were going out to grab a bite to eat, he'd eventually catch on to where we were going. As I hit the road between my house and the casinos, we made many happy memories, and I get to replay them in my mind's eye as often as I choose.

I got my passion for baseball and the San Francisco Giants from Dad, too. We watched the games together all during the season. As we watched the Giants in a playoff game, I held Dad's hand as he let out his final breath. People like me don't show up when it's tough, *but I got to*. You may have guessed by now that family has become most important to me in sobriety.

FOR MORE THAN SIXTY YEARS

My entire life was marked by tension with my brother; we were unable to spend more than two hours together without conflict. Yet, understanding him through the lens of our distinct personalities transformed our relationship. Our conversations are now more about connection than correction. It isn't that I didn't love him for all those years because I did.

He's my brother, so of course I love him. It's just that I didn't like him very much; everything is always a debate, and he's the expert.

My brother is incredibly intelligent, the smartest person I knew growing up, and he was continually correcting me. Trust me when I say he has no problem letting me know just how smart he is. He must have the last word; he was condescending and patronizing. Me? It left me feeling incompetent, incapable, and inadequate.

Every time I opened my mouth, we fought about *something*. I was sure he didn't like me. If he did, he wouldn't have always been picking fights with me. My brother even got into a *huge* fight with my dad one time. He knew all the science, so he insisted that parallel lines will eventually meet in infinity. My brother cannot be wrong, and he blames it on his high intelligence, but his personality won't allow it. He must always be the smartest person in the room. I learned that is in his DNA.

NOTHING HAS MEANING

Nothing has meaning, but the meaning I give it. This has become a universal truth for me. It's such a simple idea, yet it took me a long time to *get it*. I began understanding that all those antagonistic things my brother would say to me, those arguments, and a lifetime of thinking his behavior and actions toward me were all about me were actually all about him. By understanding the power of the system and its tools, I realized he didn't say those things to hurt me on purpose; his behavior was just in his DNA.

When I was learning about a methodology to increase sales exponentially, that's when I learned the power of personalities. Prior to understanding the four personalities, I was left feeling helpless, hopeless, and powerless. What I've learned has been life changing, and it's all about values. My brother's intellect, combined with his personality, influences him so that he *cannot* be wrong. It wouldn't matter who he was talking to. His need to be right is as strong and unconscious as his need for air.

I spent sixty years saying everything I could think of to make him understand me if I could get him to just stop talking and listen for a minute. Life would be so much easier if he would stop correcting me and answering questions I didn't ask.

Then a miracle happened! I stopped. I just stopped. I stopped talking until I was blue in the face. I stopped expecting him to understand *me*. I began understanding *him*, learning what's important and what's not important to him.

We have happier and less contentious conversations every day. I talk to my brother the way *he* wants, directly and to the point. He doesn't like long-winded questions or statements. He just wants data, no chit-chat, so I do my best to be succinct, to the point, and use fewer words than I'm used to using. I do my best to use words that light up *his* neural network. It's like hitting a high score on a video game or the finale of fireworks on the Fourth of July. When he needs the last word or feels the need to correct me, I get it and no longer take it personally. None of these things has anything to do with me. *It's part of his personality and in his DNA. It's not personal; it's personality!*

We decided to have a home built together, and we now live under the same roof. By leveraging the communication tools and techniques, I felt a major shift in my deepest feelings. This could never have happened before. Sadly, just a few short weeks after moving in, my brother fell and broke his ankle. I've been his caregiver and chauffeur for a year. Remember, *people like me* are not supposed to be able to show up when it's tough. The greatest miracle of all is that I *want* to help when he needs me, and he said, "I love you" without prompting. I can probably count the number of times he said I love you, and always after I had said it. Then, a while ago, as he was dropping me off at the airport, and as I was getting out of the car, he said, "Have a safe trip; I love you."

Today, my life is full of miracles, and I am blessed. I've not had a drink in decades; I get to help my brother when he needs me; I've had two extremely successful careers and retired and started a business. *People like me* do deserve second chances.

EXERCISE

1. Who are three people in your life you want a healthier relationship with? It could be a family member, a friend, or a business relationship.

2. What are two values you believe are important to each of those individuals? How can you honor those values?
3. How is your personality different from these people? How is it similar?

THE CHALLENGE

I urge you to shift your perspective: seek first to understand others' unique viewpoints and personalities. By embracing this approach, you can transform your relationships and foster deeper connections. Make this *your* big audacious goal; make the people in your world matter. Let them know how important they are, and do it in ways that are important to them. Light up their neural networks like the Fourth of July. Hint: you can do this by learning what's important to them and why.

THINGS TO REMEMBER

Communication is about the message. It's about the message you wish to transmit and the message that's received. You want those messages to be identical, but too often they're not. That's because everyone has their own unique life experiences and backgrounds. Those experiences are our filters. Because of these filters, we hear the same words and messages differently. Also known as miscommunication.

For as long as I can remember, I've been taught to speak to others the way I want to be spoken to, to treat them how I want to be treated. The Golden Rule works if the person across from you is just like you. Your personalities are a match. *The Platinum Rule*, now that's different. The Platinum Rule allows you to treat people the way *they* want to be treated and to speak the way *they* want to be spoken to.

EVERYTHING IN LIFE IS A CHOICE

How long will you let your relationships suffer because you're speaking different languages? Great relationships are built on great communication.

Everything in life is about *choice*. The decisions we make or don't make, the actions we take or don't take are all choices. If you decide not to make any changes, nothing will change. *You* get to choose how you want to communicate with the people in your world: your loved ones, friends, co-workers, employees, and employers. Unless you are in a cave alone in the world, you must communicate, so why not learn to do it effectively?

I invite you to join me in exploring how to deepen relationships that are important to you and even salvage some you have given up on. How can better communication ever be anything but a good thing? Better connection makes happier lives, happier relationships, and happier tomorrows.

Learning about the four primary personalities of the world and understanding why someone makes the decisions they make has changed everything for me. I have a friendship with my brother that wasn't possible before. Taking this unparalleled communication tool into K-12 schools means no child will have to wonder if they matter. I wanted to make more money and have an impact. What I got was so much greater. People like me don't get to have such heartfelt memories. But I do.

SUE MANDELL | KBNA

As an international best-selling author and a woman who has shared stages with Martha Stewart, Suzanne Somers, and Les Brown, Sue Mandell is one you want to show you a simple step-by-step system to becoming an ACE Speaker. She'll teach you how to grab your audience's attention and have fun while you're speaking.

As an award-winning speaker, Sue has spoken at Carnegie Hall, The Harvard Club of Boston, and The NY Bar Association. She has been honored as the Woman of the Year by a national non-profit and has been interviewed by all major news networks: *ABC*, *CBS*, *NBC*, and radio stations across the country.

Sue has her master's in business, is a Licensed Personality Communications Expert, and an NLP Master Practitioner. She's been assisting others to permanently change undesired behaviors and overcome limiting beliefs and addictive behaviors for more than four decades.

Author's Website: SueMandellInc.com

CHAPTER 33
UNLEASHING THE POWER OF BANK IN EDUCATION

BY TAMMY QUIST

> "Education is the most powerful weapon which you can use to change the world."
>
> — Nelson Mandela

Parents, how many of you have struggled to communicate with a teacher or a principal, feeling as though they just didn't understand you or your child?

Teachers, have you ever felt like you were speaking a different language with students, parents, colleagues, or your principal, even though you were using their exact words?

Principals, do you spend a good deal of time putting out fires and dealing with resistance to change?

How many times have you wished for a magic key to unlock the potential in your relationships and communicate effectively to have a positive impact in your interactions, especially in the challenging landscape of education?

Join me on a journey to discover that key—and the power of BANK. BANK is an acronym for a groundbreaking personality assessment tool based on four distinct personality codes: Blueprint (B), Action (A), Nurturing (N), and Knowledge (K). Each of us possesses all four codes, each in varying orders and levels. To be truly effective in the world of education, we must discover these unique patterns of communication and develop effective ways to listen and respond. This process is crucial for creating influence and impact in all relationships, especially within the realm of education.

MY JOURNEY

In addition to being an educator, I am a parent of three wonderful and very different children who have their own unique communication styles. My oldest, the perfectionist (KNAB), thrived on learning but resisted rules and direction. My middle child (BNKA) needed a clear roadmap—and any deviation from the "plan" often led to a meltdown. And my youngest son (AKNB) was a whirlwind of energy, constantly in action, seeking fun and opportunities to win.

Navigating the needs of three distinct codes made parenting both fascinating and challenging. My number-one goal? To help them communicate, work together, and get along!

Just like adults, children don't show their personalities and communication styles only when at home. At school, I witnessed how my kids connected (or didn't) with their teachers and peers and how that affected their love for learning and academic performance. The toughest moments for them were often rooted in conflicts with friends—days when they felt bullied, excluded, or not good enough.

I chose to be a teacher, principal, educational leadership consultant, and coach, and I have dedicated my life to empowering and impacting my own children, as well as my students, teachers, and educational leaders I have the opportunity to work with. While up for the challenge and totally committed, I was often frustrated by the lack of effective communication.... I often felt like we were aliens from different planets all trying desperately to get along. Change is hard, and implementing necessary changes in classrooms and schools is no exception. I frequently found myself spinning my wheels, disempowered and unable to connect and make a real difference that would bring about meaningful change.

Then, I discovered a new technology and methodology called BANK. It wasn't just another personality typing system; it was a roadmap to understanding human behavior and motivation on a deeper level. My own code, KNAB, illuminated why I approached challenges and interactions the way I did—why I often had to "figure things out" and "make sense" of it all. My code explained why I resonated and easily connected with some yet struggled with others.

Armed with this newfound knowledge, I developed the ability to see the world through a fresh lens. I began to share this new technology with the educational leaders and clients I serve, to arm them with a powerful tool that would significantly impact every aspect of their communication and their performance in the classroom. I was convinced that knowing people was key to improving and implementing best practices in schools and classrooms. The results have been extraordinary.

We all share a common desire to connect, inspire, and make a meaningful impact. Most of us have either attended school or have children who are or have been students. We all have a personal stake in ensuring our children receive the best education possible in a safe, nurturing environment that challenges and inspires them to become their best selves. BANK transformed my approach and revolutionized my results in education, and quite honestly, it's a game-changer for both me personally and my clients.

ILLUMINATING THE PATH FOR STUDENTS

As a teacher and principal for more than twenty years, I have witnessed firsthand the issues and outcomes stemming from a lack of understanding of who our students really are. In the bustling halls and classrooms, students grapple with academic challenges and social dynamics, often feeling misunderstood and disconnected from their peers and teachers. Each student brings unique strengths and struggles, but without a common language to bridge the gap, opportunities for growth and collaboration remain untapped.

Isolation continues to plague our students, many of whom turn to social media or other distractions to fill the void. The alarming rise in teen suicide, anxiety, and depression highlights the urgency of addressing these issues. Parents often feel unprepared to navigate these challenges alongside their children. It's pointless to ask, "How did we get here?" The question should be, "What we can do about it?"

With this new and powerful discovery, I began collaborating with educators in my work as a consultant and school board member who was willing to embark on a mission to crack the personality codes of students to better understand and empower them. Each student discovers their unique personality code and how to best interact and work with students with other personality codes. They discover powerful triggers and tripwires unique to each personality. We saw an immediate impact on how students collaborate, navigate the hallways, and connect during lunch. They engage with one another and respect the differences in their fellow students, realizing it's not personal—it's just personality.

Teachers find it easier to influence and engage students. Reports from educators indicate a significant decrease in behavioral disruptions in classrooms since implementing the BANK methodology, and students are engaging in discussions with fewer interruptions, resulting in a more productive learning environment.

Recently, I conducted an end-of-year assessment at a middle school. I entered a bustling seventh-grade classroom buzzing with energy and excitement. Students were grouped in small teams of four, each representing different BANKCODES. Leaning forward with their heads together, they were engaged and animatedly discussing a challenging problem related to a novel they were reading. Each student's BANKCODE was prominently displayed on their desk, giving insight and guiding their interactions. The teacher moved among them, offering tailored feedback and encouragement, maximizing each student's learning potential.

In one corner, a Blueprint student meticulously organized her notes, excelling as the team's scribe and keeping her peers focused on the learning target. Next to her, an Action-oriented student animatedly discussed the author's point of view, proposing creative solutions to the problem at hand. A third student, whose primary code was Knowledge, took on the role of learning monitor, ensuring the team tracked their progress using success criteria. The fourth student, high in Nurturing, facilitated the group discussion, ensuring every voice was heard and valued.

As the lesson unfolded, it became clear that BANK was more than just a tool; it was a philosophy that empowered both students and teachers to embrace their individuality and collaborate toward a common goal. I observed every student engaged in the learning process. Just two years ago, these same students were seated in rigid rows, silent and disengaged. The teacher acted as the sole provider of knowledge, while students passively received instruction.

Today, the classroom experience is transformed. Students express their love for learning, feel valued and included, and are excited to come to class. It's no surprise their standardized test scores have risen significantly over the past year.

A delightful bonus has emerged: Students are now having conversations about cracking the codes of their parents or siblings. One eighth-grade boy shared, "I thought I was a freak. My parents always wanted to be on the go, to entertain, to travel. They hassled me because I just wanted to stay home and read or do my homework. I hated being around people all the time. Now I know I'm not a freak—I'm just a Knowledge living in an Action household. When I shared this with my parents, they started respecting my code more. Now, our vacations include things like museums, and I can read or take a break when I need to. Things are a lot better at home."

Imagine a school where students interact with one another respectfully, honoring each other's personalities and communication styles.

- How would this affect bullying and issues of self-confidence?
- How would the relationships between teachers and students change, and how might that impact student achievement?
- How might these skills transfer to life outside of school, in the family, workplace, community, and the wider world?

EMPOWERING EDUCATORS

Teaching is hard; just ask any teacher. Try being a substitute teacher for a day, and you'll quickly see what I mean. Before I learned about BANK, I often found myself overwhelmed by the enormity of the job, the scarcity of resources, and the relentless expectations to meet the needs of every student. All of this was in addition to building strong relationships with colleagues and going above and beyond to impress my principal enough to keep my job. Honestly, there were moments when I considered walking away from teaching. In the early days, I worked eighty hours a week for a mere $19,800 in Southern California, and I'm fairly certain I cried every day during my first three months. It felt like being thrown into the middle of a very deep lake. Teaching is not for the faint of heart!

Fortunately, I had a passion and deep love for children, a fantastic principal, and a growth mindset. I was eager to learn, soaking up every opportunity to become a great teacher and school leader. By my third year, I was selected as a mentor teacher, and by my sixth year, I received the Teacher of the Year award for my school district. While I was proud of my efforts and accomplishments, something was missing. I struggled to persuade many of my colleagues to evolve and try new ideas and strategies. They seemed disinterested in implementing practices that would benefit both students and them. I felt disheartened, ineffective as a mentor teacher, and unable to communicate my vision or enact positive change.

The teachers I worked with often experienced burnout and disengagement, feeling overwhelmed by the demands of the profession. Many felt isolated and unheard, longing for a sense of connection and belonging. This struggle persisted throughout my career in education. As a principal and then as a consultant, I often hit a wall of resistance with some of the teachers and was simply ineffective in implementing new ideas and methods.

I was certain that something was missing...and I would not stop until I found the missing link!

That missing link was BANK. Once I discovered it, I was done with the daily struggle of feeling misunderstood and undervalued. I had a powerful tool that would change everything, give me a new sense of hope, and open the door of possibility. Through BANK, I found my voice and purpose, transforming my experiences into a message of empowerment and understanding. I learned to speak all the codes, empower people, and listen to what they valued, fostering deeper connections and achieving unprecedented levels of collaboration and success.

Now, as I work alongside teachers armed with the insights of BANK, I guide educators on a journey to crack the codes of their colleagues, fostering a culture of collaboration and innovation within the school community. By recognizing and honoring each teacher's unique BANKCODE, administrators tailor their approach to supervision, evaluation, and partnership, transforming once-contentious relationships into collaborative partnerships. Originally designed to influence buying behavior, BANK also influences "buy-in" behavior among educators.

My skills as a consultant using the BANK methodology have made a tremendous positive difference when school leadership teams collaborate to effect change. Things are still not perfect, much to the dismay of my Knowledge personality. However, I am witnessing the extraordinary transformation that occurs when we communicate with one another in ways that resonate with each individual's style.

Picture this: a staff room buzzing with tension as teachers gather for a professional development session. In the past, these meetings resembled battlegrounds, with opposing ideologies clashing. But today is different. Armed with the insights of BANK, administrators enter the room with confidence, equipped not with weapons but with understanding.

As the meeting progresses, subtle body language and tone shifts reveal the underlying codes at play. The Blueprint-driven administrator nods approvingly at the meticulously prepared agenda while the Action-oriented teacher perks up at the mention of exciting new initiatives. By the end of the meeting, a palpable sense of camaraderie fills the room as disparate personalities find common ground in pursuit of a shared vision.

Imagine a school where every staff member understands the codes of their colleagues.

- How might this impact the staff's ability to work together to improve instruction and meet the school's goals?
- Which teacher would you like to share this with, and why?

GUIDING PRINCIPLES

Leadership is defined by vision, action, and influence. Great principals have a clearly articulated vision of what is possible, how to engage in substantial action to turn dreams into reality, and how to inspire others to join the team. Unfortunately, when principals lack communication skills or emotional intelligence, they struggle to gain buy-in for their ideas or the changes needed to implement their vision.

As a principal, I never quite understood why a portion of my staff resisted engaging in initiatives we had collectively agreed upon, even when research indicated those changes were best for students. What was I missing?

I later learned the missing piece was my own lack of skill in conveying the message effectively and speaking to them in a way that landed for them. Assuming my first code (Knowledge), I thought that presenting research, data, and case studies from other schools would be enough to get my staff to embrace innovative ideas. I was wrong. Many did not care about the data. I came to understand that their codes differed from mine, and I needed to communicate with them in *their* code, not my own.

If Nurturing is their first code, I realized I must connect with them first, building rapport and approaching change from a people-centered perspective. Nurturers don't care how much you know until they know how much you care. Blueprints crave clear, step-by-step guidance for implementing change. Action-oriented individuals are open to risk and change but often struggle with lengthy emails or prescriptive protocols. As a consultant who now employs BANK-CODE with all my clients, I begin by helping them crack their code so I know how best to communicate. This approach has proven invaluable, leading to positive relationships and outcomes among leaders, teachers, and students.

YOUR TURN

- Describe a time when you felt disconnected from those around you. How did it make you feel? What insights can you glean from that experience? How might knowing the BANKCODE of others have altered that experience?
- Which educator would you like to share this with, and why?
- Contact them and encourage them to crack their code.

PARTNERING WITH PARENTS

I began this chapter discussing how parents navigate the BANKCODE of their children, both at home and at school. Parents are children's first teachers. Understanding each child's BANKCODE enables parents to support their development—intellectually, emotionally, and socially. As primary advocates, parents can communicate their child's code to teachers, ensuring that early school experiences are positive and set the stage for a lifelong love of learning.

Furthermore, when parents recognize and understand their own codes, they gain insight into their relationships with their children. It's often said that there's no greater love than that of a parent, yet no one can push your buttons quite like your child can! While we may love them all, it's not unusual for a parent to feel a stronger connection to one child due to a shared code. Conversely, some children can be particularly challenging to connect with. Understanding that our code may differ from our child's allows us to adapt our communication styles to reach them more effectively. Helping parents understand their codes, as well as those of other family members, fosters healthier and happier family dynamics.

Whether at school or at home, parents can use BANKCODE technology to enhance their understanding of and collaboration with their child's teacher, principal, and other school personnel. Pro tip: This works with in-laws, too!

CONCLUSION: THE POWER OF CONNECTION

As educators, we hold the noble responsibility of shaping the minds and hearts of the next generation. Whether you are a parent, teacher, principal, or community member, you play a vital role in nurturing the development of tomorrow's leaders. In life, as in education, relationships are the cornerstone of success. By embracing the principles of BANK, we can unlock the potential within ourselves and others, fostering an environment of collaboration, growth, and mutual respect.

I challenge you: Embrace the power of BANK in your life and work. Seek to understand before seeking to be understood. Approach every communication with the Platinum

Rule in mind, and watch as your relationships flourish and your impact grows beyond measure.

TAMMY QUIST | KNAB

Tammy Quist is not just a consultant; she is a catalyst for transformation. With over three decades of experience in education, leadership, and team development, Tammy has woven a rich tapestry of impact across diverse settings—from rural classrooms to bustling urban schools. As a teacher, mentor, principal, consultant, business owner, community leader, and school board member, she has cultivated a multifaceted understanding of the challenges and triumphs faced by leaders and teams in both for-profit and non-profit environments. Described by peers as a change agent and leadership gladiator, Tammy is fiercely dedicated to advocating for the underserved, particularly women and children.

As the founder of a transformative Leadership Academy, Tammy helps leaders and teams to set audacious goals and develop cohesive, high-performing groups that propel their missions forward. Her innovative approach to executive and team coaching, coupled with her expertise in professional development and organizational enhancement, equips clients with the tools and strategies necessary to create meaningful experiences and deliver exceptional value.

Author's Website: Change-Agent-Inc.com

"When you see an opportunity to change the world—get up and get the job done!"

— Robin Sharma

SECTION 3: THE MOVEMENT

In the previous section, my coauthors shared their incredible and powerful Make People Matter moments with you. I hope you are as deeply touched and inspired as I am to take the pledge and join our Make People Matter movement. I truly believe your best life is ahead of you if you do!

Robin Sharma, world-renowned author, leadership expert, and personal mentor said it best in his quote "When you see an opportunity to change the world—get up and get the job done!"

To me, this advice was not simply a suggestion or recommendation—it was a direct command. Not only that—it was a divine calling for me. I wasn't necessarily qualified for the job—but I was compelled in my heart and soul to share this life-changing methodology with the world—and, thus, our movement was born.

How to Start a Movement

I'll be honest, I never intended to start a movement. It's not really something you can try to start; it happens despite you—if you have the perfect scenario at play.

Movement building is organizing and motivating people to work toward a collective vision or cause that is important for a community.

According to Codebreaker AI, here's the formula to start a movement:

> To start a movement, you need to first identify a compelling cause, clearly define your message, build a strong foundation with like-minded individuals, effectively communicate your message through various channels, mobilize grassroots support, and consistently take action to gain momentum and achieve your goals, while adapting to changing circumstances and fostering a sense of community among your followers.

The Genesis of Our Movement

Once I realized that BANK worked for me, I immediately started sharing it with people I knew to help them succeed in both business and life. It worked! BANK was helping people understand other people in a way they had never understood them before, and the word kept spreading—to the point that I decided I would build it into a product and create a portfolio of tools, training programs, and technologies that could help our Codebreakers crack the code of the people in their world and connect in more meaningful ways.

BANK was not only transforming their relationships through the ideology of Make People Matter—it was positively impacting their bank accounts by helping them in business. Our Codebreakers were sharing their success stories from all over the world and from nearly every industry imaginable. BANK was truly making a difference—and at that point, I could no longer keep it a little secret.

Within the first year of sharing BANK in the marketplace and speaking at some of the top business conferences in the world, my phone and email blew up over and over with the same requests:

"When is your next Codebreaker Summit? I have people on my team I want to send!"

"Do you have an affiliate program because everyone I know wants to use the BANK system too, now that they see my results!"

"Do you have a certification program because I would like to teach BANK workshops in my area."

"Do you have a coaching program because I would like to mentor others with your methodology."

This huge response gave me an idea—what if I could take the gift of BANK and pay it forward in a way that could not only help people succeed and "self-actualize," but "self-transcend," and, thereby, improve the lives of others!

For years, I had followed Robert Kiyosaki's *Rich Dad Poor Dad* philosophy and *Cashflow Quadrant* business model. I was inspired to build a similar business model that would allow our Codebreakers to leverage our BANK system to increase their income and influence on the world by engaging and spreading our Make People Matter message.

CHAPTER 34

THE CODE BREAKER

"A code breaker is not just someone who cracks codes, but someone who unravels the hidden language of the universe, revealing secrets where others see only noise."

— KAI [Codebreaker AI]

During World War II, the Germans used Enigma, a complex encryption machine, to develop nearly unbreakable codes for sending secret messages. Enigma's settings offered 150,000,000,000,000,000,000 (150 quintillion) possible solutions, making it nearly impossible to crack.

Legendary cryptanalyst Alan Turing, the English mathematical genius, and his brilliant team of code breakers at Britain's top-secret Government Code and Cypher School at Bletchley Park, successfully cracked the code of Enigma in a nail-biting race against time, during the darkest days of World War II.

Some historians believe the cracking of Enigma was the Allied powers' single most important victory, shortening the war by several years.

Behind every code is an enigma—but the true enigma was the man who cracked the code.

YOUR MODERN-DAY ENIGMA

People are complicated, so understanding them can definitely be an enigma! The definition of an enigma is "a person or thing that is mysterious, puzzling, or difficult to understand."

More than 8 billion people are in the world, but luckily, you don't have to be a genius mathematician or cryptologist to crack their codes.

Were you ever considered the "black sheep" in your family—or possibly harassed or ridiculed for being different, marching to the beat of your own drum, or swimming upstream? Or perhaps you have even felt you were born into the wrong family?

Have you ever found people to be confusing or complicated? Perhaps your boss at work, a colleague, or a team member? Or perhaps your children, your spouse, or especially an ex-spouse?

Have you ever experienced the challenges or possibly the ending of a relationship, a career, a sale, or a partnership because of miscommunication?

Have you ever wondered if a secret hack existed to understanding people better and knowing exactly how to influence them, inspire them, and lead them?

Have you started to imagine how much more successful and happier you could become if you could just understand people in a way that unlocked infinite possibilities for the relationship?

Have you considered how much money you could earn and wealth you could accumulate if you could simply crack the code of your clients and build unlimited streams of income?

Can you begin to imagine the degree of influence you could have if you could simply master your ability to make people matter?

What if I told you that you are one decision away from having access to a superpower—one that allowed you to crack the code of every single person you met, unlocking access to immeasurable wealth, abundance, happiness, peace, and prosperity?

The decision is very simple—decide to become a Codebreaker today and join our Make People Matter movement!

HOW YOU CAN MAKE PEOPLE MATTER

When you become a Codebreaker, you are on the path to proactively making people matter. From the bedroom and family room to the boardroom or classroom, you can start today to make people matter!

AT HOME

Start by cracking the code of everyone in your family. Determine the code of your spouse, your children, your parents, your siblings, and so forth. Notice what is important to them, and start to proactively communicate with them according to their code. As you do this, you will notice small (and sometimes dramatic) improvements and meaningful shifts in your relationships.

I'm reminded here of a man named Robert who became a Codebreaker. Robert was married to a beautiful woman with whom he had three children. Robert's primary BANKCODE was Action, and it was the same for his wife and two oldest children. His youngest son, however, was a Blueprint.

One day, Robert's youngest son, who was six years old, came to his father and said, "Dad, why are you a liar?" Robert was stunned by the question and couldn't imagine why his son was calling him a liar, so he asked his son to explain. The young boy explained to his dad that every time his father said what time the family was leaving the house to go to their various activities, they never left at that designated time, and therefore, his dad was a liar!

This comment deeply hurt Robert, but it made him realize he wasn't parenting his son based on his Blueprint code; instead, he was forcing his son to accommodate to his dad's Action code.

Robert immediately shifted his mindset and became intentional with parenting his son based on his Blueprint code. For example, he made sure his son completed his projects for school long before any deadlines came due, and he had his son's soccer clothes washed, ready, and organized several days before his next game.

Robert's son started to feel that he mattered to his dad. He felt heard, seen, and understood. After six months of this intentional way of living out the Blueprint code, Robert's son leapt into his dad's arms for the first time on his own initiative, and said, "Daddy, I love you!"

This moment changed Robert's life! BANK was no longer a thing he did in his business—it was a way of conducting himself in every area of his life.

AT WORK

Start by cracking the code of everyone you work with. Whether it's your boss, colleagues, or team members—or even your customers, vendors, or partners, each one of them has a code, and that code is key to knowing how to access the best in them.

Imagine building a culture at your company or in your organization where you knew the BANKCODE of everyone in your ecosystem. You could optimize your business by making sure each person was in the right position so you could harness the power of their authentic code.

For example, maybe Tom is a Blueprint and would be an amazing project manager, keeping the projects on time and the spending within budget. Perhaps Michelle is an Action and would be a superstar on the sales team, dealing with bigger clients and negotiating profitable deals. Likewise, Mamie is a Nurturing and she would be amazing at organizing community events and leading the company's fundraising initiatives. And Paul is a Knowledge with incredible marketing genius that he uses to drive online traffic and lead generation based on important data analytics.

Having all four codes on the team creates a winning formula—as long as you respect each other's unique code and interact using emotional intelligence. Creating a Make People Matter culture will likely give you the competitive edge in your business and create a work environment that is happy, healthy, productive—and profitable!

AT SCHOOL

Start by cracking the codes of the teachers and faculty, the students and parents, and even the administration. Schools have been so focused on making grades matter that they have forgotten to make the students matter.

Dozens and dozens of stories have come to us at Codebreaker about how BANK is so needed in the classroom. We have stories of both tragedy and triumph—and the timing couldn't be more important than now to positively impact the next generation.

One of the early success stories of BANK being used in the classroom happened in Europe. One of our Certified and Licensed BANK Trainers was an elementary school teacher. The first thing she did after attending our courses was crack the code of every student in her classroom—and their parents.

Once she understood each of her students' codes, she began to teach them differently—she even assigned homework differently based on their unique codes. She understood why her Blueprint students always seemed to do every assignment as requested. She also understood why her Action students were louder and always goofing around. Perhaps they didn't have ADD—maybe, instead, they were just bored in the class and would rather be out on the playground!

Now it made sense why her Nurturing students were more kind and welcoming to new kids in the classroom—or why her Knowledge students were asking lots of questions or focused on studying for the upcoming test.

Wow! In that moment, she realized she could no longer take a one-size-fits-all approach to education. Each student had their own unique code—and she could get the best from them when she made them matter by interacting with them based on their codes.

This epiphany became a game-changer in the classroom—and yet this is just the beginning of bringing BANK into education. BANK has since been applied in several K-12 schools and even a handful of universities that have piloted our programs and experienced incredible results—and yet we are far from getting BANK adopted into mainstream education.

Imagine how we could build better humans by teaching them about the BANKCODE early in life and giving them a framework not only to understand themselves, but the people around them. Think of how this could not only improve the results in the classroom but could also reduce bullying and even teenage suicide, which has become a massive tragedy across our country!

YOU MATTER

What I want you to know, my dear reader, is that *you* matter! Whether you've been the most popular person in your circles, or you have felt completely misunderstood in life and isolated from people, *you* matter.

God made you perfectly you—and he gave you the gift of your own unique code, allowing you access to infinite potential in your life. Think about it. He gave you a dose of Blueprint so you could get yourself organized, stabilized, and have a plan for your life. He gave you a dose of Action so you could get yourself motivated, compensated, and exhilarated about life. He gave you a dose of Nurturing so you would be more kind, loving, and accepting of others. He gave you a dose of Knowledge so you would be smart, capable of critical thinking, and full of imagination. You are all four codes, and no matter what your code—*you* are perfectly imperfect—and *you* matter.

It doesn't matter if you're black or white, male or female, gay or straight, religious or atheist, Democrat or Republican, rich or poor—or anything in between—*you* matter.

People matter.

It's time for us to collectively stand up and put the human back in humanity. Together, we are strong. Together, we are family. Together, we call ourselves—the Codebreakers!

CHAPTER 35

JOIN THE MOVEMENT

"It's in your moments of decision that your destiny is shaped."

— Tony Robbins

Are you ready to live your best life ever—the one Maslow talked about where you are not only able to self-actualize—but self-transcend? Is it possible for this idea of BANK to give you the best of both worlds—where you are ultra-successful and happy too?

Tony Robbins has shared the secret formula to a successful life: "The two master skills of life are the Science of Achievement and the Art of Fulfillment."

Robbins further explained, "To live a truly rich life, you need more than just achievement. The science of achievement and success is only half the story. Fulfillment is the key to unlocking lasting joy and a meaningful life."

The Science of Achievement is all about making money, creating success, building wealth, and experiencing financial prosperity. Achievement is an important goal worth pursuing. However—it's not the only thing that matters.

Unfortunately, too many business owners and entrepreneurs get caught in the trap of hustle and grind, and solely focus on chasing the goal of winning in business and making money—at the expense of losing their health, relationships, and happiness.

This book has been filled with meaningful Make People Matter moments that showed you how Codebreakers are successfully blending the Science of Achievement and the Art of Fulfillment in ways that empower them to live their best lives ever.

Now it's your turn! When you embrace the Make People Matter mindset—you truly can have your cake and eat it too!

START NOW

If you are inspired by our Make People Matter message and you're ready to help us share this message with the world and make 8 billion people matter—then I invite you to become a Codebreaker and join our movement!

The first step to becoming a Codebreaker begins with implementing the BANK system into your daily life. You can gain numerous benefits by using BANK at home and at work. Many of our Codebreakers apply BANK in five key areas of their lives: communication, business, relationships, emotional intelligence, and leadership.

Improving communication skills and increasing your emotional intelligence can lead to better relationships, career success, and increased productivity.

These statistics underscore the significant role BANK plays in various facets of life:

1. **Relationship Quality:** Couples with higher levels of emotional intelligence experience greater satisfaction and reduced conflict in their relationships, contributing to stronger, more resilient partnerships (*Journal of Personality and Social Psychology*).
2. **Relationship Success:** Good communication is pivotal in maintaining healthy relationships. According to a study by the American Psychological Association, 65 percent of divorces are attributed to communication problems.
3. **Workplace Productivity:** Miscommunication costs companies an average of $62.4 million per year in productivity (Society for Human Resource Management, 2014). Clear communication is essential for efficient work processes and minimizing costly errors.

4. **Workplace Performance:** Emotional intelligence accounts for 58 percent of performance in all types of jobs, making it one of the strongest predictors of workplace success (TalentSmart, "Emotional Intelligence in the Workplace").

5. **Employee Engagement:** Organizations with effective communication strategies are 4.5 times more likely to have highly engaged employees (Towers Watson, 2012). Engaged employees are more productive and committed to their company.

6. **Career Advancement:** A survey found that 73 percent of employers look for candidates with strong written and verbal communication skills, more than any other quality (National Association of Colleges and Employers, 2016). Effective communicators are often preferred for leadership roles and promotions.

7. **Sales Success:** In the realm of sales, effective communication skills can increase success rates by as much as 40 percent (Sales Benchmark Index, 2015). Understanding customer needs and clearly conveying value are key to closing deals.

8. **Leadership Effectiveness:** Eighty-six percent of employees and executives cite lack of collaboration or ineffective communication as the reason for workplace failures (Salesforce—"State of the Connected Customer").

9. **Leadership Success:** Ninety percent of top performers are also high in emotional intelligence, suggesting that leaders with high EI are more effective in driving organizational success (TalentSmart, "Emotional Intelligence: Why It Can Matter More Than IQ").

10. **Training Return on Investment:** Companies investing in communication training report a 25 percent increase in productivity across their workforce (UK Institute of Business Value—"The Value of Training").

Whether you're planning to use BANK individually or collectively in your organization or company, we have the solutions and have developed the tools, training, and technology to help you optimize your performance and maximize your results.

SPREAD THE MOVEMENT

If you are like most of our Codebreakers who caught the "BANK bug" and have experience an increase in influence and income, we'd love your help to spread the word and pay it forward.

Here's a few ways you can help:

- Crack the code of everyone you know
- Recommend our books and programs
- Host us on your podcast
- Promote an upcoming event
- Invite us to speak at your conference
- Join our affiliate program
- Get certified and teach others
- Become a coach and mentor others
- Engage us to consult with your company

- Tag us on social media
- Share your stories with our community
- Recommend us to a friend or colleague
- Support our nonprofit initiatives
- Introduce us to your local schools
- Write about us in your blog or newsletter

"I always thought that I would spend the first half of my life making money so I can spend the second half of my life giving it all away. And one of the defining moments of my life was when I realized that I could do both at the same time with Toms."

— Blake Mycoskie, Founder of TOMS Shoes

SECTION 4: THE MATCH

Our story would not be complete without talking about how we created our own impact initiative at Codebreaker to make people matter.

As founders of Codebreaker, Esther and I wanted to give back in a meaningful way, but we weren't sure how. We had donated time and money to many charities over the years, and we did things like volunteer at the local food bank to feed the homeless or fund surgeries for burn victims and children with cleft palates. Each act of service touched our hearts, but it didn't connect us to our mission or purpose.

We were inspired by all the incredible stories about how BANK was making a difference in people's lives—from saving marriages to saving lives. We wanted to find a way we could blend being profit-driven with being purpose-driven.

And then it hit us! We were watching an episode of *Shark Tank* with the founders of Bombas. They talked about their Buy One Give One program—every time a customer buys a pair of socks, Bombas donates a pair to a homeless person or other people in need.

Boom! I had seen a similar idea with TOMS Shoes—where every time you bought a pair of shoes, TOMS donated a pair to kids who didn't have shoes. OMG—this was incredible!

Then we found Warby Parker, which had the same philosophy—buy a pair of glasses and they donate a pair of glasses. Brilliant!

This philosophy was the exact inspiration we needed to build our own impact initiative—and so our Codebreaker Foundation was started.

CHAPTER 36

MAKE KIDS MATTER®

"When you educate one person you can change a life. When you educate many—you can change the world."

— Nelson Mandela

EACH ONE TEACH ONE

Nelson Mandela was remarkable is so many ways. While he was imprisoned on Robben Island, he demonstrated his deep love for his people and truly exemplified the Make People Matter philosophy with his fellow inmates.

Most of the prisoners were illiterate. Nelson knew freedom would come faster if he helped his group of men become educated—so he advocated for the idea that if a prisoner knew how to read and write, that prisoner would pay it forward by helping his fellow inmates learn how to do the same. There on Robben Island, the Each One Teach One philosophy was born.

MAKE KIDS MATTER INITIATIVE

In January 2024, we launched our Codebreaker Foundation and announced our Make Kids Matter initiative at our annual ICONIC conference with all our Codebreakers.

Following in the footsteps of Nelson Mandela, and later TOMS, Bombas, and Warby Parker, we announced our Make People Matter matching program:

**EMPOWER YOURSELF—IMPACT A CHILD.
EVERY PURCHASE GIVES BACK.**

For every subscription, training course, or certification program sold, Codebreaker Foundation committed to donating the equivalent to a qualifying school or nonprofit organization.

Although we had no idea how to get started, we knew time was of the essence, and we could no longer wait to share this message around the world!

OUR FIRST HUMANITARIAN EXPEDITION

In honor of our inspiration, Nelson Mandela, a group of fourteen Codebreakers, myself included, packed our bags and headed to South Africa. We visited three schools—a primary school, a secondary school, and a high school.

Each group was filled with kids from the local townships—many of them coming from broken homes and some with no family at all. Despite their challenging economic situations, the students were filled with happiness and eager anticipation to learn the BANK system.

My heart swelled with pride and my eyes filled with tears as I watched these beautiful children and teenagers learning about BANK. We taught them about the Blueprints and why they're sticklers for following the rules. We taught them about the Actions and why they're always breaking the rules! We taught them about the Nurturers and why kindness is so important to them. And we taught them about the Knowledges and how valuable it is to be smart and a great learner.

We broke them into groups and did some experiential learning. We talked about how the different codes showed up in the classroom with their friends and teachers—and in the home with their parents and siblings. We watched them connect the dots as they were able to associate the people in their lives and the codes they had—and we witnessed their confidence increasing as they felt empowered with this new set of awareness and skills.

The local teachers and administration were over-the-moon excited and wanted to know more about how they could adopt and implement the BANK training into their schooling programs—sharing with us their hearts' desire to help these young students have promising futures.

We left each school feeling joy and happiness beyond words. Could this little four-letter word called BANK truly change the lives of people all around the world? Yes—there was no doubt about it!

YOUR MONEY MATTERS

Whether you simply purchase one of our books, subscribe to our technology, attend a training course, or even get certified with us, I want you to know your money matters!

When you invest into empowering yourself with our BANK programs, *you* are changing the life of a child in need—and that absolutely matters!

Sometimes, it's hard to imagine the ripple effect of the seemingly insignificant decision to become a Codebreaker. But let's try to imagine it for just a moment....

What if your purchase of a subscription to crack codes could help you not only understand your clients and relationships better, but it could help a school understand their students better?

And what if this school was able to crack the code of a little third-grader, who now understands why their parents are fighting and that it's not their fault. Or why their mom is being mean—when she's just a Blueprint trying to maintain order. Or why their dad seems so distant—when he's just a Knowledge and doesn't know how to connect emotionally.

And what if that leads to the child not turning to drugs, or gangs—or suicide at some point? Instead, this child makes a greater commitment to understanding people, learning about their codes, sharing it with friends and family members, and becoming an emotionally intelligent future leader in society.

Yes, my friend, the ripple effect is real, and you may never know the lives you will indirectly and positively affect as a result of your decision to make people matter. All I can say is, "Thank You!"

A FINAL NOTE

MAKE PEOPLE MATTER

"The Universe only rewards one thing—and one thing only—those who take action."

— Unknown

BUILD YOUR MAKE PEOPLE MATTER MAP

Congratulations on finishing Make People Matter. This book wasn't written just to share a few stories. It was written by a collective group of Codebreakers who truly believe in the Make People Matter mission—and now you can too!

MAP stands for Massive Action Plan. There are people in your life right now who are important to you—and I want to empower you to optimize each relationship with the power of BANK.

So, now it's time to put pen to paper and create your Make People Matter MAP. Who are the ten people you want to build a stronger relationship with—and what is one thing you can do to make them matter?

For example, my son Kai is Nurturing first, and he loves to spend quality time with me where I give him my full undivided attention (no phone or meetings with anyone). He loves to go to the beach—and he especially loves it when I take him out for ice cream!

Name: <u>KAI</u>   BANKCODE: <u>NAKB</u>
Action: <u>Take Kai on a special 1:1 playdate to the beach and then have an ice cream.</u>

Now it's your turn. Remember to crack your loved one's code so you can intentionally connect with them based on their BANKCODE. Start with something small, and then continue to create special MPM moments with them as you go. I guarantee it will improve your relationship and put deposits into your emotional BANK account!

1. Name:_____ BANKCODE:_____
Action:_____

2. Name:_____ BANKCODE:_____
Action:_____

3. Name:_____ BANKCODE:_____
Action:_____

4. Name:_____ BANKCODE:_____
Action:_____

5. Name:_____ BANKCODE:_____
Action:_____

6. Name:_____ BANKCODE:_____
Action:_____

7. Name:_____ BANKCODE:_____
Action:_____

8. Name:_____ BANKCODE:_____
Action:_____

9. Name:_____ BANKCODE:_____
Action:_____

10. Name:_____ BANKCODE:_____
Action:_____

MAKE PEOPLE MATTER MINDSET

Make People Matter is more than just a mantra—it's a mindset. Having this mindset means you proactively take people's BANKCODE into consideration, and you do your best to communicate according to their individual codes. It won't be easy—but it will be worth it.

The more you practice not just cracking the code—but speaking the code and living the code—the more doing so will become a natural way of life. Malcolm Gladwell suggested in his book *Outliers* that it takes approximately 10,000 hours of practice to master something. Therefore, it will take you five to ten years to achieve mastery—but according to Josh Kaufman's twenty-hour rule, you can learn any new skill by dedicating twenty hours of planned practice time to that skill. Simply put, forty-five minutes of BANK practice a day can lead you to learn your new Make People Matter skills in as little as a month!

My deepest wish is for all of us to collectively link arms in this Make People Matter movement. Together, we can make this world a much happier, kinder world for the 8-plus billion humans and beyond.

Thank you for the opportunity to share our mission, special moments, and movement with you. I wish you all the success and happiness in the world—and I can promise you that when you apply the principles of the BANK methodology in your life, you will forever experience life in full color!

Best wishes, my future Codebreaker! I look forward to meeting you someday and hearing more about your Make People Matter moments!

Make People Matter,

GETTING STARTED

UNLOCK YOUR ACCESS

Over the preceding four sections, we've demonstrated the incredible influence of BANK, shared stories about BANK's game-changing power from my own life and the lives of members throughout the Codebreaker community, and given you many compelling reasons to start changing your life through BANK.

At this point, you're probably eager to put these tools and systems to work in your life and business. To help you get the fastest results in the shortest amount of time, I'm offering three ways to engage with us and begin your journey to make people matter.

1. **Self-Implementation:** Gain access to the powerful tools, training, and technology needed to supercharge

your life, relationships, and business—and fast-track your success with your own initiative.

2. **Professional Implementation:** Engage a professional Certified and Licensed BANK Trainer or Coach to consult with you and lead you through the BANK implementation process, customized to your specific needs.

3. **Private Implementation:** Work directly with me and my top corporate team to develop a full BANK implementation strategy personally customized for you and your global business needs.

Visit our website to learn more about ways to engage with us, crack your code, subscribe to our blog or newsletter, learn more about becoming a strategic partner or affiliate, get certified as a BANK Trainer or Coach, schedule a private consultation, or book us to speak on your podcast or upcoming events.

If you have any other questions or want any additional help, email me directly at cheri@codebreakertech.com.

YOUR ACCESS CODE

Use this special Access Code or QR code to unlock your access to special offers, tools, reports, and more. Go to crackmycode.com/_____.
(*type in the Access Code word below in the URL).

ACKNOWLEDGMENTS

I want to give a few very important acknowledgments and express my gratitude to those who have contributed to this book and our mission and movement.

Special thanks to each of the coauthors who shared their special—and sometimes private—Make People Matter moments. You have each made our mission come alive and your stories will influence millions of people.

I also want to acknowledge our incredible Codebreaker community—representing more than 100 countries around the world. Your love of BANK and belief in our mission, mantra, and movement have inspired me to keep the vision of cracking #8billioncodes alive. Without you, this never would have been possible. Together, we will change the world!

A big shout out to the team behind this book who helped me pull together thirty-one coauthors and get us all to create Make People Matter magic together! Our team includes Erik "Mr. Awesome" Swanson, Jon Kovach Jr., Patrick Snow,

Anna Parker, Kelley Tenny, Dalia Harami, and Tom Tree. I know this wasn't an easy project—thank you for your help!

Lastly, I want to thank my amazing wife, Esther Wildenberg, and our incredible son, Kai, for giving me the support and encouragement to write this book and get our message out to the world. You both are my everything, and I strive every day to make you matter.

"People buy into the leader before they buy into the vision."

— John Maxwell, American Author, Speaker and Pastor

ABOUT CHERI TREE

Cheri Tree is a best-selling author, professional keynote speaker, and world-renowned entrepreneur and innovator. She is the Founder and CEO of Codebreaker Technologies, with Codebreakers in more than 100 countries worldwide. She is the creator of the revolutionary BANK methodology and Codebreaker's patented Personality Coding Technology and Artificial Intelligence, designed to help her clients increase their influence, income, and impact in the world.

A top in-demand speaker who has spoken to millions of entrepreneurs and professionals globally at some of the most-prestigious business conferences in the world, Cheri has been invited to speak at Harvard University, the University of California, Google, GoDaddy, and the United Nations.

Cheri is leading a technology and transformation revolution with her high-tech, high-touch Codebreaker company and community. She has been featured in numerous international publications, including Forbes.com, and has received numerous awards and nominations, including Woman of the

Year, Female Thought Leaders of the Year, Maverick of the Year, SaaS Company of the Year, Innovator of the Year, and Achievement in Technology Innovation.

Fueled by her mission to connect and empower humanity, and ultimately, to Make People Matter, Cheri's vision is to crack #8billioncodes, equating to the code of every human in the world.

BOOK CHERI TREE TO SPEAK TO YOUR ORGANIZATION

Cheri Tree has gained a reputation as one of the most powerful keynote speakers in the business world, due to her dynamic approach with BANK. When Cheri teaches BANK, she doesn't just give your organization another "trick" to close a sale better that will be forgotten soon after she leaves. Cheri instead instills the fundamentals of how to communicate more effectively, personally and professionally

A dynamic and engaging speaker, Cheri has appeared on hundreds of stages in front of millions of people around the world, teaching the secrets of success to entrepreneurs, Fortune 500 companies, and even students at top universities like Harvard University. In fact, Cheri has been featured at conferences in Asia, Africa, Europe, and North America. She has shared the stage with many celebrity speakers, including Robert Kiyosaki, Les Brown, Sir Richard Branson, Robin Sharma, and Tony Robbins.

Few speakers can entertain and inform throughout an entire keynote speech. Cheri is the rare exception, which makes her one of the most in-demand speakers in her field. Beyond just entertaining, Cheri's keynotes, speeches, and interactive workshops deliver real results. Not all speakers are equally skilled at training smaller groups or even effectively educating the audience on the topics at hand. Cheri Tree is. She knows how to balance interactive entertainment with in-depth learning experiences, so everyone comes away with the vital knowledge needed to dramatically increase their influence and income.

Book Cheri today as a keynote speaker for your next conference, in-house training day, keynote talk, podcast, or event. Whether you are looking for a featured speaker for a ninety-minute keynote or an experienced trainer to deliver a full-day workshop, Cheri Tree is uniquely qualified to provide a fun, educational experience that your whole organization will love.

BOOK CHERI TREE TO SPEAK AT YOUR NEXT EVENT OR GET MORE INFORMATION ABOUT HER KEYNOTES NOW
cheri@codebreakertech.com | (858) 997-7555

To learn more about Cheri's approach and topics of expertise, watch clips of her past speeches, or to download her media kit, visit CheriTree.com.

"This book is money in the BANK—your bank! Salespeople who use BANK will replace salespeople who don't."

— Jeffrey Gitomer, Author of
The Little Red Book of Selling

WHY THEY BUY

> "BANK is a game-changer for every business owner and entrepreneur. This system will strengthen your confidence, expand your selling skills—and dramatically increase your income."
>
> — Les Brown

To learn more about how to close more sales in less time using BANK, read Cheri Tree's best-selling book, Why They Buy. This book will unlock the secrets, the science, and the system to supercharge your influence, income, and impact. Visit WhyTheyBuy.com.

www.ingramcontent.com/pod-product-compliance
Lightning Source LLC
Chambersburg PA
CBHW051856160426
43209CB00006B/1323